Tabloid Terror

MW01486857

We live in a tabloid era, in which image outweighs substance and the partisan soundbite overwhelms independent policy. But rather than merely decrying modern shallowness or attempting to reinstate the rule of reason, *Tabloid Terror* analyzes the methods, the effects, and the mechanisms by which international relations reach the US citizen.

Deftly dissecting the interrelationships of national identity formation, the media fabrication of news and public opinion as tabloid punditry and sensationalist entertainment, and the impact of intellectuals of statecraft's populist views and publications, Debrix explains how a discourse of fear, terror, and war was deployed in US public culture before 9/11, and how such a narrative – supported by visual representations – became even more dominant and destructive as a result of the Bush administration's exploitation of danger and insecurity after 9/11. Debrix's analysis brings American popular cultural sites (war images and military ads, photojournalistic displays, popular TV shows, internet pamphlets, Fox News pundits' programs) into contact with advanced critical social and political theorists (Julia Kristeva, Michel Foucault, Giorgio Agamben, Jean-Luc Nancy, Judith Butler) and with the writings of foreign policy intellectuals and practitioners (Robert D. Kaplan, Samuel Huntington, Victor Davis Hanson, Tommy Franks) in order to demonstrate how a model of tabloidized international relations and geopolitics has been produced with a view toward conditioning the public to accept a boundless war on terror and endless scenes of violence and destruction of "evil others." The fields of International Relations and Geopolitics sorely need such analytics that examine how people in their everyday lives are made to relate to transnational (geo)political issues.

François Debrix is Associate Professor of International Relations at Florida International University in Miami.

Tabloid Terror

War, culture, and geopolitics

François Debrix

Routledge
Taylor & Francis Group

LONDON AND NEW YORK

First published 2008
by Routledge
2 Park Square, Milton Park, Abingdon, Oxon OX14 4RN

Simultaneously published in the USA and Canada
by Routledge
711 Third Avenue, New York, NY 10017

Routledge is an imprint of the Taylor & Francis Group, an informa
business

Typeset in Times New Roman by Prepress Projects Ltd, Perth, UK

British Library Cataloguing in Publication Data
A catalogue record for this book is available from the British Library

Library of Congress Cataloging-in-Publication Data
Debrix, François
Tabloid Terrror: war, culture, and geopolitics / François Debrix
p. cm.
Includes bibliographical references and index
1. War on Terrorism, 2001— Social aspects. 2. War on Terrorism, 2001—
Mass media and the war. 3. United States – Foreign relations – 2001—
I. Title.
HV6432.D433 2007
973.931 – dc22
2001006057

ISBN 10: 0-415-77290-7(hbk)
ISBN 10: 0-415-77291-5 (pbk)
ISBN 10: 0-203-94466-6 (ebk)

ISBN 13: 978-0-415-77290-7 (hbk)
ISBN 13: 978-0-415-77291-4 (pbk)
ISBN 13: 978-0-203-94466-0 (ebk)

Contents

Acknowledgments

I started to conceive this project back in 1999, at a time when the cultural politics of fear, danger, and emergency in the United States were heightened by the proximity of the end of the millennium and by the growing presence in the media of the Y2K technological scare. Yet, my concern with and interest in the tabloid production of geopolitics, terror, and eventually war fully developed in the months that followed the turn of the millennium as I noticed how (virtual or actual) bookstores in the United States started to fill up with publications by academic scholars, policy-oriented think-tank contributors, and media pundits urging Americans to be ready for the next catastrophe (and thus despite the fact that Y2K had not led to the chaos that had been announced). In many ways, in the broadly understood American media, these publications already set the discursive stage for the post-9/11 public culture in which ideas such as a war on terror, fighting evil, or limiting democratic debate to secure the homeland would become common everyday notions and realities. Although I witnessed the visual atrocity of the September 11 terrorist attacks with shock and incomprehension (like most academics in the United States I believe), the almost immediate take-over of public debate after 9/11 by tabloid type literatures, images, and rationalizations did not surprise me. In many ways, this discursive and representational phenomenon constituted a continuation (but with different inflections) of the public and popular narratives of fear, danger, and resecuritization that many US (pseudo-)intellectuals had wanted Americans to be aware of since the late 1990s. My task then (and now) would be to try to make sense of these expanding discursivities and their geopolitical consequences both inside and outside US borders. To do so, I would need to come up with an analytical perspective through which concepts (old and new) could be mobilized to critical effect. Back in 2001–02, I settled on the phrase "tabloid geopolitics" (and its derivatives, such as "tabloid terror," "tabloid realism," and so on) to provide a critical analytical perspective on these pre- and post-9/11 textualities and imageries of terror and war that international relations, geopolitics, and media and cultural studies scholars and students could find helpful in order to disentangle the intricacies of the history of "our" political/cultural present.

As I began writing this book, presented some sections of the chapters at conferences, invited lectures, and colloquia, and submitted some very early drafts of some chapters for publication in a few academic journals, I benefited greatly from the comments, critiques, and suggestions of many colleagues and friends. At Florida International University (FIU), where I currently teach, I presented an early version of Chapter 1 ("Cyberterror and Media-Induced Fears") at a Symposium on Culture and Politics in the Transnational Polity organized by the Department of International Relations in February 2001. I gave a lecture based on Chapter 2 ("Tabloid Realism and the Reconstruction of American Security Culture") in the context of the Faculty Colloquium Series of the Jack Gordon Institute of Public Policy and Citizenship Studies in April 2002. And I also sought the critical feedback of my departmental colleagues a year later, in April 2003, when I presented to them an early version of Chapter 3 ("Discourses of War, Geographies of Abjection") at the occasion of a Department of International Relations Colloquium. At FIU, I received helpful comments, constant encouragements, and a general sense of intellectual support from several colleagues, in particular Clair Apodaca, John Clark, Damian Fernandez, Harry Gould, Lui Hebron, Gail Hollander, Paul Kowert, Mohiaddin Mesbahi, Rod Neumann, Nick Onuf, Patricia Price, and Lisa Prugl. My gratitude also goes to the College of Arts and Sciences and the Office of the Provost at FIU whose generous funding over the years allowed me to find the time to conduct research on the project and write several of the chapters. From the College of Arts and Sciences, I obtained a Summer Stipend Award in the summer of 2002. From the Provost's Office, I was granted a one Semester Sabbatical Award in the spring of 2006, which helped me to finish drafting the last two chapters of the book.

Beyond Florida International University, I have had the opportunity to present many versions of the various chapters in this book at several regional, national, and international conferences. There, I benefited from the important feedback of colleagues such as David Blaney, James Der Derian, Kennan Ferguson, Larry George, Kyle Grayson, Nicholas Kiersey, Mark Lacy, Debbie Lisle, Wolfgang Natter, Scott Nelson, Jean-François Thibault, Pablo Toral, Julie Webber, and Geoffrey Whitehall. I owe a special debt to two colleagues, Simon Dalby and Tim Luke, with whom, over the years, I have organized several conference panels on which I got a chance to refine and clarify my arguments for this book. From the moment I came up with the idea of writing a book on the topic of tabloid geopolitics, both Simon and Tim have been tremendous supporters of the project, and their comments (as well as their own work) have helped me to elucidate some analytical, conceptual, and organizational difficulties I encountered in the process of putting the book together. Since 2000, I have also had the privilege to be invited to lecture on diverse aspects of this book by prestigious universities and institutes. I have given presentations at Ritsumeikan University in Kyoto (Japan), at the University of Lancaster (United Kingdom), in Tokyo for the Japan Center for Area Studies and the Human Security Studies Project, and at the London School of Economics in the context of the 2005 conference of the journal *Millennium*. I am grateful to the following individuals for inviting me, organizing the lectures, and offering me some invaluable advice on the parts of the book that I had a chance to present to them, their colleagues and their students: Annika Bolden, Douglas Bulloch, Mick Dillon, Makoto Kobayashi, Hidemitsu Kuroki, Chika Obiya, Kosuke Shimizu, Mireille Thornton, and Hiroyuki Tosa.

Two of my most dedicated readers, supporters, and friends – Clair Apodaca and Cindy Weber – read and commented on all the book chapters, and they were willing to do so again when the book was in its final stages. It is to both of them that I owe my greatest debt of gratitude.

Very early, shorter, and often conceptually different versions of some of the chapters' studies appeared in various publishing venues. Parts of the analysis contained in Chapter 3 appeared in *Third World Quarterly* (Vol. 26, No. 7 [2005], pp. 1157–72) as a long review essay. I thank the journal's editor, Shahid Qadir, for his interest in my research. A preliminary approach to the conceptual and critical issues tackled in Chapter 4 was presented at the "Political Violence and Human Security in the Post-9/11 World" Symposium organized by the Japan Center for Area Studies and the Human Security Studies Project at the United Nations University in Tokyo in December 2004. The proceedings of this conference were later put together in a volume edited by Chika Obiya and Hidemitsu Kuroki and titled *Political Violence and Human Security in the Post-9/11 World* (Osaka: Japan Consortium for Area Studies, 2006). Finally, early versions or portions of some chapters were published in the following journals and appear here with permission: an initial draft version of Chapter 1 appeared as "Cyberterror and Media-Induced Fears: The Production of Emergency Culture," *Strategies: Journal of Theory, Culture and Politics*, Vol. 14, No. 1 (2001), pp. 149–68; a different version of Chapter 2 appeared as "Tabloid Realism and the Revival of American Security Culture," *Geopolitics*, Vol. 8, No. 3 (2003), pp. 151–90; parts of Chapter 5 appeared as "The Sublime Spectatorship of War: The Erasure of the Event in America's Politics of Terror and Aesthetics of Violence," *Millennium: Journal of International Studies*, Vol. 34, No. 3 (2006), pp. 767–91. I thank the editors of these three journal issues for providing me with the critical input necessary to clarify my writing and my use of concepts.

Finally, I want to thank Craig Fowlie at Routledge/Taylor & Francis for his unwavering support of the project, his dynamic and creative approach in dealing with editorial and presentation matters, and his important encouragements in the final stages of the book. I also wish to recognize Natalja Mortensen at Routledge/ Taylor & Francis for her crucial assistance with editorial, organizational, and technical matters.

This book is dedicated to two individuals who make my life, writing, and intellectual endeavors meaningful and complete. The first person to whom I dedicate this book is my wife and colleague Clair Apodaca, whose love, support, and dedication are constant sources of inspiration. The second person to whom I wish to dedicate the book is my grandson Jeremy White whose cheerfulness, joie de vivre, bursting energy, and unrelenting eagerness to learn more and more new things are constant reminders to me of the importance of treasuring the simple joys and pleasures of everyday life.

The author and the publishers thank the following for permission to reprint materials:

Geopolitics and Routledge/Taylor & Francis for permission to reprint "Tabloid Realism and the Revival of American Security Culture," *Geopolitics*, Vol. 8, No. 3, 2003.

Millennium: Journal of International Studies for permission to reprint "The Sublime Spectatorship of War: The Erasure of the Event in America's Politics of Terror and Aesthetics of Violence," *Millennium: Journal of International Studies*, Vol. 34, No. 3, 2006.

Routledge/Taylor & Francis for permission to reprint "Cyberterror and Media-Induced Fears: The Production of Emergency Culture," *Strategies: Journal of Theory, Culture and Politics*, Vol. 14, No. 1, 2001 (www.tandf.co.uk/journals).

Every effort has been made to contact copyright holders for their permission to reprint material in this book. The publishers would be grateful to hear from any copyright holder who is not here acknowledged and will undertake to rectify any errors or omissions in future editions of this book.

Introduction
From images of terror to tabloid geopolitics

Being unable to make what is just strong, we have made what is strong just.

Blaise Pascal[1]

[O]nce a nameless and spontaneous reaction has been named and classified, and named over and over again so insistently by all the actors of the public sphere, backed up by thinly veiled threats and intimidation, the name interposes a stereotype between ourselves and our thoughts and feelings;. . . what we feel are no longer our own feelings anymore but someone else's, and indeed, if we are to believe the media, everybody else's.

Fredric Jameson[2]

Primal scenes of terror

Back in October 1993, American military forces received the order from their central command to launch a raid on rebel clan leader Mohammed Farah Aidid's compound in Mogadishu, Somalia. The anticipated overwhelming success of the operation (capturing Aidid, dismantling his network, restoring order to Somalia) would put an end to the in-fighting between rival clans, an internal struggle that had forced the United Nations and later the United States to intervene. Getting rogue clan leader Aidid, dead or alive, had become a priority for the US military command in Somalia and for US President Bill Clinton so that stability could be restored in the region and humanitarian organizations and the United Nations could deploy their peacekeeping and nation rebuilding mission.[3] In the euphoria of the post-Gulf War world, what promised to be a final onslaught against Aidid and his men turned out to be a disastrous mission.[4] But, more importantly, it became one of the most horrendous visual spectacles of the United States' post-Cold War interventionism throughout the 1990s, a sight that would haunt the rest of the decade. As Sidney Blumenthal noted, "within hours, horrifying pictures materialized on television screens: the corpses of American soldiers dragged through the streets of Mogadishu and burned by jubilant crowds, and a bloodied and bruised American hostage reciting his name and job in a monotone terror."[5] American audiences, who were just getting re-accustomed to foreign policy success and scenes of US triumphalism since the Gulf War victory appeared to have buried once and for all Vietnam's quagmire images, were clearly not prepared for these brutal images of dead and mutilated US soldiers streaming from Somalia. American politicians too were taken by surprise and were left unable to provide an appropriate spin to the visible events. Even Clinton, who up to this point had supported the US interventionist mission in Somalia and backed the strategy of going after Aidid, remained speechless. Again, Blumenthal recalled: "The appearance of a hostage turned Clinton into one himself: it was a picture of impotence and defeat, recalling, without any commentary necessary, the fate of the last Democratic president."[6] At the time, US television networks, starting with CNN, were really not too sure how they should handle those pictures: should they show them again and again, as they had done with the images coming from Baghdad during the Gulf War? Or should they hide them from sight, once and for all?[7] In the hours that followed this failed military assault, both strategies were adopted by the media. The images would eventually be pulled from most US news networks, but they would quickly return, albeit in a still, freeze-frame fashion, as front covers and often color shots in daily newspapers and weekly magazines.[8] In any case, it had been too late: there was no longer any buffering of the public from what had been seen by so many. In fact, the images started to speak for themselves. The US sponsored brave new world (order), championed by George H.W. Bush after the victory over Iraq in 1991 and later reprised by Bill Clinton, had come to an abrupt stop.[9] What were supposed to be the dominant images of the 1990s, the humanitarian decade – images of new American military heroes standing side by side with UN peacekeepers, or often as UN peacekeepers, and paving the way for a more humane and democratic world – suddenly gave way to the vision of tortured American troops, caught in a war that may not have been in America's vital interest to fight. On that day, October 3, 1993, in Mogadishu and hours later in the rest of the world, unexpectedly gruesome images of warfare and military violence interrupted the global flow of humanitarian and interventionist images that had filled TV screens so far, and rendered far less acceptable the political ideologies and military strategies that such a visual flow hoped to legitimize.

Eight years later (give or take a few weeks), another trauma, another set of images, and another American war. Slightly before 9:00 a.m. EST, on September 11, 2001, an American Airlines jetliner collided head-on with one of the World Trade Center towers in New York City's lower Manhattan. Although most Americans did not catch what would later be known as the "first terrorist attack" in real time, fifteen minutes later, as CNN and other cable networks had already dispatched camera crews into the area or on rooftops of buildings in midtown Manhattan, a second airliner slammed into the second World Trade Center tower, impaling the building from one side to the other, and almost immediately unleashing a devastating fireball as the kerosene-filled aircraft exploded inside the tower. Everybody saw that one, even those who had missed the first hit. Everyone who was glued to his/her television screen that morning after the announcement had been made that a first plane had collided with the first tower could not miss that second hit. People at work or on the street were told about it and rushed to the first TV screen they could find.[10] Although clearly not prepared for the images their cameras would capture that morning, all the major cable news networks made sure they had caught the live scene of the second aircraft hitting the second tower. But reporters and broadcasters were incapable of finding words that could make sense of what we all had just seen.[11] In the hours and days that followed, every American who was not present when the live image jumped onto the screen would be given many more opportunities to revisualize, record, and relive this unfathomable sight, from every possible angle, with accompanying still shots if necessary. Video footage of the first collision that had not been caught live by most TV networks would be hunted down, found, released to the public, and broadcast over and over.

The subsequent endless replay of the initial visual shock was far from sur-prising. In a sense, this obscene visual rehash was expected, not only because it guaranteed viewership to the networks, but also because it served for many as an emotional relay allowing people to cope with the unreality of the event. Moreover, as Fredric Jameson's opening quotation suggests, the visual repetition of the September 11 attacks, far from being a case of *Schadenfreude* (as with most media coverage of disasters, conflicts, car crashes, poverty, etc.), reflected a desire to name and classify, to organize so as to better rationalize and recuperate. From this perspective, what is interesting, in a way that is also reminiscent of the initial moment of hesitation in the media that followed the images of the tortured US soldiers in Mogadishu, is the virtual silence and absence of commentary and meaning on the part of the media networks as they showed the event live and as the initial hit continued to produce unexpected and cascading visual effects (the collapse of both towers a few hours later, the news of a plane crashing into the Pentagon and another one in a field in Pennsylvania, the false information about bombs exploding near the State Department and the Capitol buildings in Washington, and so on). For a few moments, the image was allowed to roam free, to operate without a name, outside of classifications. It was allowed to speak for itself and splash its disseminated meanings onto people's screens, at home, at work, in the street. Of course, all these meanings were overwhelming and in-comprehensible for the public and politicians alike. The media and their talking heads were just as clueless. As James Der Derian remarked: "There was no initial attempt by the media or the government to transform these images of horror into responsible discourses of reflection and action."[12] Of course, comprehension, ra-tionalization, and later revenge would soon take over. But, as suggested above, for these images to be understood, they would need to be replayed over and over until finally some sense of intelligibility could be drawn from them (with the ultimate closing message, pronounced by the President and accepted by the population, that America was at war).[13]

In Mogadishu on October 3, 1993, and in Manhattan on September 11, 2001, a live, incomprehensible image, a moment of terror beyond expectation, calculation, or even despair, an event as event took (its) place in the public sphere, interrupted regularly programmed media representations, and forced a temporary stoppage of public discourses by politicians, pundits, technocrats, pseudo-experts, intellectu-als, and ideologues that, for many years, had filled the cultural landscape with imagined scenarios just like this one (which they nonetheless had not predicted). The image of terror that seems to resist discourse, this event that appears to be able to impose a silence and that postpones what ultimately will return as justifications to go to war, is the reality of what might be called the "primal scene." The term "primal scene" is derived from Marshall Berman's study of Charles Baudelaire's prose poems as critical social tableaux of 1870s Paris.[14] The power of the primal scene is precisely to reveal how "a repressed reality creaks through" even when all seems to be going well for those in the political establishment, for the social elites, for those who are part of the media universe, in a nutshell, for all those for whom control over the meaning of the image and its message appears to have been settled.[15] In this context of cultural and social normalcy, when a certain set of political and economic relations are discursively and, by extension, materially taken to be the way things are, primal scenes can be brutally ironic and destabilizing. They may reveal meaninglessness behind the excesses and flourishes of dominant media representations at a moment when the public is least prepared for such a lack of meaning.

Yet, at the same time as the silent and traumatic reality of the primal scene is about to take its place in our field of vision, perception, and understanding, many non-events rush back in to fill our global mediascape, and they often become the bread and butter of our contemporary dominant and ever-encroaching discursive and public representations. In fact, when the shock and terror of the primal scene finally recede, it is often because media non-events have managed to regain control over the discursive and visual landscape of everyday public/political life. Desirous to stifle the occurrence of the unexpected/unplanned event (and its possibly lasting silence), media productions re-establishing banality and normalcy in public life return to "globally swarm" (to borrow Der Derian's turn of phrase) our daily field of perception and understanding. The goal of such media productions is to not allow us to perceive or experience any reality that has not been previously massaged, manufactured, or operated by the medium itself.

This book seeks to critically detail and untangle the discursive reality of those mediated and mediatized representations, of those textual cultural mediations that talk to the public about all sorts of possible forms of destruction, terrorism, violence, insecurity, and war prior to or with complete disregard for the advent of a primal scene, any primal scene, as if the all-encompassing simulacrum of the media-saturated public sphere was all that could count as cultural, social, and political meaning. In the face of shocking images of beaten-up US soldiers in Mogadishu, of collapsing Twin Towers in New York, or more recently of tortured Iraqi prisoners in Abu Ghraib, Iraq, these dominant media representations, these authorized public voices, always return full of rationalizations, justifications and, as previously indicated, with ready-made scenarios (often war scenarios) to neutralize whatever fledgling effect the primal scenes might have had on the mesmerized audiences and on their emotions. This book spends much of its time analyzing how these mediated discourses seem to be able to break the silence, to restore and impose meanings where none appears to exist anymore (if only for a fleeting moment) and, in the context of this search for rationalizations of the image, to give revenge a "name" ("war on terror," for example).

Throughout much of this volume, I refer to these discursive mediations whose buzzing non-events eventually find a way of fending off the reality of the primal scene as a matter of tabloid geopolitics. Tabloid geopolitics is the result of mediatized discursive formations that take advantage of contemporary fears, anxieties, and insecurities to produce certain political and cultural realities and meanings that are presented as commonsensical popular truths about the present condition. Tabloid geopolitics is the form taken by the medium and its discourse, particularly in the United States, in the early twenty-first century in matters regarding national security, the survival of the state (the United States first and foremost), war, and global terror. Tabloid geopolitics is a medium – perhaps *the* medium in matters of international politics and foreign affairs today – but, first of all, it is a discourse. As such, and as will be shown below, all those who claim to represent the "public interest" in one form or another, or who pretend to speak in the name of the American public, can and often do partake of it. As will be seen in this study, tabloid geopolitics is a discursive public enterprise that seeks to proliferate narratives and images intended to saturate and satisfy (and satisfy by saturating) the global cultural landscape, or what is left of it. Yet, by hiding deeper and deeper under layers of mediated non-events that are meant to be taken for events (for a reality that can still surprise), these tabloid geopolitical discourses cannot prepare the so-called public, American individuals and perhaps global citizens too, for the tragedy that arrives as or with the primal scene. Instead – and it is as much of a tragedy indeed – tabloid geopolitics ends up deploying vengeful and destructive strategies (and destructive for the global public too, starting with American citizens' lives) against enemies or "evil" figures that, it convinces itself, have to be the real cause of the terror witnessed in the primal scenes. By tracking the courses, recourses, and discourses of tabloid geopolitics, its institutions (in the media often), and its agents/actors, this book offers an account of the tragedy that is and has been "our" condition of global terror from around January 1, 2000 (also known as Y2K), through the 9/11 terrorist attacks and the subsequent American wars against terrorism in Afghanistan and Iraq, and all the way to the upcoming wars that have yet to/may or may not/will have already come (as non-events) in Iran, for example, or in Lebanon and Israel, or in any other place in the Middle East at about the midpoint of the first decade of the twenty-first century. In this first decade of the new century, with "our" public figures' discursive inability or unwillingness to deal with and respond to the images of terror with anything other than many of the same old twentieth-century geopolitical ways of acting (war, political terror, good states versus bad states, and so on) and ways of thinking (aggression, otherness, imperialism, and so forth), "we" once again find ourselves demonstrating Blaise Pascal's point that "we" are indeed only capable of making (and claiming) "what is strong just."

Tabloid culture

Contemporary popular culture is a tabloid or trash culture. It is so in the United States and, by way of what is taken to be globalization, in the rest of the world too. Labeling a culture tabloid or trash is not a pejorative dismissal. It is not a rejection of so-called "everyday lowbrow or middlebrow culture" and its modes of expression, representation, and entertainment on behalf of an allegedly higher, elite, refined or bourgeois culture. Contemporary literatures that talk about tabloid/trash culture recognize this. In many of these literatures, the tabloid status of today's popular cultural productions and consumptions is a descriptive and expository notion that refers to a certain moment or mood in what Jean-François Lyotard (and others) have referred to as the postmodern condition.[16]

The tabloidization of everyday culture takes place when the media and their programming and fictional realities become the all-encompassing dimension of a vast majority of people's daily lives. Although tabloid culture is often associated with the kind of television viewership that developed in the United States in the 1980s and 1990s, with talk-shows, "real-life" dramas, and on-the-scene live investigative reporting news, cultural studies scholar Kevin Glynn notes that tabloid culture actually "entails a variety of intertwined discursive formations that occupy a mobile space where journalism and popular culture intersect" and that, as such, "it includes a highly mixed bag of typical forms, thematic concerns, image repertoires, tones of voice, and narrative patterns, many of which are traditional for television but have been reworked in specific and sometimes striking ways."[17] The plurality of messages, the hybridity of forms, and the eclecticism of styles that seem to characterize tabloid TV extend well beyond the television medium and affect many other popular cultural genres that, in the 1990s, increasingly defined themselves against the background of television's upbeat real-time mode of information and entertainment. Thus, from special reports in weekly news magazines to videogames' graphics, from blockbuster films to internet blogs, much of popular culture becomes subject to tabloidization, which, as Glynn mentions, is more to be thought of as a discursive formation (that can evolve through many different forms) than as a specific genre with a single format.[18] The tabloid discourse becomes the dominant mode of communication (between individual beings), representation (of social and political events), expression (of artists, intellectuals, and ideologues), and entertainment (of the overall public) in 1990s postmodern America and later, by extension and through mimesis, in the rest of the world. Tabloid culture fulfills Lyotard's criteria about postmodern culture since its "eclecticism is the degree zero of contemporary general culture: one listens to reggae, watches a western, eats McDonald's food for lunch and local cuisine for dinner, wears Paris perfume in Tokyo and 'retro' clothes in Hong Kong; knowledge is a matter for TV games."[19] In a tabloid postmodern context, the quick, unattached, ever-changeable message that tabloid discursive formations produce offers the public sufficient doses of information, comfort, and often emotions. Or, as trash culture specialist Richard Keller Simon remarks, "[f]or people with inquiring minds but short attention spans, our stories of suffering, fall, and recognition now come in short, easy-to-read fragments as a kind of fast-food tragedy to-go, but the fragments themselves contain nearly all of the essential elements of dramatic tragedy."[20]

As a discourse, tabloid culture appears to exhibit two main discursive traits or rules of formation: intertextuality and self-referentiality. Intertextuality is the product of the postmodern eclecticism sought in culture in the 1990s and described by Lyotard above. But it is also a trait that has always been characteristic of tabloid presentation, and particularly was closely tied to the tabloid journalism and tabloid newspapers that emerged in the United States in the 1920s. In the 1920s to 1930s, tabloid literatures made up of some pulp novels, snuff stories in popular magazines, and what was often known as yellow journalism caught the public's eye with texts (rarely visuals, with the exception of a few photographs or drawings here and there) whose aim was to sensationalize everyday reality.[21] This textual style of reporting reality or "telling the truth" was popular among the working classes. It made use of bits and pieces of real events gathered from all sorts of narrative sources (news reports printed in national newspapers, political pamphlets, situations depicted in early Hollywood films, common beliefs or anxieties derived from popular folklore, and so on) to create a coherent, believable, and often awe-inspiring or emotion-stirring story that relied on an appearance of truth. Without this intertextuality, this blending of different narrative bits together, the tabloid story would have had to relinquish its claims to veracity and thus would have been indistinguishable from a work of fiction (which it often stylistically mimicked).

The rule of intertextuality already present in 1920s to 1930s tabloid texts and still defining of tabloid culture today, albeit in a blatantly more visual fashion, also guarantees the self-referentiality of this cultural genre. Because the tabloid story is made up of fragments of information collected from very different narrative origins, grounding the produced tabloid report into factual evidence, historical accuracy, or a truth claim is an impossible task. Instead, the tabloid genre creates its own rules of evidence, its own historical events, and its own "truth" as referentiality and meaning are mainly internal to the story itself (which only bears a passing resemblance to so-called real life and soon substitutes itself for it) and its production process. Thus, in today's tabloid culture, tabloid discourses have abandoned any meaningful intention of corresponding to a "real world" outside of the tabloid media world itself. What matters for the tabloid story today is to figure out how "events out there" can be infiltrated into the tabloid universe where they are manipulated, played with, shared between different media actors, replayed, and finally given meaning with an appearance of truth, factuality, and historical accuracy. If one were to use Jean Baudrillard's now famous language, one would have to say that tabloid culture is concerned not with fiction (which seeks only to imitate the truth even when it wishes to imagine an alternate one) but indeed with simulation since the objective is to generate a "reality" that is totally self-referential and yet "more real" than the so-called reality derived from any truth claim.[22] Taking television as today's epitome of the tabloid simulacrum, Glynn presents the self-referentiality of tabloid culture in the following fashion: "television's generic territories . . . constantly play off of, and mutually constitute, one another, for television's intergeneric universe is fluidly interpenetrating."[23] Glynn then generalizes (beyond television) about tabloid stories by stating that "media texts are always interdiscursive: they are continuously constituted and reconstituted by (and thus dependent on) the shifting relations of meaning that make up the intertextual networks within which they exist."[24]

Although not traditionally interested in producing discourses about politics (and even less about international politics),[25] contemporary tabloid culture finds itself at the heart of many so-called social, political or even economic debates. Since the tabloid cultural turn of the 1990s, "high politics" has been brought down to the level of sensational TV reporting, afternoon talk-shows, information-as-entertainment (or infotainment), documentary-dramas as TV series or even as feature films, and of course internet browsing. Today, "high politics" is filtered to us, the public, the global citizenry, through the simulacrum of tabloid culture. And the social problems that make politics what it is, that give it meaning and purpose (as Murray Edelman would suggest[26]), are presented to the public as a succession of tabloid discourses, often through television and by means of the main media actors, but sometimes also by way of other agents or institutions (many of which still call themselves political in order to be differentiated from the media) that partake of what Jameson once again calls the "public sphere" and are already embedded into the tabloid universe (and as such, whether they like it or not, are part of the tabloid media too). Tabloid culture at the turn of the twenty-first century is ubiquitous and, more importantly, its discursive styles, forms, and apparent modes of content are fashionable and seductive to many – and not just the audiences – because these discursive formations once again present themselves as an endless horizon of human experience. Thus, tabloid culture is always already political or, rather, politics (high or low) is always already a matter of tabloid discursive production, representation, and mediation.

Of late, and particularly since the turn of this century, international politics has become a preferred subject matter of tabloid discourses. There is no doubt that the images of terror of 9/11 (once their primal shock and silence subsided and rationalizations in the media and among politicians took over) played a substantial part in bringing traditional geopolitical issues – war, national security, military defense and strategy, deterrence of terrorism – into the domain of tabloid popular culture. But this new trend was announced a few months prior to the terrorist attacks when the United States and the rest of the world prepared for the global technological, economic, and socio-political catastrophe that was supposed to be Y2K, or the turn to the year 2000. Then already, previewing many of the tabloid media narratives and images that would follow 9/11, issues regarding terrorism, national insecurities, inter-state violence resulting in the destruction of relied upon global networks, and possibly war were the bread and butter of the media's tabloid culture and of all those experts (in government, in computer technology, in insurance matters, and many other sectors) who contributed to the sensationalistic discourse of fear and danger that is often the mark of a successful tabloid story. With Y2K, and even more so after 9/11, the reality of global threats and local dangers became that which tabloid culture produced and reproduced. In the preparations for what many thought (because it made good sense inside the self-referential tabloid discourse) was going to be Y2K's subsequent terror and chaos, geopolitics was recruited as a prime popular cultural and political topic in the new century.

Geopolitics in a tabloid context

Geopolitics, as John Agnew reminds us, has traditionally been used "to refer to the study of the geographical representations, rhetoric and practices that underpin world politics."[27] Despite the scientific pretense kept up by some initial geopolitical thinkers like Halford Mackinder or Friedrich Ratzel,[28] the study of geopolitics has always been far from objective or value-neutral. On the contrary, geopolitics has historically been tied to the way dominant and powerful sovereign nation-states have tried to make sense of and represent their global spatial environment (starting with their neighboring states) with a view to facilitating their foreign policy making. Thus, geopolitics is closely tied to the idea and practice of territorial and cartographical imagination of modern political forms, starting with the modern state.[29] Historically, it was often through such geopolitical imaginations that subsequent foreign policy, hegemonic, and, sometimes, imperial ambitions were developed.

Crucial to this powerful way of imagining the political world is the belief that power, control, and domination can be spatially pre-determined, territorially engraved and inscribed in texts and, often, in visual forms too. Among the textual and visual materials that become privileged sources of imagination/knowledge for the geopolitical specialist are maps. Geopolitical discourses can "frame world politics in terms of an overarching global context in which states vie for power outside their boundaries, gain control (formally and informally) over less modern regions (and their resources) and overtake other major states in a worldwide pursuit of global primacy."[30] Furthermore, with the assistance of maps, world politics can become "actively spatialized, divided up, labeled, sorted out into a hierarchy of places of greater or lesser 'importance' by political geographers, other academics and political leaders."[31] All in all, Agnew concludes, the different methods, approaches to knowledge, and textual and mapping techniques that make up geopolitics as a field of study can be understood as "a *system* of visualizing the world."[32]

The success of this system of political visualization of the world requires that knowledge be produced as a result of reading political texts and consulting geographical maps. Although these writings and cartographical drawings appear to provide geopolitical knowledge, they often merely reproduce and normalize beliefs (about the state, its enemies, its foreign policy objectives) that have already been affirmed by some, generally political leaders, prior to any textual or pictorial inscription. Put differently, geographical categories typically exist before the geopolitical discourse or presentation is unveiled. Susan Schulten's richly documented study of the development of the cartographical industry and imaginary in the United States from the late nineteenth century all the way to World War II reveals that, in the American context, mapmakers and world atlas producers already knew how they wanted their maps to look and what they wanted their geographical texts to describe and narrate even before the American public had a chance to express preferences or reveal interests. More often than not, those American-made maps and geographical compendia followed closely, in fact anticipated, domestic and international political categories that were meant to serve the United States' global interests or needs. In particular, the newly affirmed international place of the United States as an imperial power (particularly after the Spanish–American war) in the late nineteenth century had to be cartographically explained and justified. Thus, Schulten concludes, as early as the 1880s for the United States (the practice had started earlier in Western Europe), maps, atlases, and their accompanying geopolitical texts "legitimated what was controversial, made scientific what was historical, and naturalized what was human."[33] As a result, what Schulten calls "a metageography" was created that provided American citizens with "a normative view of both the world and the map."[34]

The text and the map, then, become confirmations or verifications of what some (cartographical industrialists, capitalist entrepreneurs, government officials, and so on) already hold to be true, necessary, efficient, and normatively binding. To use Simon Dalby's formulation, "[g]eopolitical reasoning, that is, using geographical categories as part of the practices of representation among foreign policy makers and politicians, specifies the world in particular ways that have political effects."[35] In the process, though, as Dalby further mentions, different and complex social, political, and cultural realities have to be reduced and simplified, often for strategic purposes. Once again, the (geo)political treatise, the atlas, and the map are ideal instruments of simplification and reduction of knowledge, and of further naturalization, extension, and reproduction of such knowledge.

Yet, despite this semblance of simplicity, precision, clarity, and useful transparence, geopolitical discourses and representations are much more complex, hybrid, polymorphous, and pluralized than they appear. Although it would be convenient to limit the production of geopolitical knowledge to a few texts by some political geographers or a few geometric and pictorial drawings by some cartographers, many practices and ideas in society, in everyday culture, partake of the construction of geopolitical imaginaries too. Geopolitics, this allegedly scientific modality of visualization of the world (and generally of the place and role of one or one's chosen state in the world), mobilizes all sorts of live forces in the social and cultural domain that, often unbeknownst to them, are recruited to put their daily activities to good and efficient geopolitical representational use. Gearóid Ó Tuathail's analysis of geopolitics follows this line of reasoning. Examining the turn to geopolitics that took place in Europe at the end of the nineteenth century, Ó Tuathail writes:

It [geopolitics] names not a singularity but a multiplicity, an ensemble of heterogeneous intellectual efforts to think through the geographical dimensions and implications of the transformative effects of changing technologies of transportation, communications, and warfare on the accumulation and exercise of power in the new world order of "closed space." Like other forms of geo-power, these writings were governmentalized forms of geographical knowledge, imperial rightings from an unquestioned center of judgment that sought to organize and discipline what was increasingly experienced as unitary global space into particularistic regimes of nationalistic, ideological, racial, and civilizational truth. Circulating within the developing media of civil society (which ranged from elite markets for scholarly books to the yellow journalism of jingoistic newspapers), these discourses were motivated attempts to frame the spectacle and flux of the new global political scene within the terms of imperialistic and militaristic agendas, agendas actively cultivated and pushed by political, economic, and bureaucratic interest groups within the states-societies of the Great Powers.[36]

Thus, Ó Tuathail suggests, it is better to understand geopolitics, not just as an elite discourse or representation controlled and produced by a few experts (geographers or others) to achieve calculated political results, but also as an open and pluralized "discursive event" that turns to a rich cultural (often popular cultural) background in the societies where the geopolitical discourse is deployed in order to produce a desired political knowledge.[37] Only by treating geopolitics as what Ó Tuathail calls a "problematic," as that which needs to be problematized, opened up, and untangled (and not as a sealed domain of expert imagination), can one start to appreciate, and perhaps challenge and unsettle, the cultural work that is required to turn a given visualization of the world into a dominant or hegemonic political strategy.

The study of geopolitics, then, can and perhaps ought to start with many public texts and other narratives (and many of them pictorial and visual) that seek to present, affirm, and simplify a political vision of the world. If, as Ó Tuathail intimates, geopolitics is a discursive event and a cultural production, modes of writing and representation used to convey public messages (political or not) are of necessity the media through which the geopolitical discourse circulates. Several critical geopolitical and international relations scholars have already paid much attention to these media or modes of representation that propagate a geopolitical message and perhaps create a certain geopolitical reality. David Campbell's pathbreaking study on the politics of identity creation through insecurity and danger has showed how the US government's Cold War foreign policy texts – many of them elite or expert documents (like National Security Council documents), but also others with much intended public effect (like George Kennan's 1946 "Long Telegram" for example) – "established the discursive boundaries of United States foreign policy" around a series of "self versus other" delineations and exclusions.[38] Campbell's genealogy of American foreign policy as national identity reveals a geopolitical imaginary that, from the Puritans' landing to the end of the Cold War, has turned to varied popular cultural narrative sources (Christopher Columbus' own writings and mappings, early settlers' diaries and notebooks, religious pamphlets and jeremiads, political speeches, advertising campaigns, and indeed government documents) to anchor danger and insecurity in (inter)national politics around the idea of "otherness." Michael Shapiro's work of late has also been driven by a desire to bring to the fore the geopolitical assumptions that can be found in modern and contemporary cultural genres that, from music and painting to photography and film, seem to be far removed from traditional geopolitical questions (but as such, through their "non-political" appearance, display an extremely powerful and lasting force of geopolitical normalization and persuasion).[39]

A few critical minds have even started to think in terms of what they have called "popular geographies" or "popular geopolitics."[40] Joanne Sharp indicates that popular geopolitics, as a problematic (to use Ó Tuathail's terminology), assumes that "there is not a distinct division between elite and popular: elite texts are intended for popular consumption, and members of a distinctively elite institutional locale contribute to and consume popular media."[41] If there is indeed a blending in contemporary society of expert or elite geopolitical texts (National Security Council documents for example) and popular, perhaps even tabloid or trash, cultural literatures and image productions, then the choice of limiting the study of geopolitics to what are typically labeled as official (governmental) sources of geopolitical knowledge would amount to nothing less than a safeguarding of geopolitics as a disciplinary domain inside which sacred and stable political meanings and representations are likely to go unchallenged. Moreover, as Shapiro's work introduced above reveals, ignoring the role and place of popular cultural texts and representations in the making of geopolitics would mean that much of the way discourses of geopolitics manage to establish, normalize, and reproduce foreign policy beliefs, attitudes, and courses of action would go unquestioned and possibly unnoticed. Sharp's own study leads the way in mobilizing popular geopolitics as a problematic by showing how the American middlebrow and direct mail magazine *Reader's Digest* provided American citizens during the Cold War with some of the most influential ready-made explanations (and cartographical depictions) of the Cold War strategies, the Soviet Union, and the "communist enemy." As Sharp notes, "[t]he *Digest*'s geographical imagination links the individual reader to the destiny of the United States, and to the operations of foreign powers, most significantly of course those of the Soviet Union, the Cold War enemy whose character the *Digest* is often credited with helping to create."[42]

As mentioned above, since the year 2000, international political matters typically represented or imagined by geopolitics have found their way into tabloid cultural discourses provided by contemporary media. This has been the case in the United States first and foremost. In the American context, so-called lowbrow or middlebrow publications (like the *TV Guide*, *People's* magazine, *Vanity Fair*, the *National Geographic*, and so forth), daytime talk shows on national television (with iconic TV stars like Oprah Winfrey, but also with newly rising pseudo-psychologists and feel-good gurus like Dr Phil), syndicated radio broadcasts or cable TV networks' "current topics" programs with seemingly straight-shooting, opinionated, and often populist and culturally conservative hosts (like Rush Limbaugh or Don Imus on the radio, or Bill O'Reilly or Pat Buchanan on cable TV) have all made national security, US foreign policy, terrorism, and war some of their primary subjects of concern. These media sources of tabloid discourse have done their best since 2000 (and probably before too, but with much lower intensity) to represent to American citizens what their world is about, where danger is likely to come from, what cultural posture and possibly political identity they need to adopt, and why often embracing war is the only justifiable way of defending the nation. The images of the terrorist attacks of 9/11 further exacerbated this tendency, particularly after the many journalists, talk-show hosts, pundits, and political experts working on TV or for print media finally found a language to explain what, once again, they had failed to anticipate (the attacks) but could now make sense of.

Thus, the problematic of geopolitics today cannot ignore tabloid culture. If, as Sharp suggests, the geopolitical imaginary of a nation unfolds as a series of cultural interventions that once again she refers to as popular geopolitics, the geopolitical cultural interventions of the early twenty-first century are clearly tabloid. But what is implied in claiming that today's popular geopolitics is necessarily tabloid is not just to suggest that this particular moment or mood in postmodern culture provides contemporary discourses of geopolitics with new cultural vectors through which their political simplifications and normalizations can take place. What the idea of tabloid geopolitics today also signifies, more crucially, is that the intertextual and self-referential tabloid genre of presentation of truth, factual events, and historical accuracy becomes the dominant style of geopolitical discourse. Put differently, whether they work for (tabloid) media or not, all those "actors of the public sphere" – starting with political leaders and going on to policy advisors, technical experts on specific aspects of international politics, and often academics – who write about, speak of, or try to imagine geopolitical realities, particularly in the United States, find themselves producing and reproducing a discourse that is eminently tabloid in both style and content.

Here and throughout the book, I suggest that we need to return to the notion of tabloid culture as a discursive formation. It is common for critical scholarship in the social sciences and humanities to make use of Michel Foucault's notion of discursive formation.[43] In many of these critical literatures, discursive formation is often taken to be synonymous with the term "discourse." Even though both terms are generally used interchangeably, Foucault operated a conceptual distinction between them. In order to grasp the meaning of tabloid geopolitics as a discursive formation whose very task is precisely to produce certain discourses, I believe that it is useful to keep in mind the Foucaultian nuance. For Foucault, discourse (often used by him where others would speak of language[44]) is anything that can be and is said, or written, or represented by someone or some institution with or without a specified objective. A discursive formation is a principle or technique of organization, calculation, arrangement, or redistribution of discourse or language.[45] Thus, discursive formations are interventions, directions, or specifications at the level of discourse/language with a view to attaining or realizing certain preferred meanings or representations.[46] Although thinking tabloid culture (as Glynn did above) and tabloid geopolitics (as I do here) as discursive formations places an emphasis on the methods, techniques, and textual or visual tricks that are deployed by those who wish to mobilize or use cultural or political discourses to achieve a certain type of knowledge (and, by the same token, try to negate other ways of producing meaning), this approach nonetheless does not ignore the specific formats or media through which these discourse-knowledge practices are operating. But this critical way of thinking and analyzing geopolitics and tabloid culture still recognizes that the produced tabloid discourse is more than the discourse of specific tabloid media that have embarked upon a sensationalistic style of information and so-called truth-telling. As a discursive formation, tabloid geopolitics is a generalized modality of knowledge production in today's culture, and the discourse of tabloid geopolitics can thus be created, transmitted, redirected, recycled, appropriated, and proliferated by a wide variety of public actors who find a utility (and often derive much power) in the operationalization of this discourse's truth- and knowledge-effects. Thus, the fashionable debate that is still ongoing in media studies and cultural studies today over whether the form (or the medium) should matter more than the content (or the message) in the determination of meaning and/or truth needs to be transcended and perhaps forgotten altogether. In the case of tabloid cultural and geopolitical discourses, both form and content matter. But they matter not so much because one can influence social or political meaning more than the other, but because both together, hand in hand, are necessary instruments in the making of a story or reality that, as explained above, must have the appearance of truth. Inside the discursive formation that is tabloid geopolitics, both content (what is actually said or shown) and form (what sort of media intervene to reveal some kind of reality) work together to intertextually and self-referentially generate truth-effects that will catch people's attentions, play with their emotions, and often become the main sources of what many consider to be the materiality of everyday politics.

In the ever-expanding media universe – a conceptual as much as technical domain whose limits tabloid culture keeps on expanding by bringing more and more public actors into the mix as media consultants, information providers, pundits, or truth-tellers – the discourse of tabloid geopolitics provides people in the United States and throughout the world with explanations, rationalizations, and predictions about events, images, or scenes (often primal scenes of terror) that can now make geopolitical sense. In a cultural context where the distinction between being inside actual media forms or networks or outside them no longer matters because it is no longer possible to ascertain what is part of the mediascape and what is not, the popular geopolitical discourse of the tabloid simulacrum is still an important cultural and social discourse, one that is loaded with powerful political effects. Whether it emanates from a Fox News special investigative report on the US war in Iraq, for example, or from a geopolitical treatise about America's post-9/11 security strategies provided by famous contemporary intellectuals of statecraft like Robert D. Kaplan, Samuel Huntington, or Victor Davis Hanson, whose books and op-ed pieces openly mimic a tabloid style of imagination and visualization of world political realities, the discourse of tabloid geopolitics seeks to generate some meanings and truths in (inter)national politics by sensationalizing and spectacularizing world politics at all costs.[47] Often recognizable because of the language and imagery of fear, danger, and destruction that they typically mobilize, geopolitical "issues and problems" introduced by tabloid geopolitical agents (media networks or intellectuals and academics of statecraft) are depicted in such a fashion that it now appears to the public that these so-called geopolitical problems can only be solved by means of military violence. Not coincidentally, the military violence privileged and offered as a logical outcome by most tabloid geopolitical discourses is that which a few states only, starting with the United States, have been deemed capable, willing, and justified to wield.

Tabloid geopolitics before and after 9/11

In this book, I examine the representations of security, terror, and war that have been provided by tabloid discourses as new "geopolitical truths" since the beginning of the twenty-first century. By once again treating tabloid geopolitics as a discursive formation, I pay close attention to the interventions at the level of narrative productions (both textual and visual) that have been performed by tabloid actors – media networks and intellectuals of statecraft above all – to control meaning and achieve desirable political effects. In so doing, and as I intimated earlier, I suggest that both media networks and intellectuals of statecraft are part of the same discursive regime, that they mutually refer to and reinforce one another, and that they work in complicity (although not always consciously) to build upon and embellish the tabloid geopolitical story. Empirically, it may at times appear that this book is about neo-conservative intellectuals, pundits, or academics and their narrative strategies aimed at redirecting the American foreign policy agenda toward going to war in order to fight terrorism and combat states that have been deemed to be enemies of the United States, both before and after 9/11. Although this primary level of reading is possible, it is clearly not the only and certainly not the main intended objective of the book.[48] American neo-conservative intellectual and polemical perspectives on US foreign policy since the year 2000 matter here, but they matter to the extent that they partake of, contribute to, and, in a sense, shape the contours of the public intellectual and political universe within which tabloid geopolitical discourses are allowed (and probably encouraged) to thrive.[49] Thus, more broadly, this study is interested in exploring, making sense of, and finally problematizing the discursivities (neo-conservative or otherwise) at work in the current, mostly American, geopolitics of security, terror, and war. By approaching the contemporary tabloid geopolitical discourse as what Ó Tuathail has called a "problematic" as opposed to reducing the so-called problem to neo-conservative ideology only, this discourse can now be opened up, untangled, pluralized, criticized, and, hopefully, publicly challenged too.

The book follows a rather chronological progression, starting with the months prior to Y2K and going to roughly the end of the year 2005 and early 2006, a time when a beginning of pluralization and uncertainty seemed to be able to creep into the dominant tabloid geopolitical discourse as the spectral images of 9/11 receded a bit, states other than the United States could now bear the mantle of moral outrage and political resoluteness against al Qaeda and in the context of the "war on terror" because they too had been attacked (Spain and Great Britain in particular), the conflicts in Iraq and Afghanistan were increasingly revealed as quagmire scenarios (with exit strategies starting to be visible), and Iran was increasingly presented as a new, perhaps more insurmountable, threat to America's war against terror. Still, since this book spans a short time period (some five to six years), chronology or historical succession is not so crucial to reading and understanding the following chapters.

Chapter 1 takes us back to the months that preceded the turn to the year 2000. In a context dominated by public fears about computer collapses, network shutdowns, and cyberterrorist hacking, information and digital technologies were perceived to be the main sources of (inter)national insecurity and possibly terror. This chapter develops the analysis of tabloid geopolitics before 9/11, at a time when Y2K was the main acronym and code name for danger and anxiety, by focusing on some cable news networks' programs that came up with catastrophic scenarios in order to, as they claimed, better prepare the public for the chaos that might spread just minutes after midnight on January 1, 2000. In many ways, both in the discourses produced by new types of public intellectuals and media pundits used as experts on the Y2K (non-)event and in the rise to prominence of new media actors (the internet, Fox News, and so on), the seeds were planted for tabloid geopolitics and its mode of imagination of the world. Chapter 2 examines how, in the months or even years before the attacks of September 11, 2001, a tabloid geopolitical discourse had already emerged. Mobilized by intellectuals or academics desirous to influence the course of American foreign policy making at the end of the 1990s, this discourse first focused on an attempt at restoring political realism since it had been argued by some, in international relations theory circles in particular, that the end of the Cold War had marked the demise of realism.[50] Realism's emphasis on national security, defense, containment, deterrence, and military might became crucial to this revived (tabloid) realist discourse. This reconstruction of American security culture took place, up to 9/11, by means of a political and cultural strategy that, in this chapter, I call "tabloid realism." In many ways, tabloid realism is the immediate precursor to the more generalized geopolitical discourse of tabloid terror that comes into full effect in the fall of 2001.

Chapter 3 offers a critical reflection on the meaning of the sentiments of revenge, rage, hatred, but also fear felt in the United States in the months that followed the terrorist attacks in New York and at the Pentagon. This chapter highlights how the need for the United States to move away from a post-9/11 sense of despair justifies the passage, in tabloid culture and politics, from tabloid realism to a full-blown tabloid discourse of war and abjection. Julia Kristeva's theory of the abject is an important critical filter that I use here to try to make sense of the language and imagery of retaliation, hatred, and destruction employed and championed by many American intellectuals of statecraft to justify why America must be at war and constantly be found fighting new forms of "evil" after 9/11.[51] In this chapter, the war in Afghanistan initiated by the United States in October–November 2001 is the contextual backdrop for much of this abject (and abjectifying) tabloid discourse. Kristeva's theory of abjection – an elaboration and extension of prior theories about desire, identity, and disgust[52] – is also crucial because it pushes us to notice the cultural, social, and ideological consequences of tabloid geopolitical discourses (such as those deployed in the United States in the fall of 2001). In this sense, Chapter 3 operates a transition in the book from an analysis of the narratives that produce tabloid terror to the effects of such discourses in terms of the cultural, social, and ideological imposition and normalization of war, destruction, and death as acceptable everyday realities.

Chapter 4 continues the analysis of the representations and discourses of war and terror found in (mostly American) tabloid geopolitical circles after 9/11 with a more direct focus on the consequences of such narratives and images (as indicated above). Here, the emphasis is on the institutionalization of war and war-making (or what I take to be a certain dimension of agonal politics) as ready-made realities of American public life and culture in the first decade of the new century. In this context, the US invasion of Iraq in March–April 2003 forms the empirical and political backdrop of this chapter. In Chapter 4, the interplay between everyday culture and American war-making is key. Popular cultural productions (advertising campaigns by the US Army), personal narratives (the autobiography by General Tommy Franks, the main military commander of the war in Iraq), and pseudo-academic or scholarly tabloid pamphlets and studies by American conservative pundits and intellectuals like Samuel Huntington or Lawrence Kaplan and William Kristol are brought together into the text in order to arrive at a theoretical reconsideration of the relationship between sovereignty and war in an era when absolute warfare is normalized by tabloid discourses. In this chapter, the effects of tabloid geopolitics on the political are directly addressed, and I conclude that the relinquishing of total authority to the American war machine (in Iraq above all) advocated by tabloid texts and images gives rise to a new conceptualization of sovereignty (what I call "agonal sovereignty") that, far from being concerned with the protection of the institutions of the state or even with preserving a certain way of life, is only interested in constantly finding new enemies, whoever they may be, and fighting new wars, wherever they may take place.

As Chapter 3's turn to Kristeva and abjection already announced, part of the analysis of Chapter 4 also starts to engage contemporary (often French) post-structural and critical theories. In this chapter, Gilles Deleuze and Felix Guattari's notion of the war machine is mobilized, and recent critical and post-Foucaultian interventions about biopolitics and the state of exception are introduced too. As the following chapters will confirm, post-structural theories and writings – and their close attention and dedication to language and to the textual production of identity – still have much to offer. In particular, mobilizing post-structural writings allows one to enable ruptures of commonsense and introduce suspensions of imposed meaning inside contemporary public/political culture where representations of and identifications with terror, war, and destruction all too often prevail. Thus, I object to Rey Chow's recent argument that suggests that the "self-referentiality of poststructuralist theory" dooms it to be of very little practical and critical relevance in contemporary culture and politics.[53] On the contrary, I hope to demonstrate in Chapter 4 and in the subsequent chapters that post-structurally influenced critical thinking (from various and varied scholars such as Deleuze and

Guattari, Foucault, or Giorgio Agamben in Chapter 4; from Lyotard, Jacques Derrida, and Jean-Luc Nancy in Chapter 5; and from Emmanuel Levinas and Judith Butler in the conclusion) more than ever needs to be studied closely, articulated, worked upon, and elaborated, especially if one cares to try to restore a cultural and political way of life and a public sphere of discussion and debate where difference is not automatically excised in the name of larger-than-life demands to defeat terrorism, fight evil, or destroy ever newly created enemies in whatever future war appears to be on the horizon.

Chapter 5 returns to the spectacle of terror, destruction, and war that was presented at the onset of this introduction. It does so in order to force a critical examination of the connection between tabloid geopolitical discourses of war and terror and the notion of the sublime. Benefiting from the assistance of texts and concepts derived from the thoughts of political philosophers like Kant, Lyotard, Nancy, and Derrida, this chapter seeks to place the meaning of the tabloid geopolitical discourses and representations of the Iraq war and its aftermath of guerrilla warfare, local resistance to US occupation, tortured Iraqi prisoners, and growing anti-war sentiments in the United States in the larger perspective of the relationship between sublime visual representations and the justification for violence. As a manifestly visual (through actual visual media) or imagined (through tabloid intellectuals' texts with high imaginary appeal) mode of production of geopolitical realities, tabloid geopolitics, in Iraq and beyond, bears a fundamental responsibility for the deployment of extremely violent ways of thinking, viewing, and practicing international politics today.

The conclusion to the book pulls together some reflections on the power and purpose of tabloid geopolitics and its production of tabloid terror by bringing the critical focus more closely toward the end of the year 2005 and early 2006, a time when (as suggested above) uncertainty may have started to creep up in apparently unchallenged and unchallengeable tabloid geopolitical representations. This concluding chapter "updates" the tabloid geopolitical debate and discourse of some contemporary (often imperialist) intellectuals of statecraft, and it contrasts their writings and presentations to the critically persuasive analysis provided by Judith Butler. Using Butler's recent argument about the production and representation of violence in the public sphere and its meaning for identity, human vulnerability, and life in general,[54] I suggest in this concluding chapter that one form of resistance to the violence and war normalized inside tabloid discourses is to find ways of rescuing the event from the tabloid production, of thinking the political outside of the dominant discourses, representations, and mediations of (inter)national politics (an argument already anticipated at the end of Chapter 5).[55] As was postulated at the beginning of this introduction, and as recent post-structurally influenced contributions to critical thinking (such as Butler's) have been eager to point out, this attempt at liberating the event may entail a return to the image of terror, to the primal scene, not so much because terror, any terror, is to be praised as such (in fact, quite the contrary), but because the silence or lack of rationalization that accompanies such a scene or event may have a chance of breaking the cycle of tabloid geopolitical discourses that continue to propagate war and, in so doing, are also responsible for keeping the terror alive.

1 Cyberterror and media-induced fears

The tabloid production of emergency culture

Paranoia is fashionable.

Anonymous graffiti[1]

We must protect our people from danger and keep America safe and free. Our vulnerability, particularly to cyber attacks, is real and growing.

President Bill Clinton[2]

From WWIII to Y2K

In his short story "The Secret History of World War 3,"[3] J.G. Ballard describes an apparently futuristic, although in many ways quite familiar, scenario: World War III took place on January 27, 1995, between 6:47 and 6:51 p.m. . . . and nobody noticed it. The fact that an event of this magnitude could have remained unknown to most people is indicative of what the condition of postmodernity is for Ballard. In the early 1990s, in a half-imagined, half-real America, President Ronald Reagan is called back to serve a third term and drag the country out of a devastating economic and social crisis, the worst the United States has gone through in the past century. A constitutional amendment is passed to allow the retired Californian to return to office and take America back to the glory days of the 1980s. Immediately upon Reagan's return, the economic situation improves drastically, as if by magic. In a strange displacement of popular support toward a political leader, the US population decides to focus on Reagan's health, which from now on becomes the barometer for how well the nation is doing as a whole. When his health is good, the economy thrives. When his health is poor, the specter of the crisis resurfaces. National TV networks are monitoring the President's health 24 hours a day. If his temperature goes up by a third of a degree, newsflashes interrupt sitcoms and other regularly scheduled programs, and doctors are brought on the set to explain the medical situation and reassure the public. Some networks have even decided to insert printouts of the President's heartbeat and blood pressure readings that scroll at the bottom of the screen. Meanwhile, the Cold War still rages on, and US troops are getting ready to engage a Russian nuclear submarine that has entered US territorial waters off the coast of Alaska. Reagan and his military advisers decide to launch three sea-based nuclear missiles, and the Russians reply by sending two of theirs. There are several casualties on both sides. A few minutes after the exchange of fire, Gorbachev (who has become President of Russia) calls Reagan and an armistice is concluded. The Third World War, a nuclear conflict, lasted no more than 245 seconds. Nobody in the United States noticed the war as everyone was glued to their TV screen, desperately waiting for the next report on Reagan's irregular heartbeat. A few news-anchors briefly mentioned the war, in passing. All in all, it was lost in the flow of information about the President's health. Once the President's heartbeat became normal again, public anxiety immediately subsided.

Ballard's mini-fiction about America in the 1990s is prophetic, and not simply because of his identification of the President with the TV screen (although it is unlikely that a war story would only be mentioned in passing these days). Ballard's short story is an apt allegory for the condition of uncertainty that appears to best describe late twentieth-century America. In the late 1990s and early 2000s, when social situations are explained through the filter of information networks, when individuals desperately seek to identify with televisual icons, and when anxiety is virtually produced and controlled, there is no possibility of ascertaining whether the next world war has already happened or not. For all we know, the nuclear holocaust may have taken place a hundred times over. What remains once uncertainty has taken hold of society (and has deprived individuals of their ability to sort out what is real from what is false) is a sense of generalized anxiety, a common panic, so to speak, that settles on some of the most readily available media and tabloid manipulations, such as Reagan's endless but irregular heartbeat on screen or on the front page of news magazines. As Brian Massumi has put it, "beyond the pale of our accustomed causal laws and classification grids," we live in a world dominated by a multitude of dangers, coming from nowhere and everywhere at the same time.[4] Real or virtual, imagined or experienced, these perceived dangers, and the fear they provoke, are the result of our inability to ground meaning in any fixed category of knowledge or any stable belief system. A generalized sense of panic is what human bodies cling to in an age of uncertainty. At least, it is so until tabloid discourses and representations come in to try to provide a sense of direction and a mode of rationalization to these fears and anxieties.

The production of uncertainty in late modern society cannot be dissociated from the role and impact of the media. As Ballard implies, common anxieties are intricately tied to the media, to what they show, and to how they try to explain social relations. As Marshall McLuhan discovered, "the medium shapes and controls the scale and form of human association and action."[5] For McLuhan, a loss of human identity and of personal values generally followed the advent of the information age. In McLuhan's universe (our late modern universe), human beings surrendered to the media – their vectors of knowledge, pleasure, and convenience – so that they could achieve cultural comfort and develop social interactions on their behalf. McLuhan insisted, however, that this relinquishing of modern subjectivity to the media (their objects, their sounds, their images) came at a cost. By turning to a fully mediatized society, human beings accepted being driven by realities that stood beyond their control. New structural powers, institutional authorities, and semiological codes were thus able to take over the conduct and meaning of the social. They were given full range to recondition the human subject to social effects that were mostly deployed to guarantee the continued domination and control of society by the media. This, for McLuhan, was not a paranoid version of a future that had yet to come. It was rather a half-real and half-prophetic interpretation of the transformation of social life at the hands of the media and their networks of power in the latter part of the twentieth century.

The fateful consequence of this media take-over was for McLuhan the gradual spread of what he called "social numbness." "By putting our physical bodies inside our extended nervous systems, by means of electric media, we set up a dynamic by which all previous technologies that are mere extensions of hands and feet and teeth and bodily heat-controls . . . will be translated into information systems. Electromagnetic technology requires utter human docility and quiescence of meditation such as befits an organism that now wears its brain outside its skull and its nerves outside its hide," McLuhan wrote.[6] Although some of McLuhan's prophecies and analyses turned out to be incorrect,[7] his thought on social numbness is still meaningful in the light of some recent technological innovations. Yet, what is perhaps the most crucial lesson to be retained from McLuhan is his insistence on studying the media more from the perspective of their effects than from their inherent meanings or intentions. As McLuhan suggested, what the media "mean" to the human subjects (the affects linked to the alleged choice of mediatic vectors), or even to the media operators themselves, is beyond the point. It is rather what the media do, how they operate, and what social outcomes they enable once they are allowed to produce meaning-effects that matters. This, in short, can be referred to as media ideology, and McLuhan can be seen as one of the first critical theorists/sociologists of this ideological mode.[8] In a sense derived from McLuhan's analysis, it can be said that the media possess the (technological) capacity to fabricate their version of social reality. This insight forces social and cultural critical analysts to stop worrying about attributing agency to selected media actors, institutions, or users that supposedly possess a capacity to manipulate media messages.[9]

Since McLuhan, this approach to the media and their conditioning work has been developed further, amplified, and popularized (see Ballard's short story for instance). The contemporary social critic and theoretical provocateur Jean Baudrillard has certainly done his share to up the ante in this domain of analysis by going so far as to postulate that the media have an objective life of their own. In the midst of a system of objects where no place is left for human agency, the media freely run the show.[10] For Baudrillard, it is the social itself that has disappeared in the shadow of the conditioning, reality-making world of the media. The media have substituted themselves for the social. What this new "social" domain is populated with are mesmerized audiences, "silent majorities," whose function is to quasi-mechanically respond to the stimuli (soundbites, videobites, databites) emanating directly from the media.[11] Whatever social knowledge or human interactivity appear to be produced in this fashion is completely self-referential. Meaning comes from the media and returns to them. Any capacity of judgment becomes useless, obsolete. According to this generation of meaning referred to as information, the relevance of events and phenomena that are being broadcast is impossible to determine. An event in the information world is at once true and false, real and fictional. Baudrillard calls this condition of undecidability of the event and uncertainty of meaning "hyperreal" modernity.[12] Hyperreality sets in when the medium has used its technical capacities to appear more true-to-life than the objects and/or subjects it purports to represent.

Once again, the exacerbated operation of social numbness and intensified construction of uncertainty are not without power effects. Social numbness and amplified uncertainty facilitate the deployment of a media-induced ideology that seeks to place the media and its institutions at the heart of the new power assemblage. This was clearly diagnosed by Jean-François Lyotard, who indicates that contemporary power manifests itself in the ability to produce meaning-effects. Power, Lyotard contends, is the capacity to fabricate information as knowledge.[13] What this statement implies is that power in the media age has become a matter of devising the most eye-catching scenario, of plugging in the most novel code, or language, or game that will succeed in capturing, if only for a fleeting moment, the attention of the silent majorities. Blinded by the ideological glare of the media, deafened by the white noise of all sorts of informational gimmicks, the inert masses blissfully subscribe to the lifelike reality-(re)making of these late modern social institutions. Lyotard calls this condition not late modern, but rather postmodern. The postmodern condition for Lyotard denotes the passage of social knowledge into media-conditioned and released information. This condition is postmodern, not only because of its temporal emergence, but also, and more importantly, because it revises some of the basic foundations of modern life. Belief systems are made improbable. Human subjectivity is rendered indeterminate. Social meaning is undecidable. And all sorts of potentially conflicting realities are made both immediately available and simultaneously realizable. Additionally, as Ballard suggests, a generalized, illogical, and often unspecified sense of panic is facilitated in this postmodern environment where all scenarios can and often are played out. But this generalized sense of panic is no longer akin to the centralized fear that emanated from the power of the sovereign in the modern era.[14] Rather, it is an evanescent sentiment that anything can happen anywhere to anybody at any time. This postmodern fear is not capable of yielding logical, reasonable outcomes. All it does instead is accelerate the spiraling vortex of media-produced information. All it does is give way to emergencies and emergency discourses that are often the point of departure, both practically and epistemologically, for the tabloid geopolitical representations introduced above (see introductory chapter).

In their own singular ways, Ballard, McLuhan, Baudrillard, and Lyotard help us to understand how media-generated or -infused tabloid discourses about popular fears and emergency responses to perceived dangers become our everyday realities in a highly mediatized society. These discourses are symptoms of the contemporary dominance of media ideology, an ideology that is not steered by one master subject or does not seek to discover or reveal any one truth. These tabloid discourses and representations about fears, dangers, and insecurities to be found in the media universe (and perhaps only there; but is there really an outside to this media universe?) point to the power of and take-over by the media, as McLuhan suggested. They also force us to realize that the meaning of ideology (and its purpose) in a media age has radically been changed and that ideology today, in the media and in tabloid discourses, is not about consistency, certainty, and truth. It is rather about the production (mobilizing and conditioning to be sure) of consistency-effects, certainty-effects, and truth-effects in an era when appearances are key.

The Y2K panic is a case in point. The Y2K (non-)event or appearance of an event was also one of the first cases of the use and abuse of tabloid geopolitical productions of terror as a result of a media-generated fear and emergency. By hammering in the danger of the Y2K bug, multiplying scenarios of what would happen if, for instance, computers were to suddenly read 2000 as 1900 (air traffic would have been paralyzed, banks would have run out of money, telephone service would have been interrupted, VCRs would have stopped recording "real-time" events, national defense computers would have become vulnerable to all sorts of hackers), constantly running programs on TV or on the radio that were meant to provide the viewer or listener with detailed checklists of what s/he needed to do in order to be Y2K ready, and updating everyone on how well or poorly government agencies were dealing with the anticipated glitches, the media made Y2K into a powerfully conditioning event. But the media also unleashed the opportunity for a discourse of danger, emergency, securitization, and terror that precisely sought to provide a sense of direction and a mode of rationalization to the alleged uncertainty and indeterminacy that came along with these new media-induced fears. In this manner, much of the Y2K discourse, both in its tabloid popular cultural mode of presentation and in its reactive and often conservative content, anticipated and announced the tabloid geopolitical texts and imageries that would fill popular and political culture (in the United States mostly) after the September 11 attacks.

Y2K was a media event (or a non-event as it turned out to be) that was based on a combination of emergency (the risk was imminent, the countdown to the millennium became the equivalent of a death threat) and common anxiety. In the wake of such a media frenzy, every statement regarding the phenomenon was made to sound plausible: yes, people across the globe would suddenly find themselves totally disconnected; no, there would be no possible way of retrieving lost data after the Y2K bug hit home computers; yes, people would be out of electricity or water for several days, possibly weeks; no, you would not be able to go to any hospital if you needed to during the first days or weeks of the year 2000, and so on and so forth.[15] Panic and emergency, fueled by the media, helped breed more uncertainty in the public about this entire Y2K phenomenon. The only thing that people soon became convinced of is that there were good reasons (because the media had said so) to be fearful. This was indeed quite reminiscent of Ballard's pre-World War III universe (and of McLuhan's prophecies, Baudrillard's theories, and Lyotard's diagnoses as well). Only this time people were watching Y2K programs on TV, and not live reports on the President's health. Soon, all sorts of experts, technicians, pundits, analysts, intellectuals, and academics – often emerging through the media networks – would join in the panic and would come equipped with a language whose purpose would be not so much to reassure the members of the public, but rather to explain to them why indeed these media-presented dangers and anxieties were not to be doubted. The language and terminology they would use to explain and justify the Y2K scare would make it abundantly clear that emergency scenarios and security measures would be the only possible and rational responses. In the context of Y2K, the key term that these emerging tabloid geopolitical scholars/expert public figures would mobilize would be "cyberterrorism." And the specter of cyberterror (and Y2K now redefined as a cyberterrorist event) was something that could not be messed with.

The next Pearl Harbor will not take place

An investigative special report on the Fox News cable TV network in the fall of 1999, just a few months prior to Y2K, made it its objective to present to the American people what Y2K was really about. The program's purpose was to convince American audiences of the unambiguous reality of what otherwise was quite a sensationalistic report on Y2K. The reality/truth vividly and fearfully introduced in this program was that the next Armageddon was indeed upon us, that there might still be a bit of time left to organize our necessary forces to try to defeat this new terror, but that, in the end, this might not be enough to save us all. This Fox News program, "Danger on the Internet Highway: Cyberterror" (narrated by John Scott),[16] started by offering some basic platitudes about the imminent possibility of cyberterror: the "cyber frontier is the next venue for war;" cyberterrorism is "taking the internet to its most lethal level;" the American supremacy in the domain of information technology is also America's Achilles heel. These were clearly some terrifying warnings that did not really aim at explaining much about cyberterrorism (or even cyberwarfare as the program did not hesitate to call it). The point was rather to mobilize the public through fear and to do it in the flashiest of fashions. The attention of the American public had to be grabbed at all costs. And what could be better able to grab the American public's attention than the revelation of an impending terror coming from one of today's most familiar, user-friendly, necessary, yet technological and somewhat mysterious still household objects: the home computer? "Danger on the Internet Highway" thus needed to convey the danger sharply and efficiently: we had no choice but to look at our PC as "a bomb waiting to explode," the program stated. Lest the viewer had any doubt about the veracity of this prophecy, John Scott, the narrator, repeatedly came back to assure him/her that what s/he was about to witness was "not science fiction!" To further demonstrate the reality and urgency of the situation, the Fox News network producers turned to John Arquilla, a US Navy postgraduate fellow and one of the most prominent experts on cyberattacks and counter-cyberterrorism, whom they used as their main reference and source of authority on this terrifying topic.

Based almost exclusively on Arquilla's "pioneering work" in the field of counter-cyberterror, the program went on to describe a simulation exercise run by Arquilla himself and one of his colleagues. The simulation was intended to determine the effects of a cyberterror attack (very much like what could happen on Y2K) on the nation's main infrastructures. Similar to the "How to Prepare for Y2K" videos that were on sale in department stores in the months before the turn to the millennium, this simulation detailed step by step what damages a planned and systematic cyberterrorist attack would do to the United States. But, unlike some of the Y2K videos, the manufacturers of this made-for-TV program/simulation had no ready answer or safety tips to offer to the consumers/viewers. What the viewer was left with instead was the certainty that something similar to this simulated attack would take place (although it was highly uncertain when and where it would) and that many Americans would die in the process. Again, short of remedies that, hopefully, such a program would help to develop (after all, the American public had the right to know that its government was ill-equipped to respond to such a drastic danger; the American public had the right to demand protection, the Fox News network intimated), fear was really all the viewer was left to hold on to. The simulation of the world's first cyberterrorist war started with an admonition: our government probably would not know when or if the world's first cyberwar had started, but our adversaries, whoever they were, would undoubtedly let us know! And, as a matter of fact, this is exactly how the simulation started. In the summer of 2000, an unknown militant group targets several of the most frequently used websites and servers to display its manifesto asking for the withdrawal of all US military personnel from (where else?) the Middle East. In cyberjargon, this is the equivalent of a "spam attack." A few hours later, computer screens in all Federal Aviation Administration track-on facilities go blank: obviously, the cyberterrorists have chosen to target the US airways first. From a strategic point of view, this move was well calculated. Within a few minutes air tragedies are reported from all the corners of the nation. The first American victims of this cyberwarfare attack die in airplane crashes. Shortly afterwards, air transportation has to be paralyzed. All non-essential air traffic is grounded until further notice. The President appears on TV, trying to reassure the public. Meanwhile, the Pentagon's cyberwarriors are already devising strategies to counter the enemy and put an end to "the hack of the century," as the program calls it. But, as Arquilla interjects, "anonymity on the internet makes it difficult to identify the enemy." In the uncertainty that reigns, it becomes convenient to assume that a rogue nation may be behind the attack. Day 1 of the world's first cyberterror war (a war on the United States only, by the way) ends with a few hundred US civilian casualties. On Day 2, the cyberterrorists have decided to push their assault further. They are now aiming at the supercomputers that control the heart of the country's infrastructure. Principally, they are targeting the computers that regulate the electric power-supply grids. These are controlled by passwords, but the terrorist hackers have been able to decode them. Using "ping attacks" this time (a randomly performed barrage of aimless data that diverts or overloads the digital circuits and systems), the terrorists are able to hit the main computer of a large power plant in the state of Washington. A series of power failures all over the west coast ensues. There are also reports of phone connections being down from Oregon to California. In turn, the rupture in the power grids is responsible for several car accidents and heart attacks. The amount of civilian casualties is rising. All of a sudden, a nuclear power plant in the Midwest has gone critical. Can this be because of the cyberattack? Two trains in Cleveland, Ohio have collided. Did the cyberwar cause this too? Rumors are starting to spread that the Pentagon's main computers may be affected too. Is this true? Nobody knows for sure. The public worries. Panic has taken over the country. As a result, Wall Street takes a major tumble. Meanwhile, at the White House, the President and his staff are still trying to determine who is behind the attacks. Are these the Russians? Some Middle-Eastern group? As Arquilla reminds us, this is almost impossible to figure out since, after all, "there is no geography on the internet." On Day 3 of the world's first cyberwar, civil unrest has spread throughout the country. But finally the counter-cyberterrorists have a breakthrough. The CIA, FBI, the Pentagon, and other intervening factors (including, as the narrator mentions, "plain old dumb luck") have been able to identify the source of the attacks. It is all coming from a little-known country that, up to now, was thought to possess very little information technology. But, after all, as John Scott notes, "there are a lot of disgruntled information technicians out there who, after the Cold War, are looking for jobs and are willing to offer their services to rogue nations." Having identified the enemy, the White House must decide how to retaliate. Will the response be through the vector of internet technologies or will it be more conventional? The narrator suggests that, in all likelihood, the United States will opt for a more conventional retaliation, sending special forces to the invading country to place cybertaps on the power lines of the enemy.

The simulation ends here. What happens next, both in terms of the more conventional war (since the enemy has finally been identified) and in terms of rebuilding the country's information infrastructure, is beyond the scope of the simulation. It is, as the program mentions, "anybody's guess what comes next." But what the simulation showed for sure, however, was that "cyberwarfare is an impending threat." This was now beyond any doubt. Cyberterror would be the type of war in use in the twenty-first century, and it might even come as early as January 1, 2000.

The cyberterror simulation presented in this Fox News program was not representative of most cyberattacks that indeed did (and still do) take place everyday in the United States. Most of these attacks were (and still are) more benign or limited in range, even if some have already affected the CIA's and even the Pentagon's computers. Yet, the simulation presented on Fox News was quite "real," and the dangers it displayed were supposedly immediate. At least, this was the intended message. This kind of simulated scenario was aimed at convincing the American public that cyberterrorism was imminent and would be extremely destructive. Its point was simply to show America what the "next Pearl Harbor" would be like. The next Pearl Harbor would be an attack that would hit America both everywhere and nowhere at the same time. Its target would not be the US military or defense system but, instead, the US public and its post-industrial, highly informatized lifestyle. What was for the time being a tool of comfort, an object of leisure, or a necessary support for work (information, computer technology, the internet) would soon become the world's deadliest weapon. And, this time, being hit at its core, the US public would have a difficult time recovering from this inevitable Pearl Harbor of the future.

Ironically, the "next Pearl Harbor" would indeed take place less than two years later, although not quite in the manner envisaged in this Fox News program. Terrorists attacking both everywhere and nowhere at the same time would hit the United States on September 11, 2001, and other "objects" of American everyday culture would be utilized by the attackers (airplanes this time, not computers). More importantly, beyond this somewhat eerie resemblance between the "Danger on the Internet Highway" show and 9/11, the Fox News network special report placed a certain type of geopolitical and security discourse at the heart of Americans' daily life concerns. From Y2K on, fears and panics in the media would necessarily be accompanied with tabloid discourses and representations such as this one, featuring all sorts of experts (and their studies, research, exceptional insights, or simulations) who, far from providing answers or solutions, would mainly be interested in preparing the public to respond to these new unquestionable dangers and insecurities in manners that could not always be rationalized. These would be the truths (as truth-effects once again) and rationalizations (as simulacra of rational answers) that those tabloid experts' discourses would want to produce. I now turn to some of these so-called rationalizations or truth-effects that appeared in those fledgling tabloid geopolitical discourses of terror around the time of Y2K and that sought to bring cyberterrorism into public focus.

Net wars, ping attacks, and digital casualties

The idea of the media today needs to be understood in a broad sense. This is the way McLuhan intended the media to be understood. For McLuhan, the media were an "electric galaxy" composed of multiple objects or material supports (from the telephone to the radio, from comic strips to cinema) that mattered more for the various effects they had on the social environment and for the way they recombined (and at times "retribalized," as he put it) the culture of "modern man."[17] The media today, then, are not just to be thought of as specific objects but also as vast networked assemblages of information-producing technologies. The media universe that makes our everyday culture at the turn of the millennium is as much about TV networks that produce programs such as "Danger on the Internet Highway" (and, in the process, turn academics and technical experts into new public figures of danger and terror) as it is about the multiple pamphlets, manifestos, or reports issued by organized networks of specialists, communities of intellectuals, or governmental agencies' advisers and researchers that detail the alleged threats and go through great lengths to announce the impending collapse of society, in part or in whole, once these threats materialize. These pamphlets, manifestos, or reports are mediatized and become media (just as Fox News is, for example) because they shape the cultural domain around the fears, anxieties, and insecurities of everyday life. They are also tabloid (in the sense developed in the introduction to this book) because they are discursive formations that build upon such fears and anxieties to produce certain geopolitical "realities" that claim to be undebatable popular truths and convincing commonsensical rationalizations. These media and discourses of fear that give (cyber)terror a textual basis take various forms: newspaper articles, books, academic conference papers, websites, essays posted on the internet, email messages or blogs, videos, TV programs, films, and so on. What makes these materials cyberterror-producing media is less their formal mode of appearance (visual, written, or digital) than their ideological, and, once again, tabloid, motivation. Indeed, these tabloid media/discourses operate a literal *mediation* between individuals (the public, human bodies) who receive the messages/images they provide and the cultural environment in which individuals interact/interface. As suggested above (by Ballard in particular), these tabloid media/discourses become authority-wielding and authoritative systems of knowledge and truth that intervene in culture to explain to uncertain individuals what it is that they see, hear, fear, feel, experience, love, or hate.

The alleged novelty of cyberterrorism as an object of knowledge and truth is by and large the result of this kind of media-work. Once again, multiple mediatized and tabloid supports and materials are involved in the production of cyberterrorism as a taken-for-granted reality of today's information age. From sensationalistic TV shows that create the concept by supposedly reporting it to the public to a plethora of texts (most of which are immediately made available on the internet) on post-Cold War national security by actual or would-be representatives of the defense or security community, these tabloid media have the cyberterrorist event (and its fear- and emergency-producing effects) pretty much under control. Despite giving the appearance to the public that nobody knows where the new threats come from, when the new terrorists will strike, and who the victims of those attacks will be, the cyberterror-making media have all the keys to the fabricated problem. They have the appropriate language to make sense of it; they have identified the key players; they have devised the main moves and counter-moves. In short, they have established all the sufficient parameters of cyberterrorism as, once again, a discursive formation in a game of simulated reality where the successful outcome is to create or maintain fear, emergency and securitization. Beyond this result, the game/discourse has no obvious purpose (as we saw with the Fox News show above).

Taxonomy

Cyberterrorism, as it emerged in tabloid media and discourses around 1999, was not an evanescent, chaotic threat, even though many media sources liked to convey that image to the public. On the contrary, media/tabloid discourses organized cyberterrorism into categories, strategies, typologies, and methodologies that made it possible to talk about it (as a threat, a fear, a virtual danger) and to produce more knowledge/truth about it (but mostly as an anticipated sense of ever-present emergency, planning, and security). One may in fact suggest that what may be called a media-based taxonomy of cyberterrorism developed in the months prior to Y2K.[18] This taxonomy of cyberterrorism was supported and often embellished by a technocratic language, supposedly adapted to the threat, that sought to give the impression that there was truly something unique about this danger, and that a community of media experts and tabloid intellectuals was best able to address the population about it. Both the taxonomy of cyberterrorism and its specialized language added to the drama (as we started to see in the Fox News program).

Back in the months that preceded Y2K, the taxonomy of cyberterrorism was established upon the following reasoning: (1) not every cyberterrorist act had to be a threat to national security; (2) not every security-threatening cyberterrorist attack would lead to cyberwarfare; and yet (3) all forms of cyberterror had the potential to turn into a major national catastrophe. The first part of this reasoning served to operate a distinction between "amateur cracking" and willful cyberterrorist disruption. These were two possible modalities of what was (and still is) known as "hacking." As Barry Collin, member of the Institute for Security and Intelligence, noted: "A great deal of 'cracks' are committed for the purposes of anarchy, humor, or as often stated by the perpetrators, to be annoying."[19] This cracking terrorism was not to be seen as the number one worry of the security and defense community of cyberterror experts. After all, these experts claimed, these types of attack were often acts of teenage loners, dorky adolescent punk wannabes, who found an escape from their social isolation or ineptitude by playing with what they knew best: computers. These "cracks" could nonetheless become serious if they escalated, but they could also be dismissed quickly. Their range of action was often limited. Scare the kids, and they would not do it again! This type of hacking was not, according to the cyberterrorism-producing tabloid/media discourses, to be construed as a "genuine" cyberterrorist act. It found its place only in the margins of the cyberterrorist taxonomy.

By contrast, the second case-scenario was supposedly more daunting. The "real cyberterrorists [would] remotely access the processing control systems of a cereal manufacturer, change the levels of iron supplement, and sicken and kill the children of a nation enjoying their food,"[20] we were told. Now, this was more serious stuff! Unlike the cracking loner, the "genuine" cyberterrorist wanted to harm, weaken, possibly kill. The dangerous cyberterrorist had a long-range strategy of action placed at the service of a cause s/he wanted to promote. This type of cyberterrorist was clearly presented as a threat to America's national security, and the public had to realize it. In fact, this type of cyberterrorist may well have had the nation at his/her mercy, and Y2K may have been a prime target/opportunity for it. Thus, this was s/he that the nation needed to fear the most. The cybergeek prankster could be disciplined. But the cyberterrorist criminal had to be profiled, identified, contained, possibly annihilated, these new experts were telling us. Such was the first distinction upon which the cyberterrorist taxonomy constructed by the cyberterror-producing media operated.

But not all serious and dangerous cyberterrorists would make it to the level of cyberwarriors, that is to say, would want to launch a sustained and tactical assault on the nation, its culture, and its values. Consequently, a second distinction needed to be established in those tabloid discourses of cyberterrorism. This second distinction suggested that, on the one hand, there were cyberterrorist criminals who would use computer technology for their own purpose. They would hack info technology to steal credit or calling card numbers, to obtain somebody else's digital records, to access private databases. In short, they would seek to enhance their personal position (power, wealth). This was what was sometimes referred to as "Personal Information Warfare" (PIW). As a bulletin on Personal Information Warfare posted on the internet in 2000 stated, this type of cyberterrorist attack "does not seem to be a potential threat [to national security], but can easily destroy someone's identity."[21] The Personal Information Warriors could serve their own interests, or they could work for a larger organization, such as a cybermafia, or a private corporation intent on spying or obtaining valuable information about a competitor. On the other hand, there were the real cyberterrorist activists and practitioners who were more terrorist in spirit than the hackers. They were traditional terrorists from rogue nations or transnational networks of terror (Bin Laden's al Qaeda network, for instance) who had finally discovered how technology could be used to fulfill their main cause, namely, destroying the American nation. These were the true warriors of the internet, the ones to be feared by the public. They were able to upgrade their arsenal of terror from conventional weapons to digital armaments, our terror experts told us. This last group of (cyber)terrorists had clearly stated political motivations. These were often referred to as "postmodern terrorists"[22] or "rogue state warriors,"[23] whose ability and, more importantly, intention was to cause huge casualties. These cyberterrorists and the threats they represented to the state (mostly the American state) were really what the above-mentioned apocalyptic scenarios and simulations were about. These were the paroxysmic versions of a cyberterror scale that started from the local teenage hacker and went all the way to the America-hating (cyber)warrior. While these different levels of threats and conditions of cyberdisturbance needed to be distinguished by the public in order to establish a gradation of fear, all of them nonetheless had to be treated as very sizeable risks, particularly in the uncertain context of Y2K. The degree of emergency could vary according to the location of the cyberterror threat on this constructed scale. But the nation as a whole, and its people (that is, the media audience), could not afford to let their guard down. Constant preparedness and growing securitization were presented as the main defense weapons.

Netwar

The cyberterrorist taxonomists were concerned with the cybercriminals identified through the first distinction, and the agents of what was often diagnosed as "netwar" profiled through the second opposition. In fact, these two groups were sometimes combined in the pre-9/11 discourses on (cyber)terror. The two basic distinctions also had the tendency to converge on the profiled identity of the criminal cyberterrorist netwarrior. Having cleaned up the field of cyberterrorist activity by putting to the side the pranksters, the hacking thieves, and other corporate spies, what the cybersecurity tabloid media and experts were now left with were networks of terror (the term would return in a slightly different context after 9/11) that at times claimed allegiance to certain nation-states or otherwise simply wished to identify themselves with "nonstate, paramilitary, and irregular forces" across the globe.[24] Netwar, what these networks of terror were said to be preparing for, was what the cyberterror-making media and experts spent a great deal of time detailing.

Netwar was defined as "an emerging mode of conflict and crime at societal levels, involving measures short of traditional war, in which the protagonists use network forms of organization and related doctrines, strategies, and technologies attuned to the information age."[25] Moreover, it was assumed that "these protagonists are likely to consist of dispersed small groups who communicate, coordinate, and conduct their campaigns in an internetted manner, without a precise central command."[26] In a redundant fashion, it was argued that the two defining characteristics of netwar were the presence of terrorist networks and their ability to use advanced information technologies. Never clearly specified in such a taxonomic schema, but always implied in the classifications, was netwar's final intent: to produce an uncontrollable large-scale disturbance to an existing socio-politico-economic order. This "total disturbance" outcome of netwar could be slightly modified depending on the terrorists' more specific objectives. Again, the objectives of netwar had to be contained in a taxonomic table. Four possible objectives were advanced: exploitation, deception, disruption, and destruction.[27] These objectives were certainly not unique to netwar and its agents. Similar objectives have been classically attributed to more conventional forms of terrorism and even to belligerents involved in "real" warfare. What was supposedly different about those four possible goals of netwar was that they were accomplished by means of not yet fully mastered technologies (the public could not fully grasp the strength of info technology yet; by and large, the public had not been physically or even digitally victimized by these technologies as the Fox News program reminded us) and, more importantly, that their proponents, as loose networks, were not easily identifiable. Once again, the public was repeatedly told that there was "no geography on the internet" and, thus, that the source of the attacks could be both inside and outside the nation-state. In truth, the cyberterrorist netwarrior operated across nation-state borders. And this was precisely what gave credence and legitimacy to simulated scenarios like the "Danger on the Internet Highway" program on the Fox News network.

Ping attacks and other cyberweapons

Instead of pondering over this transversality of netwar attacks, the taxonomists of cyberterror took for granted netwar's challenge to territorial sovereignty. From this point, they moved on to categorize the different modes of attack that assuredly presented an as yet unstoppable threat to the state, its territory, and its population. Existing or virtual modes of attack in netwar situations were the flashy and exciting aspects of cyberterrorism, at least for these tabloid media experts and intellectuals. This was also what turned cyberterrorist attacks into sensationalistic TV shows. Forms of cyberterrorist attacks and their weapons were clearly what the media wanted to highlight. And so the taxonomic deployment of cyberterror knowledge/truth continued. Four categories of attacks were typically identified. These were data attacks, software attacks, hacking attacks, and physical attacks.[28] Each attack also had its own subset of strategic weaponry. A data attack consisted of inserting new, fraudulent, junk, or spoiled data into a healthy information system to provoke its malfunction or, instead, to facilitate its functioning in an unexpected manner. Spamming, swarming or ping attacks, we were told, were typical subsets of such attack strategies. Software attacks were similar in their operationalization to data attacks, except that they aimed at destroying the infected system. In software attack situations, the weapons of choice were viruses, worms or Trojan horses.[29] Hacking, as described above, was not peculiar to netwar. It consisted of taking control of an existing information system, often by cracking its codes or breaking its passwords. Finally, physical attacks were conventional assaults (bombs, military operations) on facilities that were suspected of housing crucial information or data.

Digital casualties

Such were then the assumed conditions and circumstances that allegedly made an electronic Pearl Harbor an impending threat to American society around the Y2K timeframe. The purpose of this multi-layered taxonomy was supposedly to better prepare the US population. The nation's people would indeed be the target. They would be the main casualties of this inevitable war. Although many casualties would be human (the children of the nation, as was mentioned above), more than likely the more common victims would be the part of us that had become essentially dependent upon information technologies to live. In the information age, the split between the human body and the world "out there" was no longer a dominant dichotomy. To this previous, modern, division, another dualism had been added. The body was now additionally split into two components: its physical part, still necessary for the human being to function (eat, sleep, breathe); and the digital body, which relied upon mostly computerized technologies to "live well" in this day and age.[30] The digital body was that part of the human that turned to email to communicate, went online to find meaningful relationships, shop, have sex, or simply experience image flows (on TV, on the internet, in video arcades) as a substitute for everyday life. The digital body could not exist without its physical complement. But the physical body would be aimless without its digital extensions. As Manuel Castells argued, digital life was the product of the emergence of an information network society.[31] As network society developed new forms of material existence managed through flows of interdependent information, digital beings were created. But the risk that digital beings could vanish because of a rupture or disruption in the information flows was a growing concern. In short, information networks could bring new forms of existence and disappearance too. Digital casualties were seen as one main form of disappearance in the information age. In a sense, yesterday's hapless victims of gunfire and bomb attacks were about to become today's digital casualties of cyberterrorist data swarming and ping assaults.

Cyberterrorism may sometimes have had the "real" body as its target. But, by and large, cyberterrorism was taking aim at the digital body. Often, to get to the physical body, cyberterrorist warriors had to decide to eliminate the digital components of the individual first, knowing that the physical would not last long without its digital extensions. When Graeme Browning of the *National Journal* was asked by the publishers of the US government agencies' newsletter *The Daily Fed* to detail the potential casualties of terrorist cyberattacks, he mentioned telephone lines, bank computers, and the Pentagon's data files.[32] The victims that had already fallen prey to cyberterrorism in the United States had been home computers' hard drives, bank accounts online, social security numbers inside government's computer systems, and so forth.[33] For counter-cyberterrorists, protecting the digital body (of the nation, of its people) was now presented as the number one priority. At the turn of the millennium, a Cyber Threat Assessment Report by the newly created National Infrastructure Protection Center emphasized the reality of "sensitive intrusions" into computer networks, from the Department of Defense's computers to personal laptops. It urged that emergency counter-measures be taken in this crucial domain of national defense and security.[34] Not only were the digital bodies of US citizens in danger because of cyberterrorism, but the digital body of the nation as a whole (starting with the DoD's own computers) was at risk too. In the information age, the physical death of an organism/organization was apparently less significant than its digital disconnection.

This realization was symptomatic of what some cyberculture critics have called the posthuman condition.[35] The posthuman condition is based upon the following assumptions. First, information patterns are preferred over material substance, the so-called "world out there." Second, the postulate of human consciousness gives way to sentient machines that turn the thinking subject into a "minor sideshow." Third, the body is an original prosthesis, and nothing more than this. It is a prosthesis upon which other prosthetic layers can be grafted. Fourth, through the prosthetization of the human body, the gap between body and machine can be easily overcome. The human body can thus be "seamlessly articulated with intelligent machines."[36] What results then is the fabrication of a posthuman environment populated with digital bodies (DBs) and artificial intelligences (AIs). We, as subjects of this environment, are left with an expanded panoply of techno-sensitive objects that allow us to interface as posthumans, or cybernetic organisms.[37] At some level, at the time of Y2K in particular, we all became posthuman. Posthuman subjects were presented as living in postsocial states whose security now had to be defined in cybernetic terms. In order to protect its posthuman citizens, the postsocial state had to rely upon an infonetwork-originated fear that kept the posthuman subjects in a constant state of anticipated disaster and collective anxiety. Again, this could be seen to take place to the detriment of the body in the present moment, and perhaps to the detriment of human social interactions in time. A postsociety of posthumans would erase unmediated experience. It would substitute for it a series of prosthetic and virtually cognitive encounters. In this (post)socio-cultural context, cyberterrorism was constructed as a (post)human threat. Indeed, according to cyberterrorist netwarriors, to win the game, digital bodies had to fall.

Inducing fear

In 1999, a National Security Agency adviser stated that "we need to know what normal behavior" is in cyberspace.[38] Determining normal behavior was crucial if we wanted to protect ourselves from abnormal activities now thought to be found mainly in the digital world. Normal and abnormal digital bodies now had to be accounted for. Once again, taxonomies created by the media and embellished in tabloid discourses of cyberterror provided necessary bases of knowledge and truth on this subject matter. These taxonomies facilitated profiling, allowed experts to detect suspicious cyberbehavior, and would help the US government to deter the deployment of delinquent cyberactivities. If counter-cyberterrorism were to be successful, the practice of cyberterrorism first had to be organized into such categories of information-gathering (and -making). If cyberterrorism were to be countered, and its digital casualties were to be minimized, a proper language addressing this specific threat had to be invented too. The mission of these taxonomists was also to provide such an expert technostrategic language. By deploying a specific language within the bounds of the taxonomy, the threat would be more easily controlled. At least, this was one of the advanced objectives of this taxonomic organization.

This use of taxonomy and technocratic jargon on the part of the cyberterror-producing media is reminiscent of the type of strategies and rhetorics that were deployed by nuclear defense specialists during the Cold War. In her seminal essay on the role of linguistic metaphors, puns, and acronyms in the field of nuclear defense strategy, Carol Cohn has shown how specific uses of language were mobilized to de-dramatize the actual threat.[39] Giving deadly weapons pet names, using a rhetoric replete with sexual innuendo and gender stereotyping allowed the defense analysts to de-realize the threat and treat it as if it were a purely technical matter. Through the production of such rhetorical signs, the nuclear threat had been domesticized. Additionally, this language was pitched at such a level of technocratic abstraction that it became almost impossible for those who employed it to grasp familiar notions such as war, death, or human destruction. For these "real-life" situations, abstracted notions such as collateral damage, surgical strike, and countervalue attack had been substituted. War, death, and human destruction no longer made sense within such a system.

The taxonomy of cyberterrorism and its specific language formed their own emergency and securitization system. For any individual still rooted in the analog world (as opposed to the digital domain), this language created a system of abstraction too. Simply, it was divorced from the real world. But, even if we still insisted on treating the taxonomy of cyberterrorism as a system of abstraction, we had no choice but to note in this case the opposite of what Cohn appeared to witness with regard to the nuclear strategists of the late Cold War era. The language of cyberterrorism mobilized by the media and its experts was quite technical for sure. But this technicality, far from de-realizing the threat, actually rendered it possible. It realized it in the mind/psyche of the public, which was now subjected to the simulated scenarios and mediations in the broader context of the Y2K anxious and uncertain social environment. The taxonomy of cyberterrorism and its technocratic language allowed the public to recognize that there *was* a threat, and that this threat, as presented to it by the media and its new experts, would surely cause serious casualties within the population.

At the same time though, the public was not supposed to gain mastery over such a highly technocratic language. The public had to receive the message from the media and its tabloid geopolitical intellectuals, but members of the public were not allowed to speak the language through which the message was spread. It was once again an expert language, a language of knowledge, security, and danger. The technocratic jargon and the taxonomy it helped to construct in a sense buffered the media, its specialists, and their discourse from the public. While the language and the taxonomy were deployed by the media and cyberterrorist experts to proliferate the fear about the threat, the media were by the same token in a position of authority vis-à-vis the ignorant and soon-to-be victimized population. The ideological buffer created by this powerful discourse, then, was really not between the population and the so-called cyberterrorist warriors, but instead between the media and the population itself. By constructing an unfathomable threat and spreading an ethereal panic, the cyberterrorism-producing media imposed themselves as the most omniscient subjects, who derived their power from their ability to manipulate the emotions of the populace. This construction of fear was in fact a terrorist mechanism too. In a sense, the cyberterrorism-producing media terrorized the public by shoving in the public's face images and discourses that hammered in the presence of an uncertain danger and the need to take desperate emergency measures. Perversely, the tabloid media and their specialized discourses used against the public the same type of cyberterrorist weapons they claimed to be condemning: data swarming, information overload, security conspiracies on the internet, and so on. Faced with such a regime of mediatized/tabloid terror, there was only one thing the population could and in fact was encouraged to do: be afraid, be very afraid.

From televisual fear to e-anxiety? The spaces and discourses of tabloid panic

More than ten years ago, the authors of the *Panic Encyclopedia* had anticipated the dominant social condition that would culminate with the Y2K scare. "Panic," they claimed, "is the key psychological mood of the postmodern culture."[40] Late modern or postmodern panic does come with the media, their community of newly discovered experts, and their conditioning and mobilizing (ideological) operations. For some time, television had remained the main reality-producing medium. Fear was thought by many to be "the political aesthetic of the medium of television" principally.[41] As the live image of the September 11 terrorist attacks would reveal, this would still be the case in the new millennium. But although fear was and still is on and about TV, new interfacial media emerged at the end of the 1990s and started to compete with television over the "control" of the production of mediatized/tabloid fear and panic.[42] The internet, for many (starting with cyberterror experts), then began to replace and displace television as the main source of panic. Y2K was once again a prime example of such a phenomenon. The Y2K panic, some claimed, was symptomatic of "the anxiety of the network society."[43] What seemed to make internet panic or e-anxiety so much more vivid and credible than televisual fear at the end of the 1990s was the fact that individuals online often lost the sentiment that their encounter with the "real" world was indeed mediated. Unlike television, which broadcasts fear but at the same time appears to buffer viewers (you could be at home sitting in your sofa watching war news), the internet gives its users the feeling of an immediacy of dangers hidden in the digital world but that at any moment could spring onto their laptop computers. With Y2K, fear was thus depicted as a "real" possibility since the immediacy of the digital/internet link was thought to replace the inter-mediacy or inter-mediation of television.

Y2K never led to the catastrophic scenarios that were predicted and projected. Cyberterrorism was not unleashed in Y2K's aftermath. Instead, more "conventional" terrors have returned since then. With 9/11, televisual fear would once again become the main vector of anxiety and apprehension for many. In many ways, as the Y2K phenomenon and the corollary cyberterror tabloid discourses around the time of the end of the last millennium revealed, TV panic and internet anxiety have been and will continue to be complementary mediatic modalities of production of fear. Visual images via cable or satellite television networks and digital data via cybernetic connections add up to the panoply of the digital/human body today. In truth, as was shown above, both television and the internet contributed to the creation of cyberterror as the next apocalyptic scenario, an apocalypse that nonetheless did not take place. In the context of the early twenty-first century version of an electric galaxy where television and the internet play off one another, combine and collaborate to bombard the (post)human body with stimulations and simulations that mobilize and terrorize, new tabloid discourses of danger, emergency, security, and war (cyber or conventional) are encouraged, develop, and in fact thrive. These discourses further exacerbate the conditioning of the public by means of panic and terror. As was suggested in this chapter, the invention and organization of cyberterrorism in the discourses of tabloid media (once again understood broadly) are terror-producing regimes that hope to create some truths and arrive at some rationalizations about emergency scenarios and security strategies. As the next chapter will show (confirming some of this chapter's findings), the lure of tabloid geopolitical discourses did not have to wait for the 9/11 terrorist attacks to find a use and be deployed by some intellectuals and academics of statecraft. In a way, Y2K and cyberterrorism were the symptoms of a tabloid discourse (called tabloid realism in the next chapter) already well advanced and developed by the time of the turn of the millennium.

2 Tabloid realism and the reconstruction of American security culture before 9/11

We are entering a bifurcated world. Part of the globe is inhabited by Hegel's and Fukuyama's Last Man, healthy, well fed, and pampered by technology. The other, larger, part is inhabited by Hobbes's First Man, condemned to a life that is "poor, nasty, brutish, and short." Although both parts will be threatened by environmental stress, the Last Man will be able to master it; the First Man will not. The Last Man will adjust to the loss of underground water tables in the western United States. He will build dikes to save Cape Hatteras and the Chesapeake beaches from rising sea levels, even as the Maldives Islands, off the coast of India, sink into oblivion, and the shorelines of Egypt, Bangladesh, and South-east Asia recede, driving tens of millions of people inland where there is no room for them, and thus sharpening ethnic divisions.

Robert D. Kaplan[1]

Tabloid culture today

Pointing to the inescapable conditioning power of tabloid press and tabloid talk-shows (and their hosts) in late twentieth-century America, culture critic Joshua Gamson once wrote: "You know you're in trouble when Sally Jessy Raphael seems like your best bet for being heard, understood, respected and protected."[2] Paraphrasing Gamson, I would like to suggest that you are equally in trouble when Robert D. Kaplan seems like your best bet to redefine geopolitical realities, diagnose foreign policy threats, and prescribe new ways of thinking about national security in the twenty-first century. In the case of Sally Jessy Raphael's talk-show and of Kaplan's endless succession of doomsday prophecies, we are witnessing a similar popular socio-cultural phenomenon: tabloid realism at its best (or worst).

As indicated in the Introduction, the notion of tabloid media is not novel.[3] In the United States (in the 1920s to 1930s), the popular impact of tabloid publications found its point of departure in the need or desire to sensationalize reality at all costs. Tabloid realism's premise was and still is that the public does not want to be told about their everyday life. Americans do not want to read or hear that they are underpaid, overworked, bullied at work, in the home, when serving their country in foreign lands. They want glamorous stories, scandals, exceptional events, news they can build dreams on or develop a sense of anger from. In short, they want to be entertained.

And yet, consumers of tabloid literatures and tabloid images do not want complete fiction either. They do not want the newspapers they read or the shows they watch to be about someone else's reality. They still insist on reading stories that somehow are about them, are related to their own life, work environment, or everyday practices. Tabloid literatures must be based on "real-life" contexts, on issues and problems that members of the public have had a chance to experience, if only in small doses, or because they know or have heard of somebody else (a neighbor, a colleague at work, a family member) whose situation appears to be exactly what the tabloid story reveals. Jane Shattuc summarizes the intention of tabloid reporting by noting that tabloid texts must have a "populist emphasis on the injustices done to the 'average' American" and, at the same time, they must display "the allure of the extremes of vividly told stories."[4] In the tabloid medium, reality must be described and truth must be revealed in a flashy, surprising, gripping, shocking, often moralizing, and generally anxiety-inducing manner. The reality of tabloid realism is a sensational one.[5] But the tabloid narrative must also be made accessible to a large amount of people. It must use images and languages that can be readily understood and easily recognized by the vast majority of "Americans."

If the tabloid genre of reporting has retained many of its initial early twentieth-century attributes today, tabloid culture has also undergone important modifications over the past ten to twenty years. The tabloid genre has gone postmodern in order to, as Glynn explains, adapt to a media "environment that is marked by such an odd yet increasingly characteristic mélange of images and discourses [which provokes for the public] a strange admixture of exhaustion and desire for the next media event long before the present one has even reached its culmination."[6] Clearly, a passion for what is sleazy, graphic, and provoking has always been part of tabloid culture. But postmodernity provides the tabloid genre with additional tools and techniques that allow the proponents and consumers of this media/literary discourse to enhance their experience. In a sense, postmodernity is the golden age of tabloid culture. As Glynn suggests, postmodernity offers four dominant modalities of analysis and experimentation that serve tabloid purposes.[7] First, in the condition of postmodernity, increased media coverage and image saturation embellish the always graphic and spectacular mode of tabloid reporting by attaching visual signs to the story. Not only is tabloid reporting to be confined to newspapers and other periodicals, but television too can become tabloid. In fact, some television shows (talk-shows in particular, but also investigative reports, as we saw in Chapter 1) become prototypical cases of tabloid "truth-telling" in postmodern times. Second, postmodern analysis (allegedly a reflection on postmodern times) offers the possibility to challenge and unsettle modern categories of thinking and representation. The very notion of "reality" is problematized as media culture provides daily material proof of the existence of multiple levels of "reality" and "representation." The world "out there" (a naturalist assumption) and the world perceived from the perspective of the rational subject (rationalism) are no longer the only existing alternatives for human cognition. Instead, and increasingly so, the world of the media and their reality-constructing effects must be considered too in order to adjudicate between different domains of experience or between different "truths." Tabloid literatures and shows in a postmodern era benefit from this ability of the media (and culture in general) to make multiple truths possible. The third modality of postmodernity/postmodernism affecting tabloid reporting is directly derived from the previous point. As claims to unique, clearly identifiable truths are being challenged, the tendency of social, political, and cultural thinkers to provide "grand narratives" to make sense of society, politics, and culture is abandoned. Rather, all sorts of stories, events, questions, and choices can be objects of worthwhile knowledge and of information production. As "grand narratives" disappear and more relativistic presentations set in, knowledge is also more fragmented, dispersed, and plural. To some extent, anything can become a "subject of knowledge," a motto that tabloid culture had already made its own well before the advent of postmodernity. This relativist attack against meta-narratives pluralizes the ways one may go about collecting information and disseminating it. This is Glynn's fourth main point about postmodernity and tabloid culture. As the "truth" is no longer held inside a sacred sphere that must remain unsoiled by popular activities (not even in "high politics"), multiple "cultural products marked by stylistic eclecticism and bricolage" can be valid tools of knowledge too.[8] An aesthetic apprehension of the world can become the main determinant for investigation and analysis. And aesthetics can be found to be a sufficient justification for politics and/or ethics (and their representation).

The result of this encounter between postmodernity and tabloid culture is a general uncertainty (and anxiety perhaps too) about the nature of the product that is being consumed by the readers/viewers of the tabloid spectacle (as we saw in the previous chapter). Yet, the consumers of this genre are generally able to transcend the discomfort produced by this uncertainty (Is this true or not? Is it credible? Is that what I want to see or not?) to embrace the spectacle, its message, and perhaps more importantly its image. The tabloid story today remains popular, not only because of the contents of the stories (by and large, they still cater to a lower- to middle-class audience), but also because of the entertaining style or format on which this cultural medium is based. As Glynn mentioned, in postmodern/tabloid culture, the next image must be consumed even when the previous one has not had a chance to reach its completion. Yet, the entertaining presentation of the tabloid genre does not limit this mode of reporting to typically "trash cultural" topics.[9] Rather, so-called serious topics can be treated as well. But when these topics are covered, they are still dealt with as a mixture of information and entertainment. As "infotainment," these "serious" issues are introduced as (media) "events" whose images linger long enough for certain cultural effects to be created, but never long enough for such so-called events to be thoroughly analyzed and judged by methods other than postmodern modalities of investigation.

Geopolitics and popular media

In an age dominated by tabloid culture and in which politics is increasingly experienced by the public as trash entertainment, international politics also becomes a prime target of sensationalism, scandal news, injustice reporting, and crude moralizing. As we saw in Chapter 1, the Y2K (non-)event and the fear of cyberterrorism already contributed to a fusion of international political matters (national security, state sovereignty, warfare) with low or middlebrow modes of cultural representation and truth-telling (via cable TV news programs, the internet, home videos, and so on). Thus, since the late 1990s, American foreign policy and those who hope to influence its formulation have not been immune from the spread of tabloid culture. Moreover, those who have written about the foreign affairs of the United States of late, consciously or not, have often found themselves adopting a style of writing and presentation that is characteristically and perhaps purposefully tabloid. They seek to shock their audience, try to take them by surprise, announce impending dangers and disasters for the American nation, develop stereotypes about the world outside US borders, and desperately attempt to construct new international relations villains.

Whereas the intervention of tabloid culture into the domain of international politics can be seen as a late modern or postmodern phenomenon, the conceptualization of international politics and formulation of foreign policies in the United States have gone through historical stages when relatively similar discourses and representations of popular or even populist geopolitics took place. The point I wish to make about tabloid culture's use in certain foreign policy and security studies circles today is not that it is a unique trend, or that it is not based on any prior discursive tradition. On the contrary, as I hinted at in the introduction to this book, the tabloid genre of writing American foreign policy draws on a rich legacy of popular cultural and middlebrow media constructions. Yet, as suggested above and in the Introduction, the tabloid (realist) genre discussed in this chapter also possesses specific traits that explain its contemporary appeal and suggest that it is not just any reproduction of previous popular geopolitics.

The desire to condition the public to certain beliefs and attitudes through the dissemination of a popular but often paranoid political discourse is clearly not novel. As Tom Engelhardt has shown in his study of American popular culture during the Cold War, the creation and reconstitution of America's ideas of triumphalism and Manifest Destiny have often been achieved with the assistance of various national media, literary genres, and art forms that, particularly in times of crisis, have tried to shape America's imaginary of the political world.[10] One might even argue that the foundation and subsequent expansion of the American nation-state were reliant upon specific early tabloid media constructions and popular representational genres that sought to tell Americans who they were, what their land was, and where their enemies stood. Engelhardt recalls that, in the early American context of the encounter between the white European (mostly Anglo-Saxon) settler and the native Indian (or "Native American," to use contemporary language), puritan sermons and captivity narratives (depicting mostly imaginary tales of white women savagely abducted by Indian warriors, a common theme of 1940s–1950s Hollywood western movies too) "did far more than simply emphasize native savagery and depredations" and, in fact, were some of the most vivid original myths of the American national story.[11] These popular, pre-tabloid narratives made sure to place "the Indians in the position of invaders, violently intruding on the settled world."[12] Such popular representations were already geopolitical in the sense that they showcased and relied upon a specific "narrative topography" and clearly established "boundaries" to the story that made it possible to determine "who was inside, who [was] out; where 'we' belonged and where the 'enemy' belonged."[13]

Although it has taken a while for popular geopolitics to be treated as a domain of critical analysis in its own right, it is not surprising to see that, of late, several critical political geographers and critical international relations scholars have made it their objective to highlight the geopolitical sources, processes, effects, and implications of popular cultural discourses, representations, and media. A recent study of geopolitical representations in Europe around the time of 9/11 has argued that, "[f]or popular geopolitics, the media are essential because they are the main channels through which most people obtain information about foreign affairs."[14] Focusing on what Sharp has called the "relationship of state elite geopolitics to popular conceptualizations of the working of the world,"[15] scholars and students of popular geopolitics refuse to distinguish between "elite" texts and so-called lowbrow or middlebrow entertainment. Of course, as Campbell has demonstrated, "elite" foreign policy texts are still "important in establishing the discursive boundaries of United States foreign policy," for example.[16] But foreign policy and other geopolitical texts are rarely meant to be accessed by the vast majority of the population. Rather, the cultural forms and media upon which popular geopolitical constructs rely present and translate "elite literatures" as materials that can and should be consumed by the general public. As Sharp puts it, "members of a distinctively elite institutional locale contribute to and consume popular media."[17] Additionally, since popular geopolitics also turns to non-political texts to produce its desired effects, "the political encoding of such texts is more subtle and more easily reproduced."[18] Popular media such as those described above offer a mode of presentation of political realities that generally remains free of jargon, is caricaturally simplified, and often juxtaposes more personal issues to current political problems. As global political events are fused and confused with more mundane stories in the media, the reader or viewer is more likely to feel that he or she is directly called in as a direct participant in the geopolitical game.

Sharp's study of the *Reader's Digest* (already mentioned in the Introduction) and her analysis of how this middlebrow American direct-mail magazine's condensed stories helped to shape American mentalities vis-à-vis communism and the Soviet Union through the use of narratives, metaphors, graphic details, maps, caricatures, and paranoid images during the Cold War is exemplary of what popular geopolitics can offer to critical analyses of international relations and foreign policy. *Reader's Digest*'s clear style of presentation of political realities, its use of selected experts detailing the threat in vivid but accessible terms, and the mode of dissemination of the magazine (it came in the mail and reached millions of

Americans) brought "knowledge" to the vast majority of the American public. The *Digest*'s subscribers were made an integral part of the construction of America's Cold War geopolitical scenery. From reading the magazine, they were given specific tasks to accomplish and received (and often accepted) specific roles that they had to play in America's crusade against communism.

In the *Digest*, the use of cartographic representations and the depiction of facts and realities (often supported by data or simple statistical figures) in conjunction with world maps, in a manner reminiscent of what atlases normally showed, helped to anchor American readers to specific but certain rationalizations about the Cold War. Schulten has revealed that maps and atlases have always played a crucial role in the construction of America's geopolitical imaginary and of Americans' understanding (and acceptance) of what the United States' political, economic, and moral mission at home and abroad is supposed to be. From the 1880s onwards, American mapmakers and atlas producers (such as Rand McNally, C.S. Hammond, or the National Geographic Society) adopted a commercial and political strategy that was geared towards the US government but, more crucially, was aimed at influencing the American public's sense of the world (and of the United States' place in it too). Popular political cartography was thus deployed as a marketing strategy (to sell maps and atlases to American citizens) but also as a (geo)political instrument of governance and public instruction (since preferred geopolitical views and preferences by the US government were emphasized in these US cartographical representations). As Schulten puts it, the American atlas "contained not just maps but narrative descriptions, illustrations, graphs, and charts to bring cosmopolitanism and nationalism into American homes."[19] Schulten continues: "Analyzing how the atlas divided, organized, mapped, and narrated the world reveals how it purported to explain and contain the world for public consumption . . . America's rise to internationalism shaped and was facilitated by popular cartography."[20]

Maps, atlases, and their accompanying narratives are undoubtedly powerful instruments of popular (tabloid) geopolitics. Using everyday, common, and familiar media (magazines, newspapers, television, film, books, or other apparently mundane and anodyne descriptions of the world), these popular representations and discourses have the capacity to normalize and naturalize certain political, economic, and often ideological preferences that, through the work of these popular media, can be taken for granted by the general public. Engelhardt effectively summarizes both the processes and the outcomes of those popular and political cartographies: "Of the generation that grew up in the immediate postwar years [in the United States], who doesn't remember the redness of the maps? As projectors flickered in school cafeterias and auditoriums, the tentacles of the red octopi slithered around globes and inky red blobs oozed across continents."[21] Engelhardt concludes: "In this visual [and clearly tabloid, one might add] horror story, the enemy – bloody and tyrannical – was known; his plan for world conquest indisputable."[22] As some contemporary critical geographers have argued, not much has changed today. Yet, as Engelhardt's earlier emphasis on puritan sermons or captivity narratives in the context of the Anglo-Saxon discovery, settling, and expansion of the American nation suggested, one also needs to understand the role and power of popular cartographies (and popular and tabloid geopolitics) in a larger sense, one in which discursive and representational cartographies, topographies, and boundaries are not just the products of maps or atlases, but rather of a vast panoply of popular geopolitical media and/or cultural tools that seek to map out, delineate, and contain new political, economic, and ideological realities. As will be discussed below, tabloid realism is a particular modality of the tabloid geopolitical discourse (introduced in previous chapters) that does rely on popular cartographies but does not just end with the narrative production of such maps. Rather, in tabloid realist texts, cartographies are an excuse (by their authors) to deploy a larger discursive assemblage that seeks to condition the public to specific geopolitical and ideological preferences (generally anchored in the revived concepts of national security, the preservation of the state and its territory, and so on). Thus, critical popular geopolitical analyses today also need to take into account what Derek Gregory (borrowing the concept from Edward Said's writing) has called "imaginative geographies." For Gregory, "imaginative geographies" refer to the many political and ideological strategies used, generally by intellectuals of statecraft, and mostly in dominant Western discourses about the non-West, to sort out, organize, and order geopolitical relations between "us" and "them," whatever the "us" or the "them" may be (mostly, these days, the "us" is Western, often American, while the "them" is non-Western, and typically "Middle-Eastern"). Of necessity, "imaginative geographies" have recourse to all sorts of popular and tabloid media and styles of presentation in order to facilitate the commonsensical cultural deployment of those political geographies that, ultimately, seek to "locate, oppose, and cast out."[23] What Gregory's important insight into imaginative geographies brings to the forefront of the critical popular geopolitical analysis is an understanding of the larger ideological dimensions involved in the deployment of any sort of popular geopolitical imagery or narrative. Ideologically speaking, popular cartographies and other tabloid cultural geopolitical representations matter because they serve as the material supports and pretexts for global imaginative geographies of power, force, and violence. As will be shown below, contemporary tabloid geopolitics (and tabloid realism specifically) is perhaps the discursive and representational formation that is best suited to reveal the intricate connection between popular geopolitics and imaginative geography.

But Gregory's analysis of popular and imaginative geographies of today's world is important to the present study for another reason. Whereas much of the currently available critical literature on popular geopolitics (Sharp, Schulten, Engelhardt, and others) mainly assumes and does present what Sharp calls an "active subject" of popular political geographies, that is to say, an individual target subject of those popular geopolitical discourses and cartographies who responds to the substance of the message made available to her or him through obvious and efficient media channels or popular cultural genres (from eighteenth-century Indian stories to *Reader's Digest*, from Rand McNally's atlases to articles and photos in the *National Geographic*), Gregory's work suggests that the form of the media's message is equally determinant in conveying a particular type of geopolitical and ideological reality to the population, and above all to the American public. Gregory recognizes that, in what I have called above the postmodern age, popular media and cultural forms have the capacity to produce imaginative or imaginary geopolitical realities that are self-referentially driven by and derived from the medium itself (and thus can try to substitute themselves for whatever material reality may be in their way in the "real" geopolitical landscape, if such a concept still has any meaning).

At the same time though, Gregory's point about the impact of the form/style of the medium, of popular culture in general, on the formation of contemporary imaginative political geographies does not go far enough in diagnosing the peculiarities (and specific rules of formation and effects) of what I have called tabloid geopolitics. Indeed, the tabloid genre of geopolitical reporting and truth-telling today is directly affected by the form of the medium. As will be seen below, the particular form of this medium is a primary reason why producers of contemporary geopolitical discourses, foreign policy analyses, and American security narratives find the tabloid genre attractive. The tabloid medium allows scholars, journalists, pundits, and all sorts of experts to deploy relatively ahistorical – but imaginative and ideological – discourses in textual and representational contexts that do not (have to) abide by rules of temporal and spatial contingency (the realities they describe are at once past, present or future, as we started to see in Chapter 1 in relation to cyberterror). Sharp, for example, had indicated that *Reader's Digest*'s production of "clearheaded facts" was crucial to the magazine's mission of educating the public.[24] The American citizen had to learn about the Cold War (as presented from a specifically selected perspective) in order to become more knowledgeable about the threats and dangers. But, as will also be shown below, the tabloid discourse of contemporary international politics (and tabloid realism in particular) does not claim to provide knowledge, and its geopolitical imageries and imaginative geographies are not meant to be instructive or educational.[25] Instead, as I already noted in Chapter 1, tabloid geopolitics intends to spread a sense of anxiety and insecurity by providing spectacular scenarios and doomsday prophecies about "realities" that are generally not tangible or sometimes may not even be immediately meaningful to the reader's or viewer's personal experience. The "dumbing down" effect of/in the tabloid genre once again gives priority to entertainment value, and it seeks to condition the public through a lack of knowledge (which often is also an excess of information). Tabloid geopolitical experts can thus be presented as and remain uncontested "authority figures" who play the part of knowledgeable intellectuals of statecraft, as the last thing the producers and operators of tabloid geopolitical media and literatures want is for their audience to know (what they are up to).

Thus, contemporary tabloid geopolitical discourses do not create the kind of "active subjectivity" that some critical geopolitical scholars have argued the reading or watching of popular texts or shows with (geo)political messages and effects supposedly require. As Gregory intimated was at play recently when US audiences consumed images and commentaries on the war in Iraq in the US media for example, the reading/viewing subject of today's tabloid geopolitics is generally asked to occupy a very passive position.[26] This postmodern version of popular geopolitics adopts a tabloid approach so that the main task asked of the reader/viewer is to sit down, enjoy the show, and, of course, remain fearful. Other subjects, agents, and authorities, the tabloid reader/viewer is being told, are doing the acting and are being vigilant on his or her behalf. Unlike some of the recommended or expected popular Cold War reactions (to the red scare visible on Engelhardt's "red maps," for example), today's consumer of tabloid geopolitical literatures and shows does not have to constantly spy on his/her neighbors since the producers of the "spectacle" are already doing this, supposedly on this consumer's or citizen's behalf. Thus, by and large, adherence to and acceptance of the tabloid narrative is the main thing that is demanded of the (now passive) "subject" of this popular geopolitical genre. At the same time, the tabloid narrative today erases any critical ability that may have remained in previous popular geopolitical enterprises, since the discourses or representations tabloid geopolitics now provides are simply to be taken at face value. Its imaginative geographies are meant to be the exact renditions of the way things really are and of the way politics and ideology ought to be. The facts, events, issues, maps, figures, statistics, and images displayed through the tabloid medium are what they are, so-called "purely objective realities" that are not supposed to be contested and do not even require active recognition or acquiescence.

Tabloid international politics

Even before the 9/11 terrorist attacks, much was made in international relations circles of the multiple transformations that were apparently affecting traditional visions of state sovereignty.[27] Notions like globalization, deterritorialization, cultural fragmentation, and the proliferation of information were advanced to suggest that the "condition of postmodernity" had reached the domain of international politics throughout the 1990s. Postmodern times in international relations were allegedly marked by changes that appeared to affect the traditionally fixed markers of international political analysis.[28] The nation-state, sovereignty, and the state's territorial claims (behind clearly identifiable borders) were no longer sacrosanct "truths," as a sense of political relativism combined with an absence of structural stability were witnessed by practitioners and scholars. It was precisely this sense of political relativism supplemented by an apparent lack of structural certainty after the Cold War that gave rise to new concepts (globalization, deterritorialization, and so on) supposedly better able to make sense of contemporary political realities. But these concepts often remained vague, imprecise, fleeting, and changeable. They were in fact as vague, imprecise, fleeting, and changeable as the postmodern realities they purported to represent.

Among so many disparate and confusing notions, conceptual clarity was lacking. Once again, before 9/11 (but also before Y2K), and as in previous times of political doubt, a rhetoric of danger, security, and national identity resurfaced in intellectual circles as a reaction to these alleged postmodern phenomena (and as a result of the media diffusion of such new "realities"). Similar to previous historical periods marked by a sense of geopolitical uncertainty, a persistent, populist, and panic-inducing discourse returned and sought to combine elements of "expert knowledge" with popular media representations. The discourse of cyberterrorism in expert, intellectual, and pseudo-academic circles (seen in Chapter 1), often filtered by the media around the time of Y2K, was representative of this trend. Emerging in the mid- to late 1990s, this new discourse of popular geopolitics claimed to make better sense of some of the diverse phenomena identified above by first returning to some of political realism's basic tenets (later, after 9/11, this renewed appeal to realism would be abandoned somewhat, but the tabloid genre/ style of presentation would remain). This rekindled realist spirit was an attempt at stabilizing geopolitical discourses in uncertain postmodern times. It allowed its proponents to argue that international politics still revealed the basic greed and desire for power in human beings. The apparent revival of political realism served as a confirmation to these newly populist intellectuals that human nature in parts of the world, and sometimes not so far from the United States' shores, had indeed turned for the worst. Realism revealed to them that, even though states at times seemed to be relinquishing their central place in international affairs, they were still to be taken into account, if only because they could fall prey to new power groupings such as ethnic organizations, new nations, civilizations, multinational economic conglomerates, drug cartels, and terrorist groups. In fact, because these new salient groupings were slowly but surely taking over the state, selfish interest defined in terms of power and often expressed in violent forms was once again becoming a global political reality. Finally, the revival of this sort of panic realist discourse allowed these intellectuals to announce that anarchy was taking over the fragile order that the Cold War had brought and the semblance of a new order that the post-Cold War period had ushered. Thanks to this reinvented discourse of (realist) geopolitical certainty and clarity, the doubts and dangers of postmodern international politics could perhaps be conquered, managed, or at least conjured away.

This return to an apparently overt realist approach to world affairs was interested in identifying clear threats and spreading a sense of urgency in dealing with those dangers. For this contemporary mode of political analysis, it was American national security that mostly was at stake and, consequently, it was the American nation-state (perhaps the last bastion of sovereign power) that was the inevitable target. Again, much of this discourse started to surface around the time of Y2K. Thus, it was essential for the American population to develop a sense of urgency. According to this re-energized approach to popular realist geopolitics, the recognition that borders were no longer inviolable, that populations were increasingly mixed and culturally plural, and that political power often had to be shared with (and sometimes taken away from) subnational groups had to give rise to a rather persistent discourse of danger, security, and popular vigilantism too. Clearly, this discourse did not need the 9/11 attacks to be deployed in American cultural and academic circles. 9/11 would merely appear to confirm and justify it.

At the same time though, this persistent discourse was more than a return to traditional realist postulates. It was also more than a return to the Cold War geopolitics of fear that could be found throughout the pages of *Reader's Digest*, for example. This discourse was more importantly a tabloid discourse. It was what can be called *tabloid realism* in contemporary international politics and culture. Found in texts authored by scholars like Benjamin Barber, Zbigniew Brzezinski, Samuel Huntington, Robert D. Kaplan, Michael Klare, John Mearsheimer, and many others, tabloid realism was also not to be understood as a uniform theoretical model.[29] Tabloid realism was not a new theory of international politics either. If anything, it was composed of fragments of realist geopolitics, American nationalist ideology, and cultural reactionism that were loosely put together to propagate shock effects in the public.

Since these texts and authors did not form a coherent theoretical paradigm, they may be best understood as what I called in the Introduction (following Foucault) a discursive formation. As Foucault suggested, a discursive formation often presents itself as a "system of dispersion." Far from demanding adherence to a unity of content, to a theoretical matrix, or to a single methodology, a discursive formation operates at the level of linguistic/discursive statements (*énoncés*) that are often diffuse, disparate, and dispersed. The point is not to arbitrarily regroup such statements but instead to emphasize their "rules of formation" (their correlations, positions, transformations over time) and see how such rules sometimes come to form (or be taken as) epistemological regularities, particularly by those who produce or wish to control the effects of such statements.[30]

The most common denominator among these varied texts was tabloid realism's constant hammering of the difficulty of the United States in adapting to the new international environment where transnational phenomena often appeared to matter more to international subjects/agents (people, nations, organizations, corporations, business interests, terrorist networks) than the state itself. This was, in a sense, the common message of the tabloid realist discursive formation that spread in the late 1990s and early 2000s. But what made this tabloid mode of reporting and explaining contemporary political realities intriguing, and what at the same time made it different from previous discourses of popular geopolitics, was tabloid realism's adoption and apparent embrace of the postmodern style of analysis. Tabloid realism was ideologically and politically reminiscent of the popular cultural geopolitical analyses of the Cold War (in the United States at least) when classical realism and right-wing conservatism merged to exclude non-American ideals and people, protect the American nation behind a rhetoric of securitization, and redraw the map of the world so that it would evidence an obvious West versus East dichotomy. But tabloid realism chose to adapt to postmodern times. It chose to deal with the postmodern realities of globalization, cultural fragmentation, human displacements, and so forth. It recognized post-industrial economic flows and post-realist geopolitical realities to better make sense of them and later cast them away through a discourse that, as previously indicated, returned to basic realist postulates. In short, tabloid realism understood (even if it did not fully appreciate) the postmodern premises about social and political conditions in the aftermath of the Cold War. As will be shown below, tabloid realism was masterful at "mimicking" a postmodern style of describing/analyzing political realities that would strike a chord with a younger generation of students and practitioners for whom the Cold War was mostly a lengthy chapter in World History textbooks.

To reproduce the postmodern story, tabloid realism chose to start from the premise of culture. It talked about cultural signs and icons, which it admitted were free flowing in contemporary world politics. Linked to culture, tabloid realist geopolitics also spent a great deal of time emphasizing the power of identity constructs. Power struggles and rivalries were embedded in identity debates. Additionally, to fit neatly in the postmodern mood, tabloid realist texts were very visual.[31] The writings were made up of short, lapidary sentences, riddled with metaphors that called for the audience to maintain a mostly visual, figurative, and imaginary apprehension of the intellectual arguments. As will be seen, maps – particularly imaginative or imaginary maps – were often the necessary technical bases for this textual genre. The tabloid realist maps were no longer the binary, simplistic, red-ink-filled cartographical representations of the Cold War. They were rather apparently fluid and flexible, multi-dimensional, or almost "holographic" projections of the allegedly new (geo)political realities. Yet, despite their apparent graphic complexity, many of these maps drawn or projected in tabloid realist texts were still containing and constraining, delimiting and self-defining. Finally, tabloid realism absorbed the postmodern genre of reporting to better capture audiences by replicating the televisual, graphic, spectacular, sensationalistic pop cultural model of trash talk-show/tabloid television truth-telling. To captivate their audience with "extreme" stories that were most likely to stir popular emotions, tabloid realism also described and explained contemporary geopolitical realities in a manner that was meant to be gripping and entertaining, even if, at the end, the reality the audience was left with (and could not act upon) was quite dramatic and often terrifying.

Ultimately, this adoption and projection of postmodern (visual) tools and (narrative) tricks in these tabloid realist discourses were generally nothing more than a façade. They were an attempt at recapturing or reinventing a safe, secure, and specifically recognizable geopolitical identity (particularly for America and Americans). While a postmodern apprehension of political realities was set up, and a semblance of appreciation for the postmodern genre was established, tabloid realism's eminently Realpolitik-driven, conservative, and reactionary narrative and representation could not hold on to the claims of political relativism, the lack of objective knowledge, the disdain for historical certainties, and the epistemological doubt with regard to truth-telling that necessarily seemed to accompany postmodern studies of politics and culture (and, as we shall see in subsequent chapters, the events of 9/11 would further demand a return to truth, certainty, and stability – or, at least, to a semblance of truth, certainty, and stability). And so, far from maintaining the postmodern trash popular cultural course they were set on, tabloid realists eventually wished to steer their geopolitical writings and cartographies away from postmodern uncertainties. They set up a specter of postmodernity, of postmodern geopolitical realities, and of postmodern literary/cultural genres to better conjure them up, exorcize them, and cast them away.

As will be shown below, behind the veil of their postmodern/tabloid/trash cultural mode of presentation, tabloid realists nostalgically and often desperately longed for the return of modern political certainties, Cold War geographical structures and schemes, national security programs, culturally protectionist foreign policies, and traditionally modern and Western ideological ways of dealing with "others."

To examine the connection between tabloid realism, the securitization of American culture at the turn of the century, and the rebirth of cultural conservatism in certain circles of geopolitical analysis (especially in the years that preceded 9/11), I spend the rest of the chapter featuring some tabloid realist authors and stories. By placing the spotlight on the tabloid realists, I wish to make visible some of the elementary political, cultural, and ideological rules of formation that constitute this mode of writing/thinking/projecting international and domestic politics. In the following pages, three popular tabloid realists and their respective texts are highlighted. I look at Robert Kaplan and his paranoid vision of a "coming anarchy." I then turn to Samuel Huntington and examine his belief that a fundamental "clash" of the world's main "civilizations" is about to occur. And I finish the presentation with former Cold War realist politician Zbigniew Brzezinski and his displayed (and displaced) anxieties about a post-Cold War world that, in his view, has gone "out of control."

Robert D. Kaplan: tabloid realism and the search for a secure national space

In his book, *The Coming Anarchy: Shattering the Dreams of the Post-Cold War*,[32] Kaplan gathered many of the articles on foreign affairs he had written for *The Atlantic Monthly* since 1994 (starting with his now famous "The Coming Anarchy" article). In this book (and the 1994 article for which the book is named), Kaplan declared that the map of the world had forever been altered. States and their borders were in constant flux. Flows had replaced scales. Dromography had replaced geography.[33] Ethno-religious disturbances and ecological disasters had replaced geopolitical order and security. Consequently, the map of the Cold War was totally obsolete. Mapping, the very need to draw maps, to chart lands and people, had to be reconsidered altogether in order to reflect these new global insecurities.

In lieu of traditional cartography, Kaplan called for a "holographic" representation of the multiple layers in motion that made up the fabric of the twenty-first century world. "Imagine," he wrote, "cartography in three dimensions, as if in a hologram."[34] Kaplan continued: "In this hologram would be the overlapping sediments of group and other identities atop the merely two dimensional color markings of city states and the remaining nations, themselves confused in places by shadowy tentacles, hovering overhead, indicating the power of drug cartels, mafias and private security agencies. Instead of borders there would be moving 'centers' of power, as in the Middle-Ages."[35] This was what Kaplan called the "last map." Indeed, the aim of this map was to be final, fatal, and apocalyptic. It would end modern civilization as we knew it. It would forever alter lifestyles, even in the West, which appeared to be somewhat buffered from the growing chaos emanating from Africa, Southeast Asia and Latin America (see Kaplan's quote at the opening of this chapter).

The problem for Kaplan was as much the map itself as what it supposedly represented. The map was doomed to remain fluid, porous, disorganized, and disorderly. It was, as Kaplan affirmed, a postmodern map. It could not fix, nor could it stabilize. It could not mark, identify, or differentiate. At best, it was able to trace paths or record flows that might have already passed on. It did not capture, but instead released. In a strange operation of cartographic cathexis, Kaplan dumped onto the new map all that he thought and feared was wrong with mid- to late-1990s international politics. His fears were not only shown *on* the map. They *were* the map!

While Kaplan tried to hide his anxiety about the new world with its disasters and plagues behind such a cartographic (or is it holographic?) screen, he still had a hard time containing his discomfort with what he had just described. His discomfort had to do with what he felt would happen to the United States in such a quickly mutating world. "It is not clear that the United States will survive the next century in exactly its present form,"[36] Kaplan revealed. In fact, one might never be able to identify the United States on such a holographic image anymore. One might find instead a few city-ethno states (the Tijuana to Los Angeles corridor; the Portland–Seattle–Vancouver Asian Pacific/Cascadian zone), several regional links stretching across oceans, rivers, and landmasses (the two sides of the Rio Grande; the Miami–Caribbean link; the Arizona desert), some left-over urban wastelands no longer connected to any political or economic core (the inner cities of what formerly was the industrial rust belt for instance), and many self-contained, self-sufficient, cleansed, and barricaded suburban communities that could be anywhere from Florida to North Dakota. Kaplan actually wrote an entire book describing (his anxieties about) this new American geography.[37]

But despite his intent to fold all that was apparently destabilizing about the post-Cold War world into new maps, Kaplan did not succeed in fending off the threats and the panic attacks they appeared to produce. The maps, holographic and postmodern as they may have been, remained disturbing to the Western (tabloid) realpolitiker in search of comfort and stability. What for Kaplan was disturbing about the new maps was that they indicated that doomsday had finally hit home. The chaos of the post-Cold War world was not, could not be, contained to the "wild zones" of the globe (Africa, the Middle East, Central Asia, some parts of Latin America) that he described in all his (travel) narratives. The contagion was spreading, and the remedy was not yet available. Containment was thus the only possibility. But not every American citizen, not every large city or small town in the good old USA would be prepared when global chaos hit. In fact, it may have already been too late: "The signs hardly need belaboring: racial polarity, educational dysfunction, social fragmentation of many and various kinds."[38] America's "domestic peace" was "further eroding."[39] The very fact that we needed to think about designing new maps to orient ourselves in this new world was a clear sign that problems were looming on the horizon.

Kaplan's obvious discomfort with this impending geographical reality is revealing. What was first designed by Kaplan to buffer "us" from this "coming anarchy" – the new holographic, three-dimensional map – was fast becoming the very symptom of disorder, the exact representational proof that hell was about to break loose. The cartographic cathexis was apparently not working well. Instead of hiding and containing, it revealed, projected, and proliferated even more fears. Instead of providing solace to the new tabloid geopolitikers, it was a constant reminder of how insecure "we" (in the West) were. Dalby has rightly critiqued Kaplan's mapping strategy by pointing out that "resurgent cultural fears about the Other" and "political angst about the collapse of order" infused his pre-apocalyptic vision.[40] Although this map of the frightening new world was labeled "holographic" or "postmodern," it was in fact driven by very traditionalist considerations about the "here" and the "there," the "us" and the "them," sameness and otherness. This peculiar cartography was a new type of imaginative political and ideological geography of America and the West before the fall, a form of geopolitical imagination that hoped to conjure away impending disasters. Thus, behind the covers of a high-tech, three-dimensional, and virtual representation of space, Kaplan was worried about the state, borders, order, and national security. Kaplan drew new maps to better contain what he clearly perceived to be "outside" threats and to try to redefine what he considered to be the core of order, power, and stability in the postmodern world, namely, the American nation. Unfortunately (for him mostly), this did not work too well, as the specter of doom lingered.

Such an approach to drawing maps, no matter how technically innovative they are made to appear, and more revealingly, the need to turn to maps to achieve geopolitical security are classic (geo)political realist concerns.[41] The attempt is to defend what the scholar considers to be the national interest at all costs, starting with the United States' borders and the protection of the American lifestyle. The problem is not with the inside, but rather with the outside. As Dalby mentions, Kaplan did note "the dangers of the criminals from 'there' compromising the safety of 'here' but never countenances the possibility that the economic affluence of 'here' is related to the poverty of 'there'."[42] To the extent that the "inside" became compromised, it was only because the "outside" had managed to penetrate the insufficiently protected boundary-lines.[43] The trouble was not and could not be with the inside, with the American nation and its changing culture. Rather, the American nation and its culture were in trouble because of what was coming at them.

Kaplan (in *The Coming Anarchy* at least) is an exemplary tabloid realist scholar who plays with postmodern terms, techniques, and images but, in the end, is bedeviled by them. Kaplan recognized the fluidity of contemporary geopolitics and he presented it in a (geo)graphic postmodern manner: the virtual map, its flows, its absence of containment and finality. But, more importantly, Kaplan understood that in postmodernity fictions can be more "real than reality itself."[44] Images are their own reality. If done well, fictions without referents can nonetheless produce desirable effects in society and culture. This was precisely the point of Kaplan's tabloid realist mapping. A simulation of geopolitics at the turn of the century,

Kaplan's geographical imagery relied upon bits and pieces of information data about the post-Cold War (dis)order, popular global news stories (environmental degradation, the growth of transnational crime, and so on), and snapshots of disasters and conflicts in the 1990s seen by everyone on CNN or on the covers of *Time* and *Newsweek* to "substantiate" his vision of an inevitable political anarchy. To further establish the veracity (or "reality-effect") of his global dystopia, Kaplan told his reader that these frightening scenes of impending chaos could not be doubted (even if the reader/viewer had no direct experience of them). After all, he, Kaplan, reporter of the tabloid story, had seen them all in his many travels. But, even with Kaplan's dramatic narrative, a reporter's story could always be doubted. Kaplan's story, however, was not supposed to be doubted or believed, accepted or rejected. It actually stood beyond "truth claims" and "historical certainty." As a postmodern story, it was a simulation of reality that could not be assessed and accessed as either true or false. Even if one were to counter Kaplan's version of post-Cold War geopolitics by bringing different factoids, news-events, and stories into the picture,[45] Kaplan's tabloid realist narrative could still hold "true" at some level because, according to his own visual and cartographical premises, no other conclusion could be derived but that of the recognition of a generalized sense of impending chaos. Ultimately, what this "coming anarchy" was built on was a self-evident and self-referential "holographic" map that, beyond facts and data, could say it all. In an age when all sorts of narratives could be produced and supported by all sorts of information technologies, the visual became the final refuge of what counted as true. In a saturated media universe, what was (still is) on TV screens stood (still stands) in for what could be positively verified. Kaplan's postmodern map was this tabloid realist's final visual/virtual evidence. The map, and only the map, confirmed Kaplan's journalistic testimonies and granted them credibility. In this simulated universe where the map created "realities" that in turn justified the deployment of the map, reality-effects and truth-effects were self-referentially constructed and, again, were neither true nor false.

But the construction of this self-referential and self-sufficient mapping was only half of Kaplan's tabloid (realist) discourse. Indeed, even though Kaplan offered his readers a postmodern simulation of geopolitical (dis)order, he still appeared to be caught by surprise and finally terrified by what he had conceived. The simulated object (Kaplan's map) obliterated any possible return to modern political order, security, and the nation-state. Caught in his own postmodern game, Kaplan then made an about face and suddenly refused to recognize the "realities" that his "holographic" map had unleashed. Instead of drawing the logical conclusions one might have been led to derive from such a chaotic, dizzying, and fluid cartographical fiction, Kaplan's tabloid realist discourse turned reactive and protective. Instead of following his postmodern premises to what could have been their fatal outcome, Kaplan chose to extol the virtues of the "inside," the nation, the state, "us," in a word (Kaplan's word), America, that had to be defended at all cost even if, earlier in his text, Kaplan had shown his reader how futile and doomed national defense and security measures were in a postmodern age.

Kaplan's deployment of a postmodern imagery of uncertainty and chaos and his subsequent rejection of it is a common case of tabloid realist self-induced paranoia. As will be revealed below, both Huntington and Brzezinski seem to display similar symptoms. Unable to "have it both ways" (postmodern yet modern, fluid yet secure, relativistic yet believable), tabloid realists provide a spectacular, entertaining, gripping, and sometimes chilling "reality" that they later must totally discard. As an exemplary symbol of this tabloid realist genre, Kaplan's map was not so original after all. Below the opaque, fluctuating, and confusing layers of his postmodern map lay the stable, orderly, and static map of twentieth-century America that was slowly but surely being obliterated. As Brian Jarvis has noted, postmodern cartographies do not always "constitute a decisive break from the dominant tradition of landscape representation."[46] Instead, in American geopolitical culture in particular, some new maps simply "represent a reworking of the raw materials that have always been central to the American geographical imagination."[47] Kaplan's postmodern cartography exemplifies this tendency since his map betrayed a profound anxiety about the integrity of the old map. After throwing away the new map, only one possible conclusion remained (no matter how illogical and incoherent this conclusion was in relation to Kaplan's original premises): the old map had to be restored. And the old map showed us that it may have been tolerable for the rest of the world (mostly the non-Western world) to live in a spatial universe made up of uncontrollable flows and uncertain identities. But this was not acceptable for the United States, which had to remain rooted in a space where sovereign power, national culture, and fixed borders were still visible and meaningful.

Samuel Huntington: tabloid realism as cultural conservatism

It may seem odd to label Samuel Huntington a tabloid realist, since his work, spanning several decades, has influenced generations of political scientists (in the United States mostly) who would not necessarily consider themselves (tabloid) realists. Still, Huntington's scholarly research has always revolved around the notions of security and political order. In his classic *Political Order in Changing Societies*,[48] Huntington sought to demonstrate that attempts at democratization in "changing political systems" could not succeed and in fact could become detrimental to the development of stable democratic regimes if they were not accompanied by institutions capable of establishing order first. The imposition of institutional guarantees and political safeguards, even if these sometimes had to take the form of authoritarian structures, was preferable to the immediate introduction of democratic values in formerly non-democratic social systems. Even though Huntington would revise this formulation in a later work (written as the Cold War vanished),[49] Huntington's approach has sometimes been labeled conservative and reactive to the extent that it places the achievement of social order before the enjoyment of democratic freedoms and rights.[50] Additionally, as an American academic writing during the Cold War, Huntington always kept an eye on the problem of order in American society. By extension, this concern with American order in an era of bipolar political and ideological struggles at times led him to consider the situation of some of America's allies and enemies too.[51]

The end of the Cold War did not abate Huntington's intellectual quest for political order, both at home and abroad. Because of the changing geopolitics of the post-Cold War era, Huntington spent a great deal of time rethinking order in relation to space. Based on what he called the "cultural reconfiguration of world politics," Huntington presented another map of post-Cold War international politics in his 1996 bestseller *The Clash of Civilizations and the Remaking of World Order*.[52] In this book, Huntington claimed that the structure of civilizations was starting to take over a world organized around the needs, interests, and prerogatives of sovereign states. State-to-state politics was quickly disappearing, Huntington believed. With the Cold War over, bipolar geopolitics no longer made sense. In fact, the vanishing of the Cold War had allowed new forces of integration and fragmentation to come to the forefront of international affairs. Religious preferences, ethnic identifications, and cultural values could now be advanced as the geopolitical and ideological dialectic between East and West was gone.

Like Kaplan before, Huntington adapted his old Cold War rhetoric of order to postmodern times. Equating the postmodern era of geopolitics with a "cultural turn," Huntington affirmed that cultural politics was the dominant reality of this new age.[53] With Huntington's vision of cultural politics came new divisions and new alliances, new fault-lines and forms of cooperation too. As culture became the determining factor in people's lives transnationally, Huntington argued, a clash of cultural civilizations was sure to follow. Geopoliticians and policy-makers would have to find ways to deal with it. Huntington was eager to prepare political leaders and foreign policy makers in the West, and in the United States above all, for what was about to come. To be prepared to face this clash of civilizations, one could no longer rely on a conception of geopolitics that took Cold War maps as a representational support. Modern international relations thinking was based on maps. These maps had shown the clash between the West and the East, Western liberalism and communism. They had told us who "we" were and where "we" stood. These old maps had served their purpose. They had averted global destruction during the Cold War. They had preserved the West and America in particular. They had brought stability and order. Finally, they had kept "us" free.

But the new international relations were different, Huntington asserted. Post-Cold War international politics required the creation of new maps, the development of what Kaplan called a "postmodern cartography" as a point of departure, so that we could know who "we" were again, and more importantly, who "they" were and where "they" stood. A map, Huntington added, was necessary to "best serve our purposes" and to provide a "simplification that allows us to see where we may be going."[54] For Huntington, maps served to show the road ahead. They traced a path to the future and directed the scholar in his/her re-envisioning of the world out there. Down the line, maps would help to preserve the integrity of the nation.

Even if the new map was representationally postmodern (as will be shown momentarily, the map partly revealed a post-statist international system), Huntington's intention was still very much modern. The temporal linearity and causal relations that Huntington hoped the new map would engender were traditional modern concerns. Similar to Kaplan, Huntington's new map was a bridge from postmodern geopolitics back to modernity and modern political order. At first glance, the map Huntington offered was much more orderly than Kaplan's. Chaos was not readily evident on Huntington's map. Rather, chaos or geopolitical instability was the threat Huntington's map would bring if states (and mostly the United States of course) did not react and adopt a necessary defensive posture. Huntington's map was multi-dimensional too: it had two main superimposed layers. The first layer was made up of nine civilizational clusters. These clusters represented the major cultural civilizations that Huntington perceived would be taking over international politics in the century to come. Latin American, Islamic, African, Sinic, Hindu, Orthodox, Buddhist, Japanese, and Western were the labels given to the civilizations, to the nine main new geopolitical players. These civilizations were self-sufficient. They included and excluded on religious, ethnic, and often linguistic bases. More importantly, they were antagonistic and sometimes mutually incompatible. These civilizations were destined to do battle with one another now that Cold War politics was out of the picture. States who fell within those large cultural clusters were also stuck. They followed the dominant cultural logic to which they had been ascribed. Thus, states' policies would have to be readjusted to exemplify civilizational claims. Continents and sub-continents were divided and reformed too in order to be in line with the major civilizational fault-lines. Africa, for example, was now divided in two at about the 15th parallel to mark the separation allegedly found there between the so-called Islamic and African civilizations.

The second layer was much more conventional. It took sovereign nation-states as its main marker and traced boundary-lines around them. As Huntington reminded us, the state was not absent from this global clash of civilizations. The sovereign state was the political unit that was most affected by the cultural redistributions exemplified by the first map. Thus, Huntington continued, it was necessary to have a secondary map that could reflect the deep "cultural" transformations at both the inter-state and intra-state levels. The second map was more classical to the extent that geopolitical divides took place between and within states. But it was still very different from the previous maps of the Cold War since the structure of the post-Cold War inter-state map was now made to depend upon a conditioning super-structural clash of civilizational clusters (as opposed to the super-structure of balance of power politics during the Cold War, for instance). Both internally and externally, "state alignments" were being modified, and this was precisely what the second map revealed.

This sub-structural cartographic layer was composed of four different categories of states. Every sovereign state on the planet fell into one of those four categories. The categories were defined by the degree of involvement, reception, inclusion, resistance, or rejection of the state (any state) vis-à-vis the civilizational cluster within which it was found. In other words, culture was the determining variable of a state's identity. The four categories were the following ones: core states, lone countries, cleft countries, and torn countries. Core states were "places which are viewed by [a civilization's] members as the principal source . . . of the civilization's culture."[55] They were often central to the civilizational cluster, and they defined the cultural politics that all the members of the civilization (states, subgroups, ethnic entities, and individuals) would adopt. China, for example, was described as the core state of the Sinic civilization, while India was the core of the Hindu cluster. The new cultural geopolitics of the post-Cold War era radiated from these different cores (more or less nine of them; one per civilization). The core states had the power to culturally permeate other, more peripheral countries within the civilizational bloc. They also had the ability to draw the main battle-lines with other civilizations. In many ways, the "road-map" of cultural clashes Huntington wanted to imprint found its point of origin in these civilizational cores.

A lone country was, as its name indicates, a country that was left alone.[56] It did not have the desire, or rather capacity, to belong to any of the nine dominant civilizations. Ethiopia was given as an example of a lone country. Haiti was supposedly another case in point. These lone countries were troublesome according to Huntington. Since they had no determining alignment, they could more easily sell themselves out to any civilization that wanted to incorporate them. But the potential problem posed by lone countries was still minimal compared to the danger that cleft countries represented. Cleft countries, Huntington indicated, "territorially bestride the fault-lines between civilizations."[57] Cleft states were multi-civilizational states, with generally two major civilizations wanting to take over that state. Cleft countries were internally divided along cultural lines. For these states, the civilizational fault-line was not outside but inside. Driven by repulsion, cleft countries were thus a constant source of geopolitical instability. Their internal disputes could easily affect the geopolitics of civilizational blocs as these countries would exacerbate the already existing cultural tensions and widen the fault-lines. Thus, it was feared that cleft countries would affect the politics of non-cleft countries. They could drag non-cleft countries, including core states, into an open civilizational war. For this reason, cleft countries had to be closely monitored, particularly by all the core states, in all civilizations. Cleft countries were the main source of division and conflict in a cultural world. What had happened to Yugoslavia throughout the 1990s was for Huntington a blatant example of the global risk of insecurity cleft countries represented.

Finally, a torn country "has a single predominant culture which places it in one civilization, but its [political] leaders want to shift it to another civilization."[58] Risks were also apparent in these countries that often "bestride" fault-lines against the will of the populations. Political leaders wanted their countries to bridge East and West, Europe and Asia, Islam and Western Enlightenment, and so forth (Huntington pointed to Turkey as an example of a torn country). But the populations, also influenced by their cultural or religious leaders, sometimes resisted the formation of the civilizational bridge recommended by the political leaders. Once again, for Huntington, this sort of forced positioning across cultures was a potential source of geopolitical disorder.

For Huntington, this multi-layered map of a world dominated by post-statist cultural allegiances was a necessity. It was the basic visual representation of what was happening "out there" in the late twentieth and early twenty-first century. All could be explained by referring oneself to this new global mapping. More importantly, whereas the first map evidenced the new dominant geopolitical reality, the second map bore witness to how unstable the new world was and would remain if no action was taken to either smooth the fault-lines or protect oneself from them. On the second map, anything went and, potentially, cultural conflicts would abound. Huntington's civilizational map projected instability and uncertainty. It did so, not by presenting itself as a fluctuating map like Kaplan's, but rather by inscribing a new order, the order of civilizations. Because of their cultural natures, these civilizations were generally hostile to one another. Because they were hostile to one another, these civilizations would lead the world into endless crises, conflicts, and human dramas, dramas similar to those the United States would soon have to face on September 11, 2001. In short, it was in the very nature of this new (cultural) order to be disorderly. Huntington's postmodern map was a necessary evil, a harbinger of doom. And doom on this map was particularly manifest on the secondary level where states had no choice but to rearrange their strategic positioning in terms of core, cleft, torn or isolated cultural categorical imperatives.

The second map was concerned with states and attempted to redraw boundaries (some strong, others quite weak) around them. For Huntington as for Kaplan before, it was clearly the state that was being threatened by all those civilizational re-alignments. The map told us as much. As Michael Shapiro has suggested, beyond the appearance of novelty, transformation, and re-mapping, Huntington was a cartographical "recidivist" of sorts.[59] Despite Huntington's attempt at painting twenty-first-century international relations as the inevitable outcome of a post-structural cartography, Huntington was also a structural recidivist who ascribed states to a specific place that had already been carved out by the preconditions of the larger super-structural order. Even when states were being (re)defined by cultural super-structural positions, state-to-state geopolitics remained the main issue. The new affiliations still conformed to "a state-oriented set of antagonisms,"[60] except that the new antagonisms were allegedly much more unpredictable (hence, more dangerous) than the previous ones.

Huntington's mapping strategy and the geopolitical analysis it enabled followed tabloid realist tenets. Indeed, Huntington combined a stereotypical understanding of postmodern political analysis with a keen sense for the dramatic and the spectacular to produce a hoped-for reaction (or provoke outrage perhaps) on the part of his audience/readership. This reaction, Huntington calculated, would bring a return to modern preoccupations with order that would focus on the always necessary and salutary presence of the sovereign state. To repeat, Huntington's arrangement of post-Cold War international space and his construction of impassable fault-lines made chaos the only possible geopolitical outcome. This, of course, was done by design and with a clear sense of what was being produced. Again, the desired effect was borrowed from the tabloid model of truth-telling and

-reporting. Huntington had to give his readers the image of a map that would inevitably lead to anarchy so that they could conjure up more effectively the prospect
of such a global disorder.[61] In particular, foreign policy makers had to react to this
mapping, rebel against it, conservatively protect their possessions, and culturally
regroup. Similarly to Kaplan, by painting a potentially disastrous portrait of the
civilizational structure of twenty-first-century international politics, Huntington
hoped to "rally the troops" around the idea of a traditional geopolitical space, a
space governed and controlled by fixed and stable sovereign states. Ó Tuathail
was on target when he diagnosed Huntington's work as a form of "neoconserva-
tive cultural anxiety."[62] Tabloid realism, despite its co-optation of postmodern cultural tools, remained an eminently nostalgic discourse. Huntington was nostalgic
for the good old past, the Cold War, its "long peace," and the maps of yore that
"imposed closure upon events, situations and people."[63]

But Huntington's model was a message too. It was a pointed warning sent
to one of the identified civilizations: the West. Huntington wrote: "The Islamic
resurgence and the economic dynamism of Asia demonstrate that *other* civilizations are alive and well and at least potentially threatening to the West. A major
war involving the West and the core states of other civilizations is not inevitable,
but it could happen."[64] Here, Huntington tapped into popular fears, thinking that
mobilizing these would yield a populist appeal to his prophecies. The security
of the West was at stake. The West was a prime target of inter-civilizational disorder. But why worry so much about the West, and the West only? The answer
for Huntington was simple, and it would be a blatant demonstration of tabloid
realism's Western ethnocentricism too. The West mattered more than the rest because it was "our" civilization, the one that had invented modern political order,
sovereignty, statehood, nationality, the rule of law, and democracy. The West mattered because it had invented modern international relations, power politics, the
balance of power, and the Cold War. The West mattered because it was (it had to
be) culturally solid and homogeneous. Finally, the West mattered because it was
where "we" were and who "we" were (on the map); it was the place from which
Huntington was writing. It was the civilization of the United States, the nation that
fed and would always feed the West its core values.

For Huntington, this crude ethnocentric message was beyond questioning. It
went without saying. It had to have mass appeal too. It helped to explain why any
cultural attack against the West was in fact an attack against the United States,
against America's culture, against America's lifestyle, against America's civilizing mission. After all, "without the United States the West becomes a minuscule
and declining part of the world's population on a small and inconsequential penin-
sula at the extremity of the Eurasian landmass,"[65] Huntington added. To protect
itself and its civilization, the United States had to solidify its cultural borders. It
had to pursue the inclusion of the Western cultural bloc. It had to keep the Western
bloc Western. Cultural renewal was clearly the answer. Cultural renewal was the
way for the United States to regain geostrategic control over international relations and recreate a sense of Western alliance, complicity, and common interest.
Huntington's brand of tabloid realist analysis was highly nationalistic and cultur-

ally protectionist. Cultural protectionism was Huntington's way of normalizing late twentieth-century and early twenty-first-century international politics and, by the same token, of securitizing domestic politics.

Cultural renewal had to start at home, in the heartland of Western civilization. Previewing some of the post-9/11 cultural conservative arguments, Huntington argued that multiculturalism, allegedly promoted by American political leaders in the 1990s, was dangerous and had to be contained before it was too late. Multiculturalism was a political abnormality, one that ran the risk of turning the United States into a cleft country and of destroying the West and its geopolitical mission of order. American leaders in the 1990s had been confused, Huntington intimated. They had failed to realize how deep the cultural fault-lines were. They should have been able to heed the warnings now visible on Huntington's map and, as a response, should have developed nationalist, territorially protectionist, and security-driven policies. As a result, today's and tomorrow's more conservative American politicians would have no choice but to protect the "homeland" so that, instead of wishing "to create a country of many civilizations," they would finally promote the "unity of the people they govern."[66] After the September 11 terrorist attacks against the United States, Huntington's culturally protectionist incantations would find many eager supporters both in the general public and in foreign policy/homeland security circles (more will be said on this in the next chapters).[67]

Once again, America was for Huntington the champion of the West. The West, infused with America's values, was a model of unity. Multiculturalism threatened this unity. Multiculturalism could cause civilizational warfare and internal divisions. The West and its people had to remember that they were valuable, "not because [the West] is universal, but because it *is* unique."[68] If retaining Western uniqueness and preserving American cultural leadership meant that other civilizations had to be declared antagonistic, so be it. At least, the average American would now know who s/he was, where s/he stood, and who the "others" were. Huntington's brand of tabloid realism clarified and cleaned up the American geopolitical landscape (and imaginary) prior to 9/11, and it would serve as a foundation for it after the terrorist attacks.

Zbigniew Brzezinski: tabloid realism as orientalist nostalgia

Two of Zbigniew Brzezinski's works, *Out of Control*[69] and *The Grand Chessboard*,[70] published in the mid- to late 1990s, are other key examples of the tabloid genre of realist writing, mapping, and projecting. But more than Kaplan's or Huntington's own texts discussed above, Brzezinski's two volumes show us the extent to which tabloid realists were (and perhaps still are) obsessed with power, its structural conditions, and the geostrategic "games" power used to allow foreign policy makers to play. Of the three tabloid realist discourses examined in this chapter, Brzezinski's is probably the one that is the least willing to adapt to postmodern times. Brzezinski was thrown into postmodern geopolitics against his wishes. He had no choice but to accept the end of the Cold War even if, as many other former cold warriors, he would have preferred to see the "long peace" stretch its stabilizing wings into the twenty-first century. Inevitably, the end of the Cold War brought a sense of melancholy among the foreign policy makers that invented, lived under, and thrived during the Cold War. Nostalgic for the strategic games of an era that apparently no longer was, realist foreign policy makers turned tabloid realists partly to relive the old fantasies and partly to cope with the new realities.[71] As a postmodern cultural genre, tabloid realism was not burdened by claims of authenticity or historical accuracy. Accordingly, in the tabloid genre, any story could be replayed and thus potentially given a different outcome. This retelling or replaying of history and its stories was precisely what Brzezinski's brand of tabloid discourse did. Tabloid realism gave former cold warriors the opportunity to re-imagine Cold War scenarios in a post-Cold War era. It allowed them to continue to fight the old struggles and, they hoped, to postpone the end of the story and history.

Brzezinski was Jimmy Carter's National Security Advisor (from 1977 to 1981). Subsequently, he served as Co-Chairman of George H.W. Bush's National Security Advisory Task Force in 1988 and oversaw most US intelligence activities up to 1989 as part of the President's Foreign Intelligence Advisory Board. Brzezinski started to work for the Department of State in the 1960s. Born in Poland and educated in the United States (Harvard) after World War II, Brzezinski was an American cold warrior with a deep nostalgia for the cultural roots he had left on the other side of the Atlantic. For Brzezinski as for many other US foreign policy makers of the Cold War, personal history was not just an anecdote. It was part and parcel of their world outlook, their understanding of ideological differences, and their passion for international politics.

While serving as National Security Advisor, Brzezinski adopted a blatantly anti-communist, mostly anti-Soviet, stance. He was credited in 1981 with normalizing diplomatic relations between the United States and China. At the same time, he positioned himself as one of the most hawkish detractors of the Soviet regime, vehemently criticizing the Soviet invasion of Afghanistan. Brzezinski responded to the Soviet occupation of Afghanistan by reviving John Foster Dulles' famous "dominoes theory": if the United States let Afghanistan fall to Soviet communism, Pakistan and Iran would soon follow. Throughout his diplomatic career, Brzezinski chose to devise a foreign policy geared toward Eastern Europe, Central Asia, and Soviet communism. Analyzing Soviet moves and advances was his first preoccupation as National Security Advisor. An effective national security policy, he affirmed, required developing an anticipated sense of what the Soviets would do next. After serving the US government, Brzezinski never ceased to remind scholars about this primary foreign policy objective. He wrote two books, *The Grand Chessboard* and *The Grand Failure*[72] (about the demise of Soviet communism), to emphasize the fact that the key to (American) geopolitical stability was Eastern Europe and Central Asia, or what in the 1990s he would reconceptualize as the heart or core of Eurasia (and often would refer to simply as Eurasia).

The post-Cold War era presented a challenge to Brzezinski's foreign policy beliefs. The Soviet Union had collapsed. Measuring American security in relation to the Soviet threat was no longer possible. Russia was still around, but building up defense strategies at home and abroad to contain the spread of communism specifically was no longer a credible option. Or so it appeared. Instead of going into pre-retirement, Brzezinski found a new motivation in the post-Cold War world. The end of the Cold War was both a challenge and an opportunity. Since no clear order appeared to have succeeded the Cold War, and postmodern times authorized multiple geopolitical scenarios to be played out, why not pretend the Cold War (or something closely resembling it) was still a contemporary reality? Why not simply point to the same old threats (Russia, Eastern Europe) and write pamphlets about the panic and destruction that would certainly ensue if the United States failed to contain the menace? This was exactly what Brzezinski's tabloid realism suggested. Brzezinski's tabloid realism anachronistically revived Cold War politics in an age when most (but not Brzezinski) believed that the Cold War was over.

Tabloid realism as a discursive genre gave Brzezinski something to do and hope for (other than teach a few foreign policy courses). It also offered him a semblance of public responsibility, provided him with the impression that he was still useful to the American government. What was left to do now, even though Soviet communism was gone, was convince the American public that it was *still* a dangerous world out there. In fact, Brzezinski argued, it was a more dangerous world now that communism had lost its grip on many third world nations. What the collapse of communism had produced was the vision that multiple nations existed and that there was a plethora of leaders and disenfranchised groups of people who selfishly sought power, legitimacy, and wealth. In the territories formerly controlled or influenced by the Soviet Union (including parts of the Middle East and Central Asia), one now found groups of individuals bearing a grudge against the United States. This anti-US sentiment was perhaps the main common attitude these groups had inherited from the old Soviet Union. Adding to the danger, many of these groups (what some today would prefer to call networks) had gained control over the weapons that were formerly owned by the Soviets, and they had the capacity to hurt the United States. Furthermore, many of these post-Soviet organizations/groups were unwilling to partake of the West's prosperity. For them, being free from communism did not necessarily mean that they would unequivocally embrace Western liberalism. As Brzezinski noted: "One billion Moslems will not be impressed by a West that is perceived as preaching to them the values of consumerism, the merits of amorality, and the blessings of atheism. To many Moslems, the West's message (and especially America's) is repulsive."[73]

For Brzezinski, Soviet communism could still be blamed for leaving "us" (the United States) with a world that was still "out of control."[74] Communism had not died peacefully. It had left its marks on the free world and still haunted America's security in the post-Cold War. Thus, there was no time for the United States to rejoice after the collapse of Eastern European and Central Asian communist regimes. Post-communism still had to be contained. The old Cold War geopolitical strategies had to be maintained. Balancing, deterring, containing, and building alliances (Brzezinski was one of the main proponents of NATO's enlargement[75]) should continue to be America's top geostrategic priorities.

Central to this reinvented Cold War Realpolitik was the need for the United States to control what Brzezinski called the "Eurasian Chessboard." The "Eurasian Chessboard" was a geostrategic zone that stretched from the shores of Brittany to the tundras of Siberia.[76] This "oval-shaped" board was going to be the "setting for the game" of geopolitics in the next century.[77] What was crucial to the "game" was the empty middle of the board. The two extremities were relatively stable (the European Union on one side; Japan and China on the other) and densely populated. But "[s]tretching between the western and eastern extremities is a sparsely populated and currently politically fluid and organizationally fragmented vast middle space that was formerly occupied by a powerful rival to US preeminence, a rival that was once committed to the goal of pushing America out of Eurasia."[78]

This vast middle space was the locus of the power vacuum left by the Soviet Union. This was where post-communism was at its worst. This was the space the United States had to occupy and control. In drawing the rules of this board-game, Brzezinski reaffirmed Eastern Europe and Central Asia's primacy to American foreign policy: "For America, the chief geopolitical prize is Eurasia."[79] History had demonstrated, Brzezinski affirmed, that a power vacuum in Eastern Europe generally led to major international crises. In the twentieth century, the United States had twice been dragged into European conflicts caused by similar types of power vacuums (in both WWI and WWII). After World War II, the United States rightly intervened to make sure that the Soviet Union would not take advantage of the Eurasian power vacuum. This led to the Cold War, but also to geopolitical stability for Europe (and the United States) for roughly 40 years. Today, such an intervention was once again necessary so that stability could be maintained. If the United States did not intervene to occupy the center of the board, the geostrategic game would be lost: enemies of the United States (from Southeast Asia to the Balkans) would certainly take over Eurasia. Once Eurasia was lost, the United States would be in direct danger. If the United States could not control Eurasia's empty middle, it would not be able to remain safe within its own borders.

Revealingly, Brzezinski's Eurasian political strategy was premised upon yet another cartographical representation of international politics. As seen above, tabloid realism often started with cartographical imageries and maps, and Brzezinski's analysis was no exception to the rule. Brzezinski took the old Cold War map and, starting with it, redrew Europe and Asia, which now formed one single geopolitical entity characterized by its structural weakness in the middle. Brzezinski's map of Europe and Asia as one, with heavy extremities but an empty core, yielded the image of a disarticulated body, one that was about to break apart. The limbs of this geopolitical body were stretching in different directions, leaving the frame of the structure to be ripped to shreds by hostile political organisms that were about to invade this weakened body. This was what the Cold War map would now look like, in the early twenty-first century. And this was precisely why the United States could not lose sight of the Eurasian Chessboard. The United States had an opportunity to strengthen the core of the structure. It had to lend its vital strengths to this apparently diseased body politic.

This particular cartographical imagery (and imaginative geography) was of course structurally constraining. For Brzezinski, it served the purpose of legitimizing America's continued control of the region while identifying the threats, pointing to the dangers, and mobilizing the necessary energies. Brzezinski called this new map the "Grand Chessboard." The point of this "Grand Chessboard" was to visually represent the United States' (inter)national interests. Brzezinski reminded us that "[t]he exercise of American global primacy must be sensitive to the fact that political geography remains a critical consideration in international affairs."[80] But, he added, "[p]olitical geography, however, must adapt to the new realities of power."[81] On this map, political geography was clearly adapted to America's desire for power in Eastern Europe and Central Asia. Without deploying this so-called "new" map, the need to fill the Eurasian vacuum could not be easily visualized by foreign policy makers whom, as Huntington did before, Brzezinski was hoping to persuade. Without visualizing the vacuum, US national security would be redirected toward other parts of the globe (the Middle East, Latin America, Southeast Asia) and away from Eastern Europe and Central Asia. Brzezinski urgently needed this map so that his tabloid realist games could make sense and eventually be played by America's foreign policy makers. No longer a foreign policy maker himself, Brzezinski could thus still "make" foreign policy by proxy. All this scheming was quite self-serving and, in a sense, self-referential. Containing the attacks of the rogues, the outlaws, and the villains – from Eastern Europe to Central Asia – who still wanted to shatter America's hegemony required Brzezinski to re-imagine the specter of a Eurasian anarchy. For Brzezinski, Eurasia was still the objective today, as it had been back then, at the time when communism was predominant in that region. In Brzezinski's tabloid realist imaginary, the specter to conjure up was really not communism then. Rather, the specter that truly seemed to haunt Brzezinski was Eurasia itself, no matter whether Eurasia was seen as being taken over by communism or perceived as a structural void.

Thus, during the Cold War and afterwards, Eurasia played a similar role for Brzezinski. Eurasia had to be controlled by the United States because, when all was said and done, Eurasia was "our" geographical buffer. Conceptually, Eurasia buffered the West from the East, the "us" from the rest. Eurasia as a buffer allowed the United States to remain unique and superior in its own sphere of influence (which, increasingly so after the Cold War, seemed to span the entire surface of the globe). Of course, the Eurasian buffer served to justify the involvement of the United States in the political affairs of another continent too. But it operated as a conceptual device that worked to preserve America's difference with the rest of the world, a rest of the world that America ought to either control or contain. This buffering/distancing effect provided by the Eurasian Chessboard was what can be called Brzezinski's contribution to orientalist ideological discourses. As Gregory has shown in his latest work, orientalist discourses and representations (still today) are often premised upon carefully crafted and purposefully designed imaginative geographies intent on sorting out the "us" from the "them," identifying the "self" from the "other."[82] Orientalism was the main ideological thrust behind Brzezinski's tabloid realist games. Orientalism was also the ideology Brzezinski had championed when he worked for the US government. Thus, what remained a constant in Brzezinski's geostrategic analyses (during and after the Cold War) was a persistent attempt to redefine the West by deploying a geopolitical discourse about the Orient, the East, the Other, in other words, that very place that Brzezinski himself had left at a young age (being born in Eastern Europe).[83]

As it turned out, the invention of a Eurasian strategy was not simply a geopolitical necessity for Brzezinski. It became a moral duty as well. And here came the popular/populist punch line of this particular tabloid realist story and imaginary. The moral symbol that *was* the United States had always stood behind a strong military arsenal and a clear geostrategy of power. This was why the West and the United States (as the West's flagship of morality) had prevailed over the Soviet Union and, perhaps too prematurely, had declared victory in the Cold War. The United States beat the Soviet Union on moral grounds by displacing communism from Eastern Europe and Central Asia. But the moral quest for Brzezinski did not end with the disappearance of Soviet communism from Eurasia. It could not. The permanent reconstruction of the United States, of its moral strength, required that Eurasia be endlessly positioned as a subaltern and inferior geographical entity, one that would be in need of constant (Western) assistance.

Because the moral battles of the Cold War had not been completely won, the West and the United States could not let their guard down. Thus, the production of orientalist discourses about the West and the United States could not stop.[84] In Brzezinski's analysis, the way the West oriented itself in relation to the East was a continued guarantee not just of global political supremacy, but also, and more importantly, of victory over moral decay.[85] It perpetuated the moral crusade. For the United States to reduce its power capacities or ignore the geopolitical games in Eurasia would be a sure path toward amoral anarchy or, as Brzezinski now called it, "permissive cornucopia."[86] "Permissive cornucopia" was the fateful moral consequence of the euphoria that had followed the apparent death of communism. The feeling that all threats were gone, that everything was possible, that money could be spent lavishly in all sorts of global commercial ventures (globalization) and in new modes of technological interactions (the internet) was a dangerous mistake. "Permissive cornucopia" was a syndrome of postmodern times, when values, truths, and historical certainties had become questioned. "Permissive cornucopia" made possible the erroneous belief (according to Brzezinski) that America's Cold War values were obsolete. And so, "permissive cornucopia" developed at the expense of national security and political hegemony. If the careless spending (of money, rationality, morality, and security) continued at the pace it had followed throughout the 1990s, the late twentieth- and early twenty-first-century Pax Americana would fall prey to the same forces that had once destroyed the Pax Romana. As Brzezinski concluded: "Unless there is some deliberate effort to re-establish the centrality of some moral criteria for the exercise of self-control over gratification as an end in itself, the phase of American preponderance may not last long, despite the absence of any self-evident replacement."[87] This was why America's preponderance once again required the deployment of an orientalist discourse of geopolitics.

Of course, orientalism was much too technical, theoretical, and critical a concept to be used in tabloid literatures such as Brzezinski's texts. Again, tabloid realism's mass appeal demanded that technical terms be excised from the discourse. Instead of orientalism, the image of a grand chessboard combined with the map of a Eurasian vacuum was mobilized to convey the same message. As with Kaplan's and Huntington's own versions, Brzezinski's tabloid realism was infused with a sense of moral conservatism and national exceptionalism. But this particular tabloid realism was further adorned with an orientalist ideology that guaranteed the continuity of the story and kept alive the geopolitical imperative from the Cold War to its confusing aftermath.

Tabloid realism, or America's hope for geopolitical therapy

Postmodern times were (still are?) opportunistic times. But, as recent studies have shown, the geopolitical opportunities provided by popular media were discovered much before the arrival of postmodernity. Tabloid culture has been around in the United States for decades. What postmodernity introduced though was the ability to use popular entertainment and the tabloid genre of reporting as generalized models of knowledge construction and truth-making or -telling. Today, even "high politics" experts can unabashedly make use of trash culture and tabloid media to give substance to their beliefs and ideologies. As we saw in Chapter 1, the apparent free flow of cultural signs and objects, the more readily accepted challenges to modernity's grand narratives, and the growing suspicion about historical certainties (all of which are characteristics generally attributed to postmodern mediatized culture) have spurred the belief among geopolitical scholars that format, style, and mastery over the medium are sufficient instruments with which (and on the formal basis of which) discourses of danger, emergency, and security can be constructed. In this chapter, I have called geopolitical scholars who apparently embrace postmodern stylistics tabloid realists. Behind the veil of their postmodern imageries and imaginaries though, tabloid realists wish to re-inject stable meanings to the nation, the modern state, Western civilization, and what they consider to be the West's messianic leader, the United States. Tabloid realism is a postmodern discursive formation, a collage of various ideological elements and rhetorical/representational techniques that, before 9/11 in fact, intended to bring back into contemporary political culture and geopolitical debates a dose of realist certainty and fixity. Still, as the analysis of Kaplan's text revealed, the only way this collage actually could stick together (and look like a coherent structure) was by functioning at the level of a simulation of postmodern geopolitics. Neither true nor false, the "new" geopolitical representations established by tabloid realist intellectuals of American statecraft like Kaplan, Huntington, and Brzezinski at the very end of the twentieth century could only function to the extent that they were built upon specific cartographical models that became the sole points of textual and representational reference for the political, cultural, and ideological situations and processes that were said to exist in the uncertain world "out there," and that allegedly made this world a dangerous and insecure one to live in. As Baudrillard has explained, a simulation is always "characterized by a *precession of the model*, of all models around the merest fact – the models come first, and their orbital circulation constitutes the genuine magnetic field of events."[88] The tabloid realist simulation of postmodern/post-Cold War geopolitics could be all the more power-ful since it did not have to be supported by facts or "real" events. Tabloid realist geopolitics offered its own facts and realities, and derived cultural effects (dan-ger, fear) and ideological lessons (passive acceptance of the model, rekindling of security measures) from them. But tabloid realist geopolitics did not stop here and, in a sense, went past the postmodern simulation it tried to establish. Far from being comfortable with the postmodern models they constructed, tabloid realists became wary of them too. Caught in their own spectacular games and ultimately frightened by the thought that no real referent might ever be recovered from their maps, tabloid realists abruptly turned their backs against their simulated exercises and hoped to show their readers that the very map they had offered had to be cast away. Paranoid about the loss of meaning and certainty (that they further ex-acerbated), tabloid realists abandoned their postmodern designs and desperately called for a return to good old modern (Cold War) politics, when America suppos-edly possessed a clear sense of its own identity and understood what or whom it needed to be protected from.

But perhaps it was not only this overtly spectacular and sensationalistic, but later reactive and conservative (in a word, tabloid), rendition of contemporary American geopolitics that attracted the public (not just other scholars) to the tabloid realist genre (many of Kaplan's, Huntington's, and, to a lesser extent, Brzezinski's books became national best-sellers). Something akin to what so-ciologists and cultural studies specialists have witnessed with people who read tabloid newspapers or watch television talk-shows was perhaps at work here too. Indeed, scholars who have examined tabloid culture have noticed that, whereas watching the *Oprah Winfrey Show*, for example, or reading the *National Enquirer* may have some entertainment appeal, there is also something comforting for the (American) public about the stories these media present and, of course, about the way they are being presented. Simply put, tabloid stories have a therapeutic effect.[89] When social and political realities do not readily make sense, when politi-cal ideologies are not immediately present to provide a sense of rationality to the events (because perhaps there is no longer any major conflict between dominant ideologies), and when a previous social order is seemingly transformed through an acceleration of styles, processes, and technologies, tabloid realism "keeps things just as they were."[90] This point may seem contradictory since the tabloid realist genre employed all sorts of postmodern visual and narrative props that ap-parently destabilized and sometimes frightened. But precisely because the tabloid realist story was a simulation, a show that could not be accepted or rejected but rather was meant to be absorbed/consumed as a whole, it gave the impression that everything, in the end, would be back to normal. In the simulated (partly true and partly fabricated, at once real and fake) universe of tabloid reality and tabloid realism, and despite the oddities, monstrosities, injustices, and disasters that were being displayed, things eventually rediscovered their ascribed, normal place. Social/political meaning was (attempted to be) recovered. Order was restored or, if it was not completely (as in Huntington's and Brzezinski's texts), simple recipes for order and security were now provided. And, exacerbating the sense of passivity that was a crucial part of tabloid entertainment, these recipes could be followed by the reader/viewer with relative ease and without much effort. The reader/viewer did not have to be constantly on the lookout, hunting for the "enemy within," as had been the case with the stories found in Cold War popular magazines. Simply, the consumers of these tabloid stories were asked to accept that the identity of the enemy that was presented to them was meaningful. There is no doubt that this genre of presentation/acceptance of certain realities would go a long way in explaining many public attitudes in the United States after the terrorist attacks of 9/11.

Tabloid realism's therapeutic remedy took the form of an appeal to order and security. Order and security, tabloid realists told us, had to be reinserted into culture and society. American politicians, tabloid realists told their readers, had to make the securitization of the nation the number one policy priority. Once again, this was a claim that had been forcefully voiced in the United States before 9/11 and that would become a normal, quasi-natural belief after the terrorist attacks. Cultural, racial, and ideological measures had to be taken to protect and solidify American society, but also, and perhaps more importantly, to morally and culturally homogenize it. Tabloid realists announced to their audience that this was what the public wanted because, as Americans, it was what they needed to fend off postmodern challenges and dangers coming mostly from abroad.[91] This conservative, protectionist, but possibly reassuring discourse was then presented as the best remedy against the world's new pathologies. Or so tabloid realists wanted their readers to believe. Even when they mobilized the specters of chaos and national insecurity, Kaplan, Huntington, and Brzezinski also wished to rally the (national) troops, regroup, reorganize, and reinscribe meaning where they feared it had been lost. Sometimes, their attempts backfired, as was the case with Kaplan's model of a "holographic and postmodern map" that, in the end, was able to breed more uncertainty than security. Most of the time, though, it would succeed. Huntington managed to retrieve a crucial role for the nation-state (mostly the American nation) in a world replete with cultural fault-lines. And, in the wake of the terrorist attacks against the United States in September 2001, Huntington would be hailed as this country's new "prophet."[92] Brzezinski also reinvented a stabilizing function for post-Cold War American foreign policy by (re)introducing orientalist beliefs and premising a new geostrategic balancing system upon such an ideological vision (which would also champion a new "colonial present"[93]).

The troubling part is that the pathologies identified by these tabloid realists were once again the direct product of their own simulated scenarios. These pathologies were the result of the geopolitical models and their images from which tabloid realists hoped to draw ideological lessons and conservatively remobilize their audience. In other words, it was these tabloid realists' self-constructed, self-referential, and self-fulfilling pathologies that made possible the need for therapeutic reme-dies. Thus, their desperate calls for a return to the "modern" ideas of the American nation, American citizenship, America's "war," and American national security were as simulated and fictitious as the conceptual models from which they were derived. Again, this is not to say that the therapies (like the pathologies to which they responded) were false, incorrect, or unsubstantiated. Some members of the public may indeed have found some of the tabloid therapies useful. The point is rather to recognize that the therapies were convenient ideological measures (with important political consequences for America if indeed they were implemented, and some of them would be under George W. Bush) that were merely the outcome of conceptual models with a capacity to fabricate reality, any reality. Placed in the hands of media theorists or cultural studies scholars, postmodern and tabloid tools and techniques may be pleasing, entertaining, and perhaps illuminating. Placed in the hands of early twenty-first-century intellectuals of statecraft (some of whom would be claiming to shape a new American ideology of war, as we will see in the next chapters), these same instruments would become terrifying and perhaps terror-producing too as, for many people in the United States and beyond, the proposed therapy would sometimes be perceived as the pathology.

3 Discourses of war, geographies of abjection

American intellectuals of statecraft and the avenging of 9/11

I guess for all of us there's that sense of how little control we have over things. And if this can happen, what's going to be the next attack? Living in a world like that is pretty disconcerting.

Reverend Bill Wade, Headmaster at St. Andrew's-Sewanee School, Tennessee[1]

Like Pearl Harbor, the events of September 11 were a terrible defeat . . . It is not only the loss of life and the physical destruction in New York and Washington, but also the effects on our economy and on our daily lives that have to be considered in thinking about the gravity of this defeat . . . A taken-for-granted sense of security in our own country has been lost, perhaps forever.

Robert N. Bellah[2]

There looms, within abjection, one of those violent, dark revolts of being, directed against a threat that seems to emanate from an exorbitant outside or inside, ejected beyond the scope of the possible, the tolerable, the thinkable. It lies there, quite close, but it cannot be assimilated. It beseeches, worries, and fascinates desire, which, nevertheless, does not let itself be seduced. Apprehensive, desire turns aside; sickened, it rejects. A certainty protects it from the shameful – a certainty of which it is proud holds on to it. But simultaneously, just the same, that impetus, that spasm, that leap is drawn toward an elsewhere as tempting as it is condemned. Unflaggingly, like an inescapable boomerang, a vortex of summons and repulsion places the one haunted by it literally beside himself.

Julia Kristeva[3]

Struggling to rebuild a war story after 9/11

America has had its share of horror, violence, incomprehension, despair, and fear since the early morning hours of September 11, 2001. From the initial terrorist attacks to the "anthrax scare," from a war in Afghanistan to a military invasion of Iraq, the landscape of American politics both at home and abroad has been dominated by the feeling that disaster, terror, and death can strike at any moment.

Politicians, religious leaders, media pundits, and academics have openly stated that, since 9/11, terror and terrorism have caught up with America. But what it means to say that terror and terrorism have caught up with America is not as obvious as it may seem. It is not simply meant to acknowledge that alien forces, unclear and shadowy enemies from beyond the land, have attacked, destroyed, and reshuffled America's sense of stability, certainty, security, control, and cultural normalcy. What is meant when so many public voices argue that terror has caught up with America is that, now, after such a visual shock and defeat, with such a glaring sense of national loss, America and Americans themselves will have to be part of the terror and of the new war that will bear terror's name.

After 9/11, once the initial shock started to fade a bit (and the moment of silence of the event receded, as I suggested in the Introduction), America and Americans were told that they had to find ways of rebuilding national identity, that once again they had to rediscover what Tom Engelhardt aptly labeled "victory culture."[4] Only a new sense of American triumphalism would be able to help American citizens overcome the trauma of the terrorist attacks. And despite the incomprehension of the new terrorist danger, for America to rise triumphant war would have to be yet again the order of the day (and of endless days to come). To fend off the terrorist attacks, both in the so-called material landscape of post-9/11 international relations and in the imaginary of America's national story, America and Americans would have to be at war against new enemies, new foes that would be called terrorists this time. This was quite simply the "true" American story after 9/11. Again, Engelhardt's words pronounced in the 1990s (with the Cold War in mind) became so pertinent and somewhat prophetic for the aftermath of 9/11: could there ever be "an imaginable 'America' without enemies and without the story of their slaughter and our triumph?"[5]

Of course, the association of the war story with terrorism – the pairing of America's triumphant and belligerent path to victory with the attacks of the terrorists – and the condensation of this association into a short symbolic phrase ("war on terror") that now should be able to encapsulate all sorts of meanings, was also supposed to have a justified point of departure. America had been attacked. Americans had been grievously harmed. Such a baseless offense could only demand American war-making as a response, as a logical outcome. As the French philosopher Alain Badiou remarked, the juxtaposition of the terrorist and terrorizing attacks to America's sense of loss and despair after 9/11 could only give way to a war sequence, to a story about the US nation and its people that would have to be (re)played through the mobilization of the military, the militarization of the nation (as homeland security), future battle scenes, and often unspecified enemies that nonetheless would have to be destroyed.[6] As Badiou put it, the once more craving to be triumphant "American imperial power, in the formal representation it makes of itself, has war as the privileged, indeed unique, form of the attestation of its existence."[7] Badiou concluded that "the powerful subjective unity that carries the Americans away in their desire for vengeance and war is immediately constructed around the flag and the army."[8]

Whether the new American war (and its story) was justified or not, whether it was fair retaliation for a vile crime, whether it was meant to recapture a clear sense of national identity and historical destiny, whether it was an attempt at defeating despair (just like after Pearl Harbor, for example), or whether it was in fact, as some have argued, part of a larger global strategy of American *imperium* that merely took advantage of the 9/11 attacks to establish "a much more ambitious unilateralism as the US ruling class acts in the confidence that it can now be the solitary global police force,"[9] the war on terror was now a common American reality. A term used in all occasions and a vague concept nonetheless accepted and adopted by most US citizens (even if they – and their politicians – did not always understand what it implied), "war on terror" had become as American as apple pie. It was in fact so American that it soon did not matter whether "we" (Americans) were replying to "their" (the terrorists') initial attack or whether "we" had started it (after all, the decision in October 2001 to attack the Taliban and Afghanistan, who were not the direct agents behind the 9/11 attacks, was unilaterally American). As Neil Smith mentioned, this time, in this latest version of the war story, "the United States stands as the original belligerent state."[10] This time, to protect itself against an enemy with no land, no political affiliation, barely a face (other than the mug shots of the 9/11 attackers and a few sightings of Osama Bin Laden), and hardly a name (if pressed, the name became al Qaeda, but the more commonly used label was "terrorism"), the crusade to revive America's identity through war would have to be active, offensive, and creative. This new installment in the American story of war and revenge would have to chart territories and concepts, design and imagine adversaries and others as if they were real soldiers or people, as if they were actually embodied military or even civilian targets. Newfangled denominations and categorizations would be created – enemy or unlawful combatants – in order to try to anchor this war, for which terror was after all the primary target, into some semblance of historical or political referentiality.

Some critical geopolitics and international relations scholars have argued that the new post-9/11 American war story was really not so novel or different from what had happened during the Cold War. As Gregory has mentioned, "after September 11 Bush was sure who 'they' were, and his newfound certainty . . . reactivated the interpretative dispositions of the Cold War."[11] According to such Cold War interpretative dispositions, the global cartography deployed in the new war on terror discourses was still very much Manichean (us/them, good/evil), and the narrative quest for victory was still marked by a "vengeful gesture" whose objective was "to reveal the face of the other *as* other."[12] I find those explanations emphasizing the continuum of an American war story that must unfold as a series of endless episodes of construction of self versus other oppositional identities – even if extreme ones – too predictable, too convenient, and probably too comfortable. Although it is undeniable that the desire to isolate, objectify, demonize, and possibly kill others was and still is at work in post-9/11 American war narratives and national imaginaries, this self/other oppositional perspective was not the final point of the new story. Rather, the American war story, I believe, started to be preoccupied with what, following Julia Kristeva, one might call strategies of abjection as ways of triumphing over complete despair at a time when enemies were no longer clearly identifiable. Rather than returning once more to the same old "us versus them" elaborations that can only take us so far in our critical perspectives on the role, power, and consequences of imagined war stories, I suggest that abjection (which, as I will explain below, is positioned beyond object/subject dichotomies) can better help us to make sense of how and why constructing a narrative of American identity and global supremacy as a way of overcoming despair also requires embracing terror, making the war on terror one's own, and in fact becoming one with terror. Engelhardt had noted that the American war story really started with the destruction of the Indian "wild west." This initial, total, and quasi-absolute "successful emptying of the land opened necessary space for the intense idealism with which the United States became associated."[13] Today, with the post-9/11 American war story, we may well be witnessing a project (whose implications are probably not clearly understood by those who champion it) that consists of emptying the global landscape through war and terror for the absolute triumph of what might be left of American idealism over despair. In this project though, there is no guarantee that the self/nation/America may still be around at the time of the hoped-for final triumph, as the absoluteness of the war/terror today does not always distinguish between self and other, home and away, subject and object.

Abjection

In a cultural and political context in which it is being argued by many American public figures, pundits, and intellectuals of statecraft (the main narrators of today's war story) that America has no choice but to be one with terror, Kristeva's theory of abjection allows us to make sense of what has happened in the public sphere where, in the immediate aftermath of 9/11, new discourses of war, new geopolitics of security, new policies of violence, and new theories of national identity were produced.[14] Unlike the traditional dichotomy between subject and object that has long been privileged by intellectuals of statecraft and that some contemporary geopolitical and cultural critics are still claiming resurfaced after 9/11, the abject is a condition or disposition of being that does not allow one to fall on either side of the subjectivity/objectivity, us/them, hero/villain, nation/enemy, or good/evil divide. The abject is both beyond us and within us. Abjection is both a rejection and a fascination. It is a condemnation through which the body nonetheless expresses itself. The abject is also not just an affirmation of the self through the opposition of an unacceptable other.[15] Rather, as Kristeva suggests in the quotation that opens this chapter, it is a "revolt of being." Being abjected, being the abject means that one fixates on a threat, a risk, a horror, a source of disgust, or a terror that seems to "emanate from an exorbitant outside or inside" and that must be "ejected beyond the tolerable or the thinkable."[16] But, in its revulsion against this unthinkable, the abject is nonetheless "drawn toward this elsewhere" that is "as tempting as it is condemned."[17]

Although not a conventional definition of being achieved through recognition of or opposition to an other than self, an objectified alter ego, or even an enemy, abjection is still "a desire for meaning,"[18] and a desire to figure out what the "I," the first person, or the individual body might become. Kristeva suggests that the "I" (of the body/self) becomes "itself" (I become "myself") through the experience of the abject. Abjection is a search for the meaning of "oneself," of one's body, without recourse to subjectivity or a need for objectivity. The German literary critic, philosopher, and theorist of disgust Winfried Menninghaus feels compelled to ask: "What sort of strange non-object and non-subject is this – one that precedes the distinction between conscious and unconscious [in the Freudian scheme, revised by Kristeva], and that always already must be 'cast out' in order that some 'speaking subject' can speak of itself as 'I'?"[19] Menninghaus pushes further the search for this abject non-subject in Kristeva's thought on disgust and suggests that, for Kristeva, the paradigmatic figure of the abject is the image of the maternal body. This Kristevean maternal body of disgust and abjection has very little to do with actual mothers. Rather, the maternal body that is and exudes abjection holds a central, defining place in the post-Freudian psychological and symbolic order that characterizes the formation of subjectivity and being, or, put somewhat differently, that shapes the contours of what the "I" will become. The image or symbol of the maternal body – that primal scene replete with so much horror and disgust that it cannot fail but to produce abjection – is what Kristeva calls an "absolute locus."[20] It is absolute, according to Kristeva, because it embodies all conditions of possibility of being at once. As Menninghaus puts it, the absoluteness of this image/symbol that must yield abjection (that is the source of the abject) "is pre-objectival; it forms no circumscribed subject; it is undifferentiated; it is nameless."[21] Menninghaus continues: "This non-object is the inaccessible ground of all (future) distinctions and the source of pleasure (jouissance) that exceeds all desire for an object and all satisfaction in objects."[22] It is precisely this pre-subjective and non-objectival image/symbol/scene of indistinction, undifferentiation, and confusion (since it refuses to set up oppositional identities, selves versus others) that is so difficult to accept for the individual body, for the "I" in search of a being. Thus, the abject is a repulsion; it must cast away. Every time it casts away objects of disgust, horror, or terror, abjection is yet another (perhaps futile) attempt to fend off this image of the unitary, inaccessible, and undifferentiated maternal body. But, at the same time, through this very repulsive motion, there is a strong attraction and libidinal attachment to that which is supposed to be so foreign to us, to that which disgusts us (because it reminds us of a primal pre-Oedipal point where our "body" was not distinguishable from others, and particularly from that absolute Other that is, for Kristeva, the maternal body). Consequently, the abject contains within its repulsion a desire to capture that which is thought to be disgusting, a desire to be one with the source of so much horror (even if the individual being, the subject in the making, often attempts to repress such a desire and struggles to establish abjection simply as rejection).

What may be some cultural, political, or even ideological consequences or applications of this otherwise psychological, symbolic, and (pre-)subjective phenomenon? Is Kristeva's abjection to be confined within the limits of the symbolic order that determines the formation of individual subjectivities or beings, or can this strange attraction/repulsion also yield some critical interpretive insight for the construction of social, political, and ideological orders (symbolic or not)? Kristeva provides us with some initial clues regarding the critical potential for thinking cultural and political orders through the concept of abjection in the following quotation: "We may call it [abjection] a border; abjection is above all ambiguity . . . [W]hile releasing a hold, it does not radically cut off the subject from what threatens it – on the contrary, abjection acknowledges it to be in perpetual danger."[23] According to Kristeva, the ambiguity of meaning, representation, and identity is what is at stake in abjection, in the repulsion/attraction that characterizes abject dispositions of disgust. Ambiguity of meaning, non-recognition of representation, and undifferentiation of identity are the dangers that the borders tenuously drawn by reactions of abjection are supposed to contain. Yet, in abjection, the boundary-lines are never so clear (they cannot be since what lies beyond the dangers is attractive too). Even attempts at imposing absolute differences through abjection are likely to fail, as the only absolute there really is, according to Kristeva, is that of the primordial condition of ambiguity, indistinction, and radical openness to all future possibilities. Thus, faced with the threat of total ambiguity of meaning and being (at a psychological, but also social, cultural, and ideological level), abjection often presents itself as a desperate search for meaning. It is a search for meaning, a desire for the meaningful, that first seeks to set up newly created subjective and objective oppositions (and identity constructs), but that soon also realizes that this will not be sufficient, or satisfactory, or resilient enough. Inevitably, the search for meaning through the abject, the need to cut off from ambiguity and lack of differentiation in order to impose a subject, to create an "I," will also find itself driven toward the incomprehensible, the irrational, the non-human, and the terror, horror, and disgust that the lack of meaning provokes. One could say that desiring meaning and identity through abjection is always already a deconstructive endeavor, even from the very moment when the abject seeks to take place as a constructive and defining enterprise. This is precisely why subject/object, us/them, or self/other dichotomies are no longer useful in explaining quests for identity and meaning that are shaped by discourses, representations, and often acts of abjection.[24] As Kristeva summarily puts it, instead of a self-as-subject defining itself by opposing an other, in abjection, "I" spit "myself" out, "I" reject "myself," and I "abject *myself* by the same motion through which 'I' claim to establish *myself*."[25] Abjection is a borderline (of identity, being) where the body's search for meaning encroaches upon itself, upon the subject, and becomes one with what is apparently disgusting and cannot be tolerated.[26] And this encroachment of the "I" upon itself (rather than an affirmation of itself) and the corollary temptation toward that which is absolutely disgusting and undifferentiated belong both to the symbolic order of the psychology of the individual and to at once imaginary and real social, cultural, and ideological orders inside and outside which collective selves/beings struggle to retrieve unambiguous meanings and identities. Kristeva herself does make the transition from the symbolic order of individual human psychology to the cultural and political orders that seek to reduce the ambiguities of everyday social existence. She notes that abject disgust is always the "primer of culture."[27]

It is indeed often with abjection that one's culture, any culture, ends and starts; it is along the tenuous borderline of the abject that one's culture is protected and threatened, safeguarded and annihilated at the same time, in the same motion.

Abject America after 9/11

In more ways than one, the post-9/11 condition of geopolitical terror in the United States seems to embrace Kristeva's analysis of the abject. The war on terror initiated as a response to the attacks of September 11 has taken the US government and its military arsenal to Afghanistan since November 2001 and to Iraq since March 2003. The war on terror, in its many inceptions (against al Qaeda, against the Taliban, against Saddam Hussein, against Sunni insurgents in Iraq), is a violent rejection of the unthinkable and the intolerable. It is a disgusting revulsion against something (that America calls "terror" or "evil") that does not make sense, that was/is still horrifying, that allegedly comes from "elsewhere" (although it was and may still be within "us"), that cannot be identified as a traditional object of geopolitics (a network, fleeting enemies whose leaders may or may not be dead, insurgent groups with multiple affiliations, masters of terror, a religion, a whole civilization perhaps), but that is nonetheless necessary for America to "establish" itself and to recover a sense of victory.[28] As media pundits and intellectuals of statecraft have reminded Americans, the war on terror is a different war, with no really distinguishable home and away fronts. It is a war in the border regions of the concept of war. It has no beginning and no end; only battles, spurts of violence along the way. As American political leaders like to repeat, it is a terror America did not want (and perhaps did not start), but that it must nonetheless readily accept in order to succeed, survive, and safeguard its own culture, in other words, to try to save itself. It is a war that America must own and, in this context, America may indeed be compelled to initiate the military attacks, invade, and perhaps terrorize too.

Media pundits, politicians, military leaders and their (tabloid) discourses after 9/11 often have taken for granted that America's war on terror needs abjection, that America has been abjected and is the abject. They have assumed that Americans are in a condition of deep psychological despair and disgust. But these discourses also affirm that it is from the depths of such desperation and horror that Americans will be able to rise again by, first, understanding the new geopolitical realities and, second, retrieving a will to fight, destroy, and eventually triumph. Clearly, many of the (war) stories produced after 9/11 have abjected the enemy, the terrorists, the "evil" states, and their "rogue" leaders who, in turn, did abject America, we are told. Thus, most Americans must abject terror, and the war against terror too. Again, this signifies that, as much as they seek to reject terror and push it away, they must desire it too, they must go through it, they will have to accept it, and, many pundits and intellectuals believe, they have to crave the social and political meaning, the sense of unambiguous, clear-cut, and differentiated geopolitical direction and meaning that supposedly will come from abjection only. Coming to realize that the protection and definition of one's culture, the re-establishment of oneself (as a geopolitical body), and the recovery of a triumphant war story will be achieved by embracing terror/horror requires a guiding and clarifying literature, one that seeks to present abjection as a form of rejection and differentiation only, in other words, as a non-ambiguous borderline of social, cultural, and political meaning. This geopolitical abjection needs a context (post-9/11 American culture and society), but it also must find a subtext. Put slightly differently, the geopolitics of abjection practiced by/in the United States since 9/11 requires the presence of what I have called tabloid discourses, that is to say, texts and other media or modes of representation that talk (to the public and their symbolic, political, and military leaders) about the terror, keep it alive, and seek to articulate it so that the public can better absorb it. The post-9/11 American geopolitics of abjection needs some masters, some masters of terror in fact, that can deploy the kind of tabloid discourses (as we saw in previous chapters), often discourses of war, that will be able to place the United States and its population on a path toward abjection, horror, and terror. "Our" contemporary masters of tabloid terror are mostly American intellectuals of statecraft who serve as relays between leadership in the media, government, and the military and the public in general. These tabloid masters of terror, these scholars of the abject, are mediators who have grown in numbers in the United States in the months since 9/11. These scholars/mediators of the abject have found many occasions in the midst of the war on terror to explain to both the population and the elites what the war is about, why America must constantly fight, why America's mission in the world requires complete victory, and in what ways violence will have to be unleashed.

Crucially, these tabloid discourses of war and abject terror are not just tabloid realist discourses anymore. Even when some former tabloid realists (like Robert Kaplan, for example) are still involved in the production and dissemination of these texts and representations, tabloid realists are no longer in control of the popular geopolitical discourse that nonetheless they initiated prior to 9/11. Realism after 9/11, even in a tabloid format, is no longer useful to these discourses and mediating productions of terror and abjection that prevail today. Realism, even in trivialized popular and spectacular renditions (such as those discussed in Chapter 2), is no longer key to making sense of the virulence and at the same time sense of despair and uncertainty found in US tabloid geopolitics after 9/11. Still, what remains crucial to these tabloid discourses – and was already developed by tabloid realists before 9/11 – is the desire to mobilize the American public by means of fear and, particularly, the desire to convince the public of the inevitability of accepting and in fact embracing war. Perhaps, as Simon Dalby has suggested, we should now label these scholars' or pundits' discourses tabloid idealist or, preferably, tabloid imperialist,[29] as many of the lessons of prudence and order contained in (tabloid) realism are quite simply rejected and sometimes mocked for being too cautious and non-unilateralist.[30] More than devising foreign policy strategies that would be based on realist tenets (to help the United States win the war on terror and to protect its national interest), these tabloid imperialist discourses of horror and abjection and their producers actually try to tell Americans *who* they are and *where* they are in the context of an unfathomable terror that requires total and unending warfare as the only possible reactive solution. As Kristeva notes, this is rather symptomatic of the abjected body or being who always struggles to situate "itself" in the borderline condition of rejection of/attraction to horror and disgust and who, by constantly asking "where am I?" (at the individual, symbolic level) or "where are we?" (at a social/cultural level), turns subjectivity – or what appears to be subjectivity – into a manifestly spatial or perhaps geographical concern.[31] Yet, this non-subjectivity that is abjection is also a paradoxical geographical posture because it seeks to demarcate a being/self but really has no need for geography. With the same movement that wishes to differentiate and delineate, abjection explodes geographical distinctions, and the abjected body politic of the war on terror pays no attention to state borders in devising its policies, ideologies, and strategies. In abjection, as the abject, America and its war story (the American war machine, as I will finally be led to call it in Chapter 4), driven by a hunger for victory at all cost, simply seek to march on across all sorts of nameless territories, in placeless locales, and toward unclear enemies. By telling Americans where they are situated in the war (they are "with us," on the side of "good"), and by describing what their role in the global war on terror is, these tabloid masters' discourses of abjection desperately search for triumphalist meaning in ways that are always about to differentiate yet further confuse, release from ambiguity yet further destabilize meaning.

In the rest of this chapter, I examine three key discourses/productions of war and terror by post-September 11, 2001, American masters of abjection. The first discourse of post-9/11 tabloid terror under consideration here, *Warrior Politics: Why Leadership Demands a Pagan Ethos* is by Robert D. Kaplan,[32] who, as we saw in Chapter 2, gained a reputation in the mid- to late 1990s as one of the most vocal supporters of doomsday visions in international politics, but also as a fierce believer in a return to basic tenets of political realism in American foreign policy in order to protect the United States against the world's growing dangers. Kaplan's *Warrior Politics* is a patchy historical survey of the important role that "warrior ethics" has played in the conduct of statecraft and particularly foreign affairs since ancient times. According to Kaplan, a return to the warrior way of ruling one's state and dominating others is desirable in contemporary times when war and violence cannot be avoided. In this text, Kaplan operates the transition from tabloid realism (and its concern for the American national interest) to tabloid imperialism (and its obsession with total victory through war). The second discourse of war and terror under scrutiny in this chapter is *An Autumn of War: What America Learned from September 11 and the War on Terrorism* by Victor Davis Hanson.[33] Hanson is an American military historian who, in the fall of 2001, after the terrorist attacks, wrote a series of reflective essays about the American war on and of terror at home and in Afghanistan. Most of these essays were published in the *National Review* (many of them online). In these essays designed to gain popular if not outright populist appeal, Hanson vents his anger and that of (as he claims) the American nation. This anger is directed at the terrorists, the regimes that support them, and also those Americans (leftist academics as he envisions them to be) who did not appear to support an all-out war. Hanson's narrative is exemplary of geopolitical abjection and tabloid terror as it demands on the part of its readers that they welcome the horror and disgust of war and vengeance and turn themselves into hatred-filled destructive beings/bodies. The final textual production examined in this chapter is *The War Against the Terror Masters: Why It Happened, Where We Are Now, How We'll Win* by Michael Ledeen, a scholar at the conservative American Enterprise Institute, a *Wall Street Journal* contributor, and a former counter-terrorism expert at the National Security Council.[34] Ledeen explains whom the American terror should be directed at, and he argues that it should be aimed at a group that he vaguely refers to as the "terror masters" (not to be confused with those, like Ledeen himself, whom I have labeled masters of abjection and terror, and who indeed often claim to be writing about so-called terror masters). Ledeen explains that his "terror masters" are not just those who attacked on 9/11, but more importantly those in Iran, Iraq, Syria, Saudi Arabia, and Palestine who have supported Middle Eastern terrorism for decades and want the destruction of America. Ledeen believes that the war initiated in Afghanistan in 2001 should be an endless one and that American forces should destroy the "terror" regimes in the Middle East until none of them is left standing. Ledeen's writing will be one key source of inspiration for US foreign policy makers to bring the war on terror to Iraq later, in the spring of 2003.

The way of the warrior

The thesis of Kaplan's *Warrior Politics* is simple. "We" (meaning Americans)[35] live in a time of war. In war, political leadership is crucial. Brave leaders in times of war must make hard choices. They must realize that war is a reality. Leaders cannot shy away from war. Brave leaders of brave nations in wartime must adopt what Kaplan calls a "warrior ethic" or a "pagan ethic." The warrior or pagan ethic is a morality based on the idea that might makes right, that political necessities demand that justice and ethics be put aside, that human nature, self-interested as it is, cannot be changed, and that war is the normal condition of humankind. So far, these characteristics are quite in line with his tabloid realism presented in the previous chapter. History, Kaplan continues to tell his reader, is full of examples of leaders who have adopted such a warrior ethic, such a "morality of consequences."[36] These historical leaders were warriors at the same time. They led their states to great victories and to great conquests. They ruled and they were respected. They kept their nations safe and secure. Not surprisingly, Kaplan's list of great names and figures of "warrior politicians" takes us back to (Western and Eastern) antiquity, when, in the person of authors and soldiers like Thucydides, Livy, Tiberius, and Sun-Tzu, he finds models of leadership that contemporary rulers should emulate. There is nothing original about Kaplan's argument so far. It is simply an age-old belief in the role and power of great leaders who are also great warriors with which many students of political realism in international relations should be quite familiar.

   Kaplan's text is a series of vignettes on several such leaders, their successes in managing politics and war, and the lessons these warriors have left us to deal with today's war. The ethics and beliefs of these allegedly great leaders are presented very sketchily. Along the way of his superficial historical and conceptual analyses of each selected leader-warrior's thought, Kaplan drops a few banal statements that, overall, are supposed to exemplify what the pagan ethic is about. One is told, for example, that "the acceptance of a world governed by a pagan notion of self-interest exemplified by Thucydides makes statesmanship easier to succeed."[37] One is also reminded that, according to Machiavelli, a successful policy-maker can be recognized by the fact that, for him/her, "projecting power comes first; values come second."[38] Kaplan also notes that, because the future is so difficult to predict in politics, the sage leader will instead turn to the past. Kaplan advocates a morality of consequences that is grounded in the success of past actions, policies, and strategies. Whereas idealizing the future is a source of danger, romanticizing the past ("our" past) is a virtuous activity. This lesson, Kaplan claims, is drawn from Livy who "shows that the vigor it takes to face our adversaries must ultimately come from pride in our past and our achievements. Romanticizing our past is something to be cultivated, rather than be ashamed of."[39] Of course, this necessary romanticization of the past generally entails romanticizing old military victories and previous wars (particularly when they have led to substantial geopolitical gains). This is what the reconstruction of today's war story requires for Kaplan. Thus, behind Kaplan's vacuous political realistic formulas for leadership lies his desire to glorify war as a political practice. Successful war, Kaplan suggests, is what brings a nation and its leaders glory. Wars do not just make nations secure. Wars make nations great.

More than a treatise on political leadership and its importance for revived realist concerns in foreign policy, Kaplan's *Warrior Politics* is a glorification of war. Because war is a glorious political activity, it cannot and must not be avoided. As Kaplan declares, "war is inherent in the division of humanity into states and other groupings."[40] Kaplan's goal in this book is not only to justify why it is acceptable for a political leader (mainly an American leader) to declare wars and conduct foreign policies geared toward winning wars, but also to make war an ever-present condition of foreign policy making and leadership (and this is also the point where the previous tabloid realist argument starts to recede). Kaplan's enumeration of cases of leader-warriors' actions and their lessons about political life is a not so well hidden excuse to carve out a space for war outside the state's borders. Although Kaplan cannot deny that America has been hit by the war inside, it is mostly outside that he wants to take the war and its accompanying terror. This is perhaps Kaplan's own therapeutic exercise, his hope that the war he himself now makes into a constant reality/story can be cast away, or at least moved away from the US territory. The war story is more likely to succeed (to bring endless victory) if it takes place in distant, foreign lands. As we saw in Chapter 2, Kaplan has a track record of wanting to fend off, expel, and abject threats, dangers, and contagions away from the American homeland.[41] Only victory must be found on US soil, not the ravages of war (which, as happened on 9/11, are not likely to yield any sort of triumphalism). Thus, war clearly beckons for American leader-warriors outside US borders, Kaplan intimates, particularly since "the birth of a warrior class as cruel as ever, and better armed" has vouched to attack and destroy the United States.[42] This "warrior class" that the new American leader-warriors will have to fight encompasses "armies of murderous teenagers in West Africa, Russian and Albanian mafiosi, Latin American drug kingpins, West Bank suicide bombers, and associates of Osama bin Laden who communicate by e-mail."[43] In case one were to doubt the veracity of Kaplan's statement about this new global war outside US borders, Kaplan typically assures his reader that he "saw firsthand the creation of warriors at Islamic schools in Pakistani slums; the children of those shantytowns had no moral or patriotic identity except that which their religious instructors gave them."[44]

Kaplan's newly envisioned space for war outside still requires sacrifices from the inside, though. Among the sacrifices that the age of terror demands is a suspension of democratic principles within the state's borders. The leader-warrior should thus be ready to push democracy aside, and not only when he and his troops fight the war against the "warrior class," but also when his own citizenry is concerned. The leader-warrior knows that this is what it takes to fight the war. Once again, political necessity comes first, and moral and democratic values come second. As Kaplan makes clear, "our responses to the outrages of these warriors are inconceivable without the element of surprise, making democratic consultation an afterthought."[45] But although democracy inside may have to be removed to make possible the war outside, the citizenry (Americans) may still find solace in the glorification of America's past history. Being patriotic, and looking back to the past to uncover proof of America's inevitable victory in the war against terror, will surely compensate for the fact that democratic principles have been erased by America's leader-warriors. Indeed, Kaplan intimates: "American patriotism – honoring the flag, July Fourth celebrations, and so on – must survive long enough to provide the military armature for an emerging global civilization."[46]

Kaplan never hides the real ambitions of his book. In the early sections, Kaplan remarks that "this is not an essay about what to think; but about how to think."[47] How to think in a time of war and terror for Kaplan means accepting the choices made by the leader-warrior and accepting the sacrifices (in terms of justice, ethics, and democracy) that come with fighting the so-called warrior class. Yet, at the same time, it is of course inaccurate and dishonest for Kaplan to claim that "how to think" has no impact on "what to think." For Kaplan's own positioning of the American nation, its leader-warriors, and its citizenry in relation to a new successful space of war allegedly located outside the state's borders demands that Americans be able to tell *what* is "evil," *what* or *who* is dangerous, and *what* their enemy looks like. Americans need to be told *how* to abject for sure, but how to abject necessarily has consequences for the postulated self and the imagined other. *How* to abject of necessity implies *what* to abject. And one way Americans can start to know *how*, *what*, and ultimately *whom* to abject is by relying on Kaplan's tabloid observations and descriptions of the world "out there" that he presents in his vignettes and chronicles. Yet another way of abjecting is, as Kaplan urges as well, to turn back to history and rediscover or revive the forms of "evil" that America once annihilated.

Chronicles of terror

Kaplan himself gave Hanson's *An Autumn of War* what, in his view, was the highest praise one could give such a book. "Reading these pieces," Kaplan wrote, "I felt less lonely about our historical situation [since] . . . Hanson shows that the War on Terrorism is part of a long story of the West's struggle against barbarism."[48] There is no doubt that, as Kaplan suggests, Hanson's book is about creating an insurmountable division between "us" (the West, America) and "them" (Kaplan's so-called warrior class, the "barbarians"). But more than helping the American population to realize who or where they are in the war against terror, Hanson's collection of essays is a series of ideological statements about America in the early twenty-first century, its global mission, its war, and its inevitable success in this new conflict. In the process of presenting such arguments, very little in Hanson's tabloid text is about political realism. With Hanson's discursive productions, we are now fully immersed into the art of tabloid imperialism.[49]

The attacks on September 11, Hanson declares, have made America an angry, vengeful, violent, aggressive, and militaristic nation. And this, for Hanson, is actually a good, necessary, and healthy condition. It is in fact so positive that, even if America and Americans did not want the war in the first place (how could they?), they have much to gain by adopting it as their own. Through the war, Americans will restore the meaning of America. America, Hanson believes, will be stronger and its values will become even more meaningful and universally accepted because America is at war, because it is winning the war, and because it is willing to prevail.

Hanson's short revenge- and resentment-filled essays are designed for Americans, for the population, for the middle classes, for the people who have felt wronged by the attacks of September 11.[50] These people must be angry, vengeful, and hateful so that America can win the war and so that American values can remain dominant wherever US soldiers are sent to fight. Undoubtedly, Hanson's American ideology of war-making is meant to have a very high populist appeal. But Hanson's ideology is not just any form of American tabloid wartime populism. Although rallying an entire nation around a cause and mobilizing the public against a common enemy is certainly part of Hanson's objective, the populist discourse of *An Autumn of War* is also one of offense, attack, and aggression. It is a discourse that implores America and Americans to start new wars and to fight them aggressively, perhaps brutally even. According to Hanson, this ideology of aggression is acceptable, justifiable, and in fact desirable because of the monstrosity of the violence that "our" enemies have unleashed upon "us." Hanson believes that this hyper-populist ideology of attack and offense does not need to be justified. It is a self-evident *truth*. In this war, the language of truth must not be avoided, particularly since the beacon of "truth" that the United States is supposed to be has been harmed.[51] Only American leftist academics and moralists, as Hanson would have it, do not believe in this kind of language. They do not want to perceive the *truth*. They want to continue to blur meanings and certainties. But they are wrong, Hanson declares, and, in the context of this extreme wartime populism, perhaps they should be perceived as traitors to the American nation.[52]

The truth Hanson wants to restore is that offense, attack, and aggression are today's American values. This is the truth our leaders must speak.[53] This is also the truth that American patriots, the vast majority of American citizens, will recognize as the only possible truth, the one truth that can revitalize America's moral strength and make it universally uncontested. As Hanson likes to repeat, America is not merely a strong, just, and democratic power. It is also "an angry and avenging power."[54] It is a nation whose power is derived from the anger, the thirst for vengeance, and the desire to attack of its people who have realized that "only that way can our children someday sleep in peace."[55] Hanson's wartime ideology of aggression has several basic premises. One such premise is that the current war is not about "us," about America. "We," Americans (sometimes some other Westerners too), do not have a problem. The problem is Islam, Hanson asserts, and Islamic people's inability to fulfill their own missionary dreams (whereas America's own missionary dreams are evident worldwide). Thus, bin Laden and al Qaeda have invented the war on terror (even if "we" took it over) to "assuage the psychological wounds of hundreds of millions of Muslims who are without consensual government, freedom, and material security."[56] Not unconnected to this first affirmation is a second ideological belief that posits that the war and its terror were brought onto "us" by people, mostly Muslim people, who actually envy "our" success, "our" prestige, "our" institutions, "our" values, in a word, "our" modernity.[57] "We" simply made this war "ours" after the fact. Somewhat reminiscent of Huntington's argument in *The Clash of Civilizations*, Hanson argues that "our" civilizational model is indeed irresistible, and that Islam cannot match it. Thus, the members of the warrior class in the Islamic world despise "us" for what "we" have and what "they" in fact jealously crave.

Another basic principle in Hanson's scheme is that Western culture is unique (just as Huntington had claimed) because it is missionary and altruistic whereas the rest of the human condition is and has always been tragic. "We" are the only civilization that has cared to deploy "efforts to ameliorate the savagery innate to all peoples at all times."[58] This has been and continues to be "our" civilizing mission, a mission that supposedly does not emerge out of imperialistic tendencies, but rather is a sure sign of "our" generosity to the rest of the world. As Hanson would have it, "we" have "our" wealth, stability, and freedom. But throughout history and still today "we" have never been restrained in "our" desire – born out of "our" moral system – to share "our" goods with other civilizations, and with Islam in particular (Hanson often likes to remark that, not so long ago, "we" came to Islam's help in the former Yugoslavia, for example). This is what makes it particularly difficult to accept that "they" could have something against "us," that Islam's people may actually have come to resent all those things the West and America have done for them. Interestingly, one of Hanson's additional basic truths is that, despite its ageless generosity toward the rest of the world (or perhaps because of it), America is also responsible for the war, or at least for not having been able to predict that Islam would attack so brutally. Indeed, America's "contemporary university" has for too long contributed to the propagation of a cynical and defeatist discourse of appeasement, accountability, and guilt vis-à-vis Islam that has led "us" to believe that "we" may actually be responsible for Islam's own problems, for the rise of fundamentalism, and for the growth of terrorist networks like al Qaeda.[59] As a cesspool of critical thinking and leftist activism, American universities have clouded "our" vision about Islam. In a sense, the war helps to restore America's vision of itself. Once again, American academics have caused much harm by accepting and even championing cultural relativism and multiculturalism. After all, Hanson affirms (reviving Huntington's view) that not every culture is on an equal footing. Thus, the war on terror is an important reminder, a measure of social and moral clarity in a sense. It reminds Americans that some cultures are superior to others and thus meant to lead the way. "Our" culture is necessarily superior because "we" have democracy. By contrast, "there is not – and never has been – a single true democracy in the Islamic world other than a sometimes constitutional, secular, and Westernized Turkey."[60]

Hanson's hyped-up and tabloid war populism is about the abjection of culture, of America's democratic culture. It is not just about encouraging "us" to fight "them." Indeed, in an apparently aberrant fashion, Hanson's ideological objective is for America to preserve itself through destruction. War is Hanson's borderline condition, the border of America's contemporary culture. As Kristeva noted about the relation between abjection and culture, abjection is the liminal condition through which "our" culture is prioritized but perhaps threatened too. It is a condition in which, faced with the extremes of horror, disgust, destruction, savagery, and death, culture nonetheless seeks to be revived, reactivated, and rearmed. This is perhaps why, in a passage where Hanson discusses the "cultural" dimension of the war against terror, he has no difficulty talking about "preserving Western civilization and its uniquely tolerant and humane traditions of freedom" and, just a few lines down, emphasizing the fact that America will have to "answer the Islamic world bluntly" by using extreme force (at the risk of destroying Islam, but also a part of the West too, starting with American lives) to make sure its culture is saved.[61] In the war on terror, saving and destroying are indistinguishable, undifferentiated, one and the same. In this abject condition of war and terror that Hanson's discourse and ideology affirm, there is no apparent contradiction between preservation and destruction, tolerance and rejection, humanity and assault. This is all part of the same body politic, of the same "human" condition, and of the same so-called moral quest for meaning. This is also the clear sign that Hanson *is* one of America's most powerful contemporary tabloid masters of abjection and terror.[62] Should one still have any doubt about this, one last statement from Hanson is sure to drive this last point home: "We are militarily strong, and the Arab world *abjectly* weak, not because of greater courage, superior numbers, higher IQs, more ores, or better weather, but because of *our culture*."[63]

Strategies of abjection

In many ways, Michael Ledeen's *The War Against the Terror Masters* picks up the argument (or the struggle perhaps) where Hanson left it. Whereas Hanson provided America with an ideological substratum needed to justify the destruction of enemies, the acceptance of war and terror, and the abjection of itself, Ledeen hopes to offer more practical lessons of strategy on how to eradicate the warrior class and particularly their leaders or, as he calls them, the "terror masters." Whereas Hanson provided abjection as a new moral compass to Americans, Ledeen takes such a moral and ideological posture for granted and prefers to worry about turning abjection into a military strategy, a strategy of action. Thus, Ledeen unabashedly asserts that "we will undoubtedly win the war against the terror masters, for we excel at destroying tyrannies."[64] Ledeen's strategy for America first consists of establishing the fact that the war against terror is not a new kind of war, at least in terms of tactics and other types of military practice. It is part of a long history of US war success. Indeed, Ledeen claims that "the main part of the war – the campaign against the terror masters who rule countries hostile to us – is a very old kind of war."[65] It is a typical kind of American war, one that should easily lead to new war victories for the United States. It is not so different from the wars Americans fought to gain their independence in the eighteenth century or to rid the world of fascism in the twentieth century. It is a war on behalf of America's "historic mission" and Manifest Destiny.[66] It is also a morally justified war, a war against "evil," as George W. Bush famously proclaimed (and Ledeen's discourse is an overt pro-Bush piece of war propaganda too). The war Ledeen wants Americans – soldiers and civilians – to fight is also a typical war in its strategic planning and its tactical design. Ledeen assumes that today's "evil doers" ("them" as he most often calls them) are no different from the previous ones America fought because they still reside in sovereign states. "Our prime enemies are the terror masters – the rulers of the countries that sponsor terrorism," Ledeen likes to repeat.[67] Ledeen wishes to minimize the recent hype in international relations and national security circles about the new forms of terror and terrorist actors (networks, al Qaeda, transnational crime organizations, cyberterrorists, and so forth) and about the vanishing of sovereign states as a result of globalization or deterritorialization. By contrast, he affirms that the new groupings of terror are important because they are closely connected to existing states that have antagonized American interests for decades. Al Qaeda, Hamas, Hizbollah, and other groups are simply to be seen as the extended arms of Iran, Iraq, Syria, and Saudi Arabia. Although America has no choice but to fight the terrorists, it must also remember that it is a handful of sovereign states that is directly responsible for the current war. Thus, America's war must directly target these states and their "terror masters" (the political, moral, and religious leaders who design the anti-American policies of these nations). Destroying these states will be arduous and long. Yet it must happen for "the glory of our victory and the rightness of our cause."[68]

To successfully fight this apparently traditional American type of war, three main tasks are required according to Ledeen: "improve our homeland defense, kill or incarcerate the terrorist rank and file, and destroy the regimes that support the new kamikazes."[69] Not surprisingly, these tasks fall in line with Bush's new security measures – at home and abroad – adopted in the aftermath of 9/11. Taking for granted that the terrorists will be thrown to jail or killed, Ledeen devotes much of his strategic planning to the issue of "homeland security" and to fighting the war against the terror masters. To secure the "homeland," Americans must first know why the nation was unprepared for the attacks of 9/11. One of the main reasons why America was not prepared is the fact that the FBI and the CIA had not been able to fulfill their tasks of protecting the country for many years. These crucial intelligence, investigative, and police agencies were no longer allowed to conduct the kind of operations that had made them (and America) so successful and dominant during the Cold War. Echoing some of the tabloid warnings that were already heard in some popular media (Fox News for example) in relation to pre-9/11 fears and terrors like cyberterrorism or Y2K (as seen in Chapter 1), Ledeen claims that previous administrations were more concerned with lifting the veil of secrecy of "our" intelligence agencies and making them accountable to the American public than letting them do their job of surveillance, spying, and infiltration of suspect groups. Ledeen adds that several key events like the Watergate scandal and, more importantly, the Iran–Contra Congressional hearings caused much damage in the intelligence community. The Iran–Contra investigations, Ledeen bemoans, "stifled independent analysis at the Agency" and caused the firing of "some of the best case officers in recent history."[70] Thus, the FBI and the CIA were not allowed to gather crucial information about Islamic and terrorist groups in America and overseas. In particular, they could not spy and help to dismantle the mosques inside the United States that served as covers for the terrorists. According to Ledeen, what our intelligence officers were not permitted to see was that "the sheiks and imams in the hundreds of Wahhabi and Shi'ite mosques in America reinforced the incantation of jihad, and supported a community of fundamentalist believers in which the terrorists could immerse themselves."[71] Because they did not receive the necessary political support to conduct these kinds of surveillance and intelligence operations, the CIA and the FBI were just "demoralized."[72] Consequently, rebuilding homeland security and restoring America after 9/11 will require that the CIA and FBI be given full powers to inquire and investigate in order to make sure that Americans are protected and not weakened domestically, on the home front of the war against the terror masters. Once again sounding like the apologist for policy decisions made by the Bush administration (the creation, adoption, and subsequent revision and reaffirmation of the Patriot Act for example), Ledeen urges Americans to accept the restrictions on privacy, freedom of opinion, and free speech that will necessarily accompany the CIA and the FBI's newly enforced means of securing the homeland. This is necessary in order for America and Americans to prevail again.

But securing the "homeland" only makes sense to the extent that the nation is at war against enemies that have found ways of weakening America. These enemies are once again the terror masters. The terror masters (again, some specific sovereign states) recognized "our" strategic weaknesses, the fact that "our" politicians had become too soft on matters of national security. Thus, the terror masters hired and/or created terrorist organizations to bring horror and destruction onto American soil. Once again, this is the very reason why Ledeen believes that Americans should not be fooled into believing that the terrorists are separate from sovereign terror masters. The way America will defeat them, Ledeen believes, is by attacking and annihilating their central core: the regimes in those "Muslim/ Arab/Middle Eastern" states that are the real source of the terror (Ledeen uses the terms "Muslim," "Arab," and "Middle Eastern" interchangeably). As previously indicated, Ledeen's war strategy is plain and simple: the US military must attack and destroy the four main "terror" regimes of Iran, Iraq, Syria, and Saudi Arabia one after another. Ledeen suggests starting with Iran or Iraq because these two states are already vulnerable. In Iran, "the driving force behind international terrorism," public riots and student demonstrations in October 2001 have shown that "the unraveling . . . has actually been under way for some time."[73] Similarly, in Iraq, "freedom is our most powerful weapon."[74] In a way that is quite reminiscent of some of former Defense Secretary Donald Rumsfeld's initial comments about Iraq in the spring of 2003, Ledeen claims that Iraqi resistance movements are anxiously awaiting American attacks to finally take over Baghdad.[75] Once Iran and Iraq have fallen, America will have to pursue the war against Syria. In Syria, Hafez al-Assad's son Bashar is "as ruthless and corrupt as his father" and runs a regime that openly supports international terrorism.[76] Because it is "every bit as important, and every bit as tyrannical as Iran and Iraq," Bashar's Syria will also have to be eradicated.[77] After Syria is destroyed, American troops will not be able to rest. Indeed, next in line will be Saudi Arabia, perhaps the greatest challenge in the war against the terror masters. Ledeen predicts that, as he claims is a growing trend, Wahhabi fundamentalists will continue to take over Saudi political, social, and religious institutions and, in so doing, will spread even more anti-American hatred. If they do so, the Wahhabi's "hate-preaching schools and mosques [will have to] be closed or fundamentally changed."[78] Contrary to what some American politicians may believe, "we" will not be able to avoid a confrontation with Saudi Arabia because "we will not distinguish between the terrorists and the regimes that support them."[79]

But while this endless war will have to be won on the ground, against states, America will also need to fight the war in the realm of ideas. As Ledeen declares, "one form of power comes from the barrel of the gun, but another flows from the human spirit."[80] Ledeen believes that, just as "we" destroyed communism in the mind of the people who, for decades, had no choice but to subscribe to and live by Marxist–Leninist doctrines, "we" will have to subvert "radical Islam" in a similar fashion. To win the war on the ground, America will have to win the ideological battle. And, in this kind of war, deterrence will not suffice. America's war, then, will require not just the destruction of "Muslim/Arab/Middle Eastern" lives, but also the erasure of Islam as an idea, an ideal, and a religion.[81] Ledeen concludes: "We will therefore need to demonstrate that radical Islamism is a road to humiliation and defeat, not a pathway to glory."[82]

Although one might be tempted to read Ledeen's practical plans of action as an extension of tabloid realist recipes (although clearly offensive ones) in the post-9/11 era, Ledeen's discourse has in fact far more to do with tabloid imperialism than with tabloid realism. Like Hanson, Ledeen is convinced that the *truth* is on his side.[83] And the truth Ledeen speaks of (or with) is of a new ideological kind, one that (despite his claims to being practical and strategic) he is not so successful in hiding behind a seemingly more conventional narrative of historical US war-making and war tactics. Ledeen's *truth* is that combating "evil" today requires America and Americans to adopt not just a protective and, if need be, offensive posture too (to prevent further attacks), but rather a downright militaristic and ag-gressive attitude vis-à-vis those whom Ledeen construes to be absolute enemies. Ledeen would have Americans embark on a holy war crusade in the Middle East to vanquish the terror masters, their states, but also their religious beliefs. It is in fact an entire civilization that Ledeen would like the United States to militarily, politically, but also culturally annihilate. Although it may appear that Ledeen's text is not so different from many other hate-spreading militaristic discourses that have been produced in American circles of statecraft for many decades (often in times of war – hot or cold – too), upon closer examination, one can notice that Ledeen's flashy and hyperbolic discourse of absolute and endless war is in fact far beyond subject construction (in this case, the reconstruction of American iden-tity through/as war). Indeed, Ledeen's discourse of terror and war is positioned beyond any subject/object dichotomy. Literally (in the military substance of the tactics Ledeen advocates), Ledeen's tabloid imperialistic discourse blasts away any cultural or political system of differentiation and subsequent identification between self and other. The meaning or identity of America Ledeen longs for is located within the abject, in a liminal space of abjection that this discourse of total war further expands. After all, Ledeen's "enemies" are rarely named or identified. They are simply regimes (with only a few names mentioned here and there) and terror masters. More often than not they are simply "them." But this "them" is an unspeakable "elsewhere," as Kristeva might suggest, a positioning deprived of any specific geographical location and perhaps geopolitical signification. They are "them" no longer as opposed to "us" any more, but rather as an incommensurable, incomprehensible, and unthinkable body of terror to which "we" must respond by means of even more terror. Indeed, Ledeen's response (to "them," to the so-called terror masters) is for "ourselves" to become the terror masters, to embody terror, in a sense, to be just like "them." Ledeen demands an ever-increasing amount of war, destruction, battle, and death so that Americans may finally be transformed into the dominant terror masters. "They" are thus only the catalysts for "our" own desire for terror. As a consequence of this kind of tabloid imperialist and abject discourse of war and terror, Americans are asked to unleash horrifying at-tacks, to be a "power of horror" (to paraphrase Kristeva), not simply to retaliate or repay the attacks of September 11 ("us" getting back at "them"), but also and more importantly to unendingly pursue what is, according to Ledeen, America's mysterious quest to "advance [its] historic mission."[84] Blindly moving toward an unspecified Manifest Destiny that is indeed "as tempting as it is condemned" (or an "elsewhere" that Ledeen can only describe as a "whirlwind of energy"), and armed with what Ledeen romantically labels "creative destruction,"[85] America is asked to take advantage of the opportunity of the war on terror to be one with aggression, conquest, and annihilation. It is perhaps not so surprising, then, if people and nations situated outside US borders – but also many Americans who explicitly or implicitly recognize that they too are in the path of war – sometimes feel compelled to interpret this American discourse of abject war strategies as a form of military and ideological imperialism (or extreme colonialism perhaps). In the end, Ledeen's tabloid text allows us to realize that America's own quest for itself, for a new triumphant meaning of itself – a quest that inevitably becomes confused with the terror and the abject – is quite possibly what troubles many people outside and inside US borders, and perhaps forces some individuals and groups to start to see themselves as America's so-called enemies. After all, as Ledeen once again affirms, "our enemies have always hated this whirlwind of energy and creativity, which menaces their traditions (*whatever they may be*) and shames them for their inability to keep pace."[86]

Subjecting American culture to abjection

Kristeva wrote that, "in a world in which the Other has collapsed, . . . 'subject' and 'object' push each other away, confront each other, collapse, and start again – inseparable, contaminated, condemned, at the boundary of what is assimilable, thinkable: the abject."[87] The three tabloid textual presentations of America's reaction to the terrorist attacks of 9/11 examined in this chapter have managed to fuse the self (the American body politic) with the other (the enemy, the terror master) to the point that, inside the "whirlwind" of terror/horror where both confront each other, neither one of them, neither subject nor object, becomes fully recognizable and identifiable. "We" become indistinguishable, undifferentiated from "them." Kaplan, Hanson, Ledeen, and their post-9/11 stories of war-making and war-justifying have launched America on a mission to allegedly rediscover itself, recover its roots, and finally uncover its *true* meaning. In reality though, their texts champion, in a sensationalistic, gripping, awe-inspiring, and overtly populist fashion, some of the most aggressive, destructive, and militarily colonizing policies, moralities, ideologies, and tactics formulated, in the United States and beyond, before and after the horrific attacks of September 11, 2001. They encourage America and Americans to dig deeper and lose themselves inside the war against/with terror. Promoting policies, ideologies, and wartime strategies designed to hate, expel, and eradicate (not just "others," but virtually anything that looks "evil" and/or anti-American, and potentially some of "us" too), these masters of statecraft, terror, and abjection offer a tabloid image and message about America that may no longer be distinguishable from the image and message of those who attacked the United States in the first place. Although Kaplan, Hanson, and Ledeen may try to convince their mostly US readers that America's power of destruction is justified, humane, or even "creative," it is still an awfully terrorizing power, one whose objective is to cause more annihilation in ever more places, no matter where those places might be (since abjection ignores geography and physical difference). Thus, as we saw with some homeland security measures after 9/11, the US territory is not exempt from these tabloid tactics and ideas either, since, after all, the distinction between home and away, here and there, is absorbed by abject representations and actions that resist subject/object dichotomies at the very moment that they seek to brutally affirm them (in the texts examined above, only Kaplan sought to preserve the idea of a distinct homeland, but even this intention was trumped by his acknowledgment that, when it comes to suspending democratic principles, the national territory would have to be subjected to the same kind of post-democratic exceptions as those in place in the lands where the US leader-warrior's troops are marching on).

Deeply ensconced in this precarious condition of abjection, America's search for new triumphalist meaning since 9/11 has actually been narrowed down and impoverished, and not reinvigorated at all. The hopes of America and Americans to recover from despair after the terrifying terrorist sights have been dashed by those tabloid imperialist and aggressive discourses and by the (populist) ability of those texts of tabloid terror and war to take command of the American public sphere. Kaplan, Hanson, Ledeen, and those in US foreign policy and geopolitical circles who readily accept their views have reduced America's quest for meaning to an abject and often disgusting desire (construed as the desire of the entire nation) to always remain one with terror and war. In the months that followed the 9/11 terrorist acts, short of any visible and viable alternative, the only practical option offered by these masters and pundits of the abject was for America to continue to expand its search for more destruction and violence. War and terror, then, became the finality, the only imagined and possibly imaginable outcome. At the same time though, and as I will further detail in the next chapter, it was a finality that was never meant to be final. The United States and its welcoming of terror always had to measure themselves against new opponents, new enemies, new warrior classes, new insurgencies, and new forms of tyranny. Interestingly, and perhaps ironically too (since some of these masters of abjection seemed to consider themselves good political realists), these masters of terror's discourses were willing to invert the Clausewitzian adage about the relationship between war and politics.[88] They were ready to reduce American politics and policy-making at home and abroad to a form of war and war-making by other means. In so doing, they also lost sight of Clausewitz's own lessons of prudence and restraint, and particularly of Clausewitz's caution about not taking war as the ultimate end in political affairs.[89] As Clausewitz might have wished to say, those who abject war and make its terror their own endlessly unfulfilled crusade eventually bring themselves and those they are supposed to protect and serve closer and closer to utter destruction.

4 The United States and the war machine

Proliferating insecurity, terror, and agony after the invasion of Iraq

I am a "War President." I make decisions here in the Oval Office, in foreign policy matters, with war on my mind.

George W. Bush[1]

The State has no war machine of its own; it can only appropriate one in the form of a military institution, one that will always cause it problems.

Gilles Deleuze and Felix Guattari[2]

Prelude: everyday culture and war-making

Over the past decade, but increasingly since 9/11, the United States military has relied heavily on advertising campaigns to try to convince America's youth to join its ranks. Television commercials broadcasting the values associated with the different branches of the US military have left the American public with images and slogans as popular and famous as those found in ads for Coca Cola, Nike, or McDonald's. Just as American youths have been told to "just do it" (Nike) or been reassured by means of a catchy jingle that there will "always" be "Coca Cola," so have these same 16- to 24-year-old Americans repeatedly learned about the life-forming merits of joining the US Marines ("the few, the proud, the Marines") or been assured that they too can "be an Army of one," just like the many other multicultural, multiracial, and non-gender specific US youths who have already joined and are profiled in these ads.

Since 9/11, the advertising campaigns of the various branches of the US military have intensified. The presence of the US Army in America's popular culture has been ubiquitous. From TV commercials about US Special Forces and full-page posters in sports magazines to mass distribution of pamphlets on American university campuses and T-shirts worn by Army recruiters and new recruits (when they are off duty and thus not wearing their traditional military fatigues), the US Army has launched a vast campaign of popular cultural saturation aimed at gaining recruits or, as some recent enlisting pamphlets have put it, designed to tell young Americans what they "can accomplish as a Soldier in the US Army."[3]

If one were not aware of the post-9/11 needs of the United States in military matters (the fact that the United States has initiated major conflicts in Iraq and Afghanistan), one could be surprised by the omnipresence of the military and its recruiting tactics in American everyday life in the early twenty-first century. Certainly, the terrorist attacks of September 11 and the subsequent emphasis on homeland security (with its corollary strategy of fighting the terrorists abroad, away from US soil) have put a premium on military security and defense in the United States. As has been mentioned in the previous chapters, a general sense of securitization, danger, emergency, and fear in US society has steadily grown since before September 2001, only to be reinforced by the invasion of Iraq in March 2003. In the fall of 2002, for example, one year after the 9/11 attacks, several American clothing outlets (Gap and Old Navy in particular) featured what they called "primary colors" in their "back-to-school" children catalogs. One such primary color was military khaki.

But the omnipresence of the military theme in contemporary American culture is more than just a fashion fad, or an immediate reaction in public attitudes to what is being talked about by pundits or intellectuals of statecraft and broadcast in the media. Lately, since the second half of 2003 in particular, the Army appears to have intensified and, at the same time, has slightly but significantly modified its advertising campaign and the themes that it seeks to convey. At a time when the US military involvement in the war on terror (particularly because of the war in Iraq) is becoming more and more costly for Americans (close to 3,000 US military deaths in Iraq as of December 2006; more than $100 billion had been spent by the United States alone in Iraq in the first 18 months after the invasion, according to some estimates[4]), when the American public is growing weary of a conflict that does not appear to have any positive foreseeable ending, and when the decisions of the American government and the actions of the US military have increasingly isolated the United States vis-à-vis its allies, the Army has embarked upon a dual campaign. On the one hand, the Army still wants to find new recruits, if only to relieve those troops (including the National Guard's men and women) whose tour of duty in Iraq and Afghanistan keeps on being extended. It also needs new troops for its Special Forces (as the constant barrage of commercials for those forces on national sports channels at half-time of football or baseball games attests) as it expects, or at least hopes, that the military operations in Iraq and Afghanistan will soon give way to more traditional spying, reconnaissance, or anti-terrorist missions for which such forces are more appropriate. On the other hand, the US Army seems to be softening its "Army of one" and "Be a soldier" rhetoric by suggesting that there are many other jobs, some of them non-combat related, that are in fact available to young Americans joining the force. Thus, around 2003, the key slogan "an Army of one" started to give way to a new more generic appellation, "Go Army," which also, and quite conveniently for those Americans in search of job opportunities, turned out to be the Army recruiting internet address (goarmy. com) for a while. According to this second recruiting track, the emphasis must be placed on the experience of the soldier as one who not only combats and goes to war but also learns a set of professional "skills" (the very word used in the ads) and becomes trained for one of the many "jobs" (potential recruits are being told that there are "over 150" of those in the active duty Army and an additional "120 jobs" in the Army Reserve) that will still be there for them once they are done serving.

Thus, increasingly these days, the Army presents itself to young Americans not just as a war-fighting and soldier-making industry, but also as an educational and professional training institution, one which, unlike most American universities and higher learning institutes, will provide its members with immediate real-life experience. From this perspective, one of the most compelling "Go Army" ads released in 2003–04 showed a black and white picture of a college-age American male, wearing a baseball cap and denim jacket. In the background was the blurred figure of an older man, also wearing a cap and a jacket. The slogan attached to the picture read: "You always hoped he would end up running with the right crowd, but did you ever think he'd also be leading it?" The message here was obviously directed at the older man in the background, allegedly a father, worried and concerned about the future of his late-teenage son who had apparently arrived at an age when a decision regarding career choices would soon have to be made. College is normally an option, but so is the military. And in this ad, unlike some other ones featuring the merits of combining a university degree with a military training by joining the ROTC program for example, the two options were shown to be incompatible. In fact, a caption below the slogan added that, in the Army, this man's son would encounter "the most challenging training," "the latest technology," and "the strongest support," qualities generally associated with a university education. This training would make him into one of "tomorrow's leaders." Needless to say, most American universities and higher learning institutions often used (and still do) the same key words and slogans to attract incoming students. Nothing in this advertising poster (placed in news weeklies such as *US News and Word Report* or *Newsweek*) predisposed the message to be about joining the Army, with the exception of the last line that stated: "Encourage him to consider becoming a soldier."

What is particularly interesting about the proliferation of Army recruiting messages, slogans, and images in contemporary American culture is how such meaning-making signs, such "mythologies" (to use Roland Barthes' terminology[5]), are capable of combining the art of building soldiers and transforming men and women into mass-killing subjects with the practice of forming tomorrow's US professionals (journalists, doctors, lawyers, bus drivers, accountants, computer technicians, car mechanics, etc.). These myths, however, have a way of naturalizing war, of normalizing the military and sometimes belligerent activities of sovereign nation-states (in this case, the United States) by convincing the American public (the potential recruits, but also their mothers and fathers) that they are just doing their job, that they are becoming America's future "skilled" workforce. What the swarming of such images and messages creates is an acceptance among the public not just of the wars America is currently fighting "out there," far away from the homeland, but also of the need to conceive of domestic American society and everyday culture as an extension (inside) of the military goals, strategies, tactics, and rationales that are being applied in America's war against terror, in Iraq and Afghanistan in particular (outside). More than just suggesting, as was the case in previous wars involving the United States, that the home front needs to prepare itself to support the troops, the sons, fathers, and husbands fighting for America's freedom overseas (the WWII American poster slogan "Remember Pearl Harbor, Purl Harder!" is emblematic of this thinking), the Army ads after 9/11, in all their different shapes and forms, demonstrate that there *is* a continuum from the war outside the borders to military preparedness and militarized everyday culture inside the borders. Put simply, there are not two Americas anymore: one at war, and one at peace; one fighting to protect the nation, and one being defended. Rather, America in its entirety, from its occupation of Iraq to its watching television programs or its buying of clothes for kids to go to school, is now one *with* war. And this abjection of oneself through war (as I put it in Chapter 3), this being one with war, means that daily cultural routines, everyday practices, normal social interactions, and, ultimately, the relationship between ruler and ruled, government and citizens need to be subordinated to the greater requirement of doing whatever it takes to win the wars that are being fought. As the tabloid and media culture of war spreads throughout America, not just among those who support one war or another, but also among all who live in the United States and are now made to experience everyday culture as an afterglow of war-making strategies and activities, America relinquishes its democratic and civic values and virtues to the war machine. As suggested at the end of the previous chapter, and to once again reverse Clausewitz's famous adage, American politics is now being turned into a continuation of war-making by other (social, cultural, economic) means.[6] The rest of this chapter extends the reflection on war and tabloid geopolitical culture already initiated in Chapter 3 and specifically interrogates what it means for American politics today to be taken over by a culture of war-making that conditions the public to accept being controlled and led by a war machine. I first turn to the work of Gilles Deleuze and Felix Guattari to provide us with some preliminary theoretical considerations on the relationship between what they call the war machine and the state.

Theoretical overture: Deleuze and Guattari on the war machine

In their seminal work, *A Thousand Plateaus: Capitalism and Schizophrenia*, Deleuze and Guattari introduce the image of the "war machine."[7] The war machine, Deleuze and Guattari suggest, presents itself as an exteriority of the state and of its sovereignty. Whereas the state has its own orderly, structural, and institutional logic, the war machine and its occupants (the warriors) are disorderly and chaotic. At least they are so from the perspective of the state form, to which, through time and across civilizations, the war machine has been a traditionally antagonistic form. Deleuze and Guattari note that, "in every respect, the war machine is of another species, another nature, another origin than the State apparatus."[8] The warrior has his/her own logic to follow, one that does not measure nor calculate violence. It is a logic of war, proliferation, and destabilization that does not stop at any sovereign structure and does not have any respect for state politics. Indeed, "the warrior is in the position of betraying everything, including the function of the military, or of understanding nothing."[9] Sovereigns, Deleuze and Guattari intimate, are painfully aware of the dangers presented by the war machine. To use the war machine without being able to control it, to turn to the warrior without being able to co-opt him/her can become fateful strategies for the state.[10] And yet, despite these risks, the state often has no choice but to run to the war machine, to borrow from it violence and energy because, as Deleuze and Guattari once again stipulate, the "state has no war machine of its own."[11]

Although Deleuze and Guattari's highly metaphorical writing is not meant to be historically contextual,[12] their notion of the war machine, particularly in its duality and/or complicity with the state, resonates with contemporary American usages of war and the military. Deleuze and Guattari's war machine is an ever-present reminder of the power of destabilization, and potentially destruction, that accompanies any attempt by sovereign states at expanding their political structures and functions by making use of what Clausewitz referred to as absolute warfare.[13] Although absolute warfare may expand a state's sovereignty (and may even turn this sovereignty into an empire), it may also turn out to be the cataclysmic undoing of that state's sovereignty and security.

Some Deleuzian scholars have suggested that the notion of the war machine found in Deleuze and Guattari's work should not be taken so literally. The purpose of the image of the war machine, these scholars argue, is merely to represent or metaphorize the idea of a "pure exteriority" of the state, of a domain/space with which the state nonetheless has to engage, but that relentlessly proliferates, pluralizes, and challenges the state apparatus, the concept of sovereignty, the state's security and integrity, and the political processes and institutions.[14] But despite some of the commentators' insistence on trying to disengage the image of the war machine from any actual war or form of warfare, the ascription by Deleuze and Guattari themselves of a terminology and imagery of war to this conceptual entity indicates that their war machine still has much to do with actual war-making and with the destructive force unleashed by warriors. I believe that there is more than just a coincidental allegorical connection between the Deleuzian war machine and the problem of war. After all, it is Deleuze and Guattari who insist on forging a genealogical linkage of sorts (hence an analytic linkage too) between the war machine and the possibility of thinking war as the absolute other/adversary of the state form (and its apparatuses). When Deleuze and Guattari start to conceptualize the idea of the war machine, their illustrative, literary, and theoretical anchoring points are virtually all about war, both as a concept and as a historical practice of extreme motion, uncontrollable energy, and boundless violence. References to the game of Go, to Shakespeare's *Richard III*, to Heinrich Kleist's writings, and to Clausewitz's political theory of war are not innocent, anecdotal, or simply imaginary linkages. Rather, these specific reference points do create analytical clusters that can be tied to actual historical ideas and practices of warfare.

Upon commenting on Deleuze and Guattari's theory of the war machine, the philosopher Paul Patton ultimately recognizes the presence of a relationship between this war machine and instances of conflict and sustained forms of violence. But Patton adds the important proviso that there is a crucial connection, not because the war machine is necessarily (by nature) belligerent, but because the state form inevitably pushes the war machine to become conflictive, violent, and destructive. As Patton puts it, "it is precisely when contact occurs between these two modes of being [the state form and the war machine] that conflict erupts and the war machine's affinity with absolute war is actualised."[15] Thus, the belligerent force of the war machine does not go without saying. It must be called forth and unleashed by the state. But once the force is released, the war machine becomes "a pure flow of violence, the goal of which is the annihilation of the enemy," any enemy.[16] The problem, however, is that, as I intimated above, the enemies of the war machine are indiscriminate according to this analytical scenario. They are not just those against whom the state mobilized the warriors in the first place, but also, and inevitably, all those who are the members and representatives of the state form, since it is ultimately as archetypal assemblages of force/energy that both the state form and the war machine recognize themselves. In a manner that may remind us of the operations of identity and/or subjectivity construction through abjection (described in Chapter 3), ideas of allies versus enemies, friends versus foes, or good states versus bad states turn out to be meaningless to the war machine, whose path of destruction is never easily controlled, assimilated, or recuperated by any sovereign presence. And, even if the war machine gets recaptured by the state and its apparatus, it is often eventually at the sovereign state's expense that it occurs. As Patton recognizes, the relation of "the war machine to the flow of pure war becomes actualised and the war machine becomes a conductor of total war directed against the state."[17] Although not every state-based military institution or armed force will inevitably turn into a war machine, the point here is that every military and every belligerent force has the potential of actualizing total warfare and producing a limitless flow of destruction and annihilation that will deny the state and its sovereign integrity. Every war has the potential to turn the political or strategic goals of the sovereign into apocalyptic violence. Or, as Patton concludes by referring to Francis Ford Coppola's *Apocalypse Now*, in every dutiful soldier lies (sometimes dormant, sometimes active) the furious energy of a Colonel Kurtz who "has surrendered to the flow of total violence and become a war machine outside the control of the military apparatus [nonetheless set up by the state]."[18]

Some contemporary theorists of the state form and its sovereignty have suggested that Deleuze and Guattari's writing is at its analytical best when it can provide international relations/geopolitical thinkers with some key conceptual insights that may be meaningful in critical appraisals of the history of the present.[19] Two such contemporary analysts (apparently eager to push the reflection on the state form to its limits), Michael Hardt and Antonio Negri, have argued that, if Deleuze and Guattari's image of the war machine is to be useful to contemporary critics of geopolitical orderings, it needs to make sense of the way the global landscape is being produced by subnational, national, and supranational apparatuses that seek to structure (or striate, to use Deleuze and Guattari's language) everyday

life. The way the world is being locally and globally produced through the stria-
tion of everyday life by state forms and other models of imperial sovereignty
or Empire (as Hardt and Negri are more likely to put it) involves the inevitable
deployment of the war machine.

Hardt and Negri's second book (after *Empire*), *Multitude*, is largely about war
and warfare. Even though Hardt and Negri's reflection on contemporary war-making in this book is not exclusively derived from the Deleuzian concept of the war
machine, it is nonetheless greatly influenced by Deleuze and Guattari's general
mode of analysis. Hardt and Negri's preferred metaphor for today's geopolitical
condition of war is not the war machine but something eerily reminiscent of it
that they call the "golem." Hardt and Negri describe the golem in the following
terms:

> The golem has become an icon of unlimited war and indiscriminate destruc-
> tion, a symbol of war's monstrosity. In the rich traditions of Jewish mysti-
> cism, . . . [the] golem is traditionally a man made of clay, brought to life by
> a ritual performed by a Rabbi . . . Creating a golem is dangerous business
> . . . [T]he one who creates a golem has in effect claimed the position of God,
> creator of life. Such hubris must be punished . . . The golem's destructive
> violence . . . proves uncontrollable. It does attack the enemies of the Jews but
> also begins to kill Jews themselves indiscriminately . . . [T]he golem is more
> than a parable of how humans are losing control of the world and machines
> are taking over. It is also about the inevitable blindness of war and violence
> . . . The violence of revenge and war . . . leads to indiscriminate death. The
> golem, the monster of war, does not know the friend–enemy distinction. War
> brings death to all equally. That is the monstrosity of war.[20]

Like the initially complicit yet eventually conflictive relationship between the
state form and the war machine, Hardt and Negri's golem is both the product
and the curse of an established political and cultural order, an order that seeks to
remain powerful or wishes to increase its power. The golem is the product and the
curse of an order that seeks to preserve itself or gain strength by creating and later
unleashing a monster whose power of violence and destruction its creator always
hopes it can master. Still, like the war machine, the golem knows neither friend
nor foe. It is a "pure exteriority" of the order (the state, a Jewish community) it
was meant to protect. The reason why Hardt and Negri feel compelled to talk
about today's global wars (of the United States, above all) in terms of a golem
is because they do not perceive any clear ending to the wars and war stories that
have been initiated after 9/11. In the era of what they call "Empire," when regimes
of state sovereignty are giving way to the global structuring, striating, and capturing power of a transnationality nonetheless controlled and governed by America's
worldwide domination and ambitions, there is "no escaping the state of war . . . ,
and there is no end to it in sight."[21] Within Empire, Hardt and Negri add, September 11 has created a new global *modus operandi*, and "war has become a general
condition" of life that is marked by the fact that "lethal violence is present as a

constant potentiality, ready always and everywhere to erupt."[22] After 9/11, global life has become a function of the war machine's potential of destruction, always waiting to be actualized by a terrorist group, a sovereign state leader eager to fight terror, or a military commander.

The logic of what Hardt and Negri call Empire, and the need for Empire (as this allegedly new modality of sovereignty that the United States today does often embody) to striate and occupy more and more space transnationally, becomes the extra-legal basis for this new sovereign structure to use war. But turning to war as a last recourse is no longer permissible. Indeed, the modern concept of political or military exceptionalism, that is to say, "the nightmare of a perpetual and indeterminate state of war, suspending the international rule of law, with no clear distinction between the maintenance of peace and acts of war,"[23] has now become the prevailing norm. Along with this state of exception from now on turned into a permanent norm, the distinction between "foreign relations and the homeland" has been removed as well.[24] It has been removed, and not just by Empire (the new state form), whose global tentacles stretch across former sovereign state territories and nations to better striate global space, but also by the war machine itself that knows no conceptual and geographical limits. The war monster blurs any clear demarcation between enemy and ally, as all in its path, along its flow, and across borders must potentially be destroyed. Since all territories within Empire have become prime targets of total war, any distinction between warrior and non-combatant has become useless too. As Hardt and Negri suggest, the modern justifications for war (to defend society, to achieve political objectives) no longer make sense in an era when the war machine has been given free reign. Rather, war becomes a "regime of biopower," a constant practice aimed at "producing and reproducing all aspects of social life."[25] Hardt and Negri add that a biopolitical war designed "to create and maintain social order can have no end."[26] The only possible end for such a war meant to create social life (by spreading death and destruction) is ironically the end of life itself, as preserving live bodies, keeping them alive, feeding them with vital energies is an unending task. To stop in this task is to condemn life itself, to doom social life to be terminated. Thus, Hardt and Negri further clarify, "one cannot win such a war, or, rather, it has to be won again every day."[27] An even greater irony, however, is that, by having recourse to the war machine, by relying upon the monster of war, those sovereign or Empire structures today that seek to aggressively preserve social life may well be about to cause the social body irremediable damage, since the war machine can never be controlled.

Despite this ultimate threat, sovereign structures in the age of Empire insist on relying upon the war machine as if it were the "primary organizing principle of society,"[28] or as if the biopolitical survival of Empire or the imperial state (again, the United States mostly) depended not so much on winning the war but, more importantly, on constantly fighting it (as we saw with Ledeen at the end of Chapter 3, for example). Thus, according to this absolutist and perhaps absurd logic, and as I suggested in the prelude to this chapter, it is not surprising to see signs of the war machine everywhere in everyday culture. Since there no longer exists any distinction between peace and war, society and politics, civilian and soldier, and life and death, it is normal for the state form to promote its strategies for maintaining or creating social order by proliferating throughout popular culture and in the media the message that indeed we are all an Army of one, or that we can be all that we can be in the military forces. While joining the military forces is encouraged, these messages tell us that it is still fine for some of us not to enlist since, no matter what, we are all part of the same war effort, of the same cultural order that must define itself as a form of war. This is precisely why, as these commercials showed us, it is no longer possible to distinguish a soldier from a university graduate, a military commander from one's boss, or war training from going about one's daily routines. Once again, these are the generally accepted and taken-for-granted signs that "daily life and the normal functioning of power have been permeated with the threat and violence of warfare."[29]

In the rest of this chapter, I take advantage of these theories and imageries of the war machine to further interrogate what might compel a powerful, perhaps imperial, sovereign state (like the United States) to turn to the war machine, to awake the monster of war, and to bring in a disorderly and chaotic force that is likely to prove destructive and fatal in the end. What logic of political order and/or cultural life may motivate a sovereign state and its apparatuses today – even if they are desperate to retrieve a story of war, a narrative of triumph over despair – to unbridle absolute, total, and unending destruction? My purpose is not to continue to figure out what the war machine could be, to identify it with precision, or to give it a name or face even (the preliminary reflections offered above suffice). It is also not to describe in a detailed fashion how the United States and its wars after 9/11 may in fact come to form a war machine (Hardt and Negri do a commendable job on this topic). Finally, my goal here is also not to determine whether the United States and its state form can turn into a successful war machine or, to put it somewhat differently, whether the United States can make use of the war machine and still master it. Although parts of the following analysis may contribute to these discussions, my main concern in this chapter is rather to make intelligible some of the reasons why political and cultural actors or agents, institutions, mediators, and intellectuals of statecraft in a presumably sovereign state like the United States today find it compelling, necessary, or beneficial to turn to an absolute and limitless form of violence and production of death in order to redefine the state (possibly as a triumphant, imperial state) and to conceptually revisit its sovereignty, even when this sovereign state has been attacked in the first place. Along these critical lines, my concern is also to interrogate if (and if so, how?) these justifications for boundless destruction through war can be reconciled at all with the desire to rebuild a successful national identity, something that seemed to be a primary objective for America and Americans after the 9/11 attacks.

In the following pages, I suggest that three reasons can be and indeed have been advanced by key voices and in dominant public yet popular cultural discourses in the United States since after 9/11 (but really more so since after March 2003, the date of the invasion of Iraq) to justify launching the war machine: the defense of the state; the rediscovery of a sense of national identity and social unity; and the desire to become one with war and destruction. Contemporary tabloid literatures and pamphlets by mostly American intellectuals of statecraft and media pundits are once again crucial texts and representations. Since the beginning of the Iraq war, some of these tabloid discourses seem to have encouraged these three different positions. Although these three propositions are probably not the only possible explanatory choices one can think of, they may nonetheless give us a good sense of what might be at stake in the desire to mobilize the war machine today, and of how this may work (or not) with the previously introduced idea of rediscovering a narrative of victory to take Americans away from despair and loss. To anticipate the argument I will develop below, these three (discursive, conceptual) possibilities offer distinct forms of sovereignty for the state (or what might be left of it), and they envision distinct relations to (geo)politics and everyday culture through war.[30] The first possible reason to unleash the war machine – defending the state – is a classical justification for war that remains within the bounds of traditional, modern, and, in fact, legal state sovereignty. From this perspective, war still is an exception, no matter how brutal or violent it is. It is a tool of state policy, and as such it should be subordinated to the traditional institutional needs of the state. The second justification – rediscovering national identity and recreating social unity through war – encourages a different form of sovereignty, one that can be referred to as biopolitical sovereignty. According to this model, preserving a social or cultural way of life as the life of the nation, of the body politic, is primordial. Finally, the justification of deploying absolute warfare in order to eventually become one with war is possibly the least logical and the least expected option since it does not appear to provide anything to the state and those who claim to be its representatives and defenders (other than their and the state's ultimate surrender to and potential destruction by the war machine). Yet, this apparently paradoxical justification is actually found in the writings of some influential post-9/11 tabloid (imperialist) public intellectuals and pundits, and, as we will see, it is not necessarily beyond a certain vision or usage of culture and (geo)politics. This last option – the relinquishing of the state/nation to the war machine without any thought about the ultimate safety and unity of the social (national) body, about the respect of the idea of law, or about what will happen to America's public culture – is what I call "agonal sovereignty." It is agonal to the extent that, in this model, constant struggle and endless fighting are actualized in a generally heroic fashion and, as such, this sort of violence becomes the acme of political success.

Act 1: defending the state

As was already noted in the previous chapters, the Y2K/cyberterror syndrome around 1999–2000, the aftermath of the presidential elections in November 2000, the terrorist attacks on the World Trade Center and the Pentagon on September 11, 2001, and the US-led war in Iraq in March–April 2003 have unleashed a flurry of media punditry and "intellectual statecraftism" in the United States. Nowadays, any self-proclaimed public intellectual figure, any cable news network talk-show host, any government official in search of visibility, any disgruntled CIA or State

Department bureaucrat, or any retired military officer feels that s/he is authorized to write and publish his/her own impressions about the war on terror and the role of the United States in it. Inevitably, these new pundits of statecraft and their tabloid geopolitical discourses reveal strong opinions about the war, whether it is desirable (some of them think it is), whether it is necessary (the majority of them believe it is in some circumstances), and how it should be fought (they often disagree on this last point). More importantly, the tabloid writings by these pundits of statecraft go a long way in trying to explain to Americans what the war means and, by extension, how the United States as a war nation is supposed to act.[31] As we saw in Chapter 3, many of these discourses of America at war are moral, ideological, and tactical conditioning mechanisms that contribute to normalizing and perhaps abjecting war as the key contemporary explanatory variable for both domestic and international politics. These discourses establish the idea that American citizens have no choice but to define their everyday life in relation to war, at home and abroad.

In this popular cultural context dominated by war punditry since 9/11 and more so since March 2003, it is not too surprising to find the main warrior of America's post-9/11 conflicts in Afghanistan and Iraq taking part in this mode of tabloid political conditioning. General Tommy Franks, the Commander in Chief of the US military's Central Command from July 2000 to July 2003, exposed his thoughts about war in a book released in the summer of 2004.[32] Although this book, *American Soldier*, is written as a biography, the vast majority of the volume (the last two thirds) is dedicated to the US military campaigns in the aftermath of 9/11. What is striking about this book and its accounts of warfare and war-making (which were General Franks' number one tasks since his appointment in July 2000) is how matter-of-factly normal, expected, and often necessary war is presented to be. Although it is certainly not shocking to read a professional soldier describe the art of war as a daily routine, an occupational task, or a job like any other,[33] it is interesting to note that Franks appears to go out of his way in this volume to affirm that war is never to be thought as limitless or absolute. Instead, Franks often intimates, war is a necessity that must always be subordinated to political and institutional interests, and principally the interest of defending the state and its sovereignty.[34] Quoting military thinkers like Sun-Tzu and Clausewitz on many occasions, Franks does not fail to remark that war is the extension of a political process. It is a political practice involving fierce violence and often causing brutal death that should be used when diplomacy is no longer sufficient.[35]

One might not have expected the creator of the "Shock and Awe" war campaigns deployed in Iraq and the supporter of the "Thunder Runs" tactics used to take over Baghdad and other Iraqi cities to talk about war as a form of political exception,[36] as something to be used when all else fails. Instead of singing the praise of war as a way of creating life (a biopolitical motif that we shall encounter later), as many illustrious American generals and field commanders of the past, from Sherman to Patton, have had a tendency to affirm, Franks refers to America's war machine as a professional enterprise. He, the Commander in Chief, is the boss. Below him are hundreds of thousands of his employees whose job it is to make the company look good and work efficiently. But the Commander in Chief himself is accountable. Franks, as he often recognizes, has his own bosses, his "company executive board" so to speak, who, from the Defense Secretary to the President, give him the objectives and goals that they would like the company to achieve. As Franks puts it: "My duty was to recommend the most effective and decisive employment of our armed forces in solving a particular problem. The civilian leadership – the Secretary of Defense and the President of the United States – would determine whether my strategic assumptions were appropriate."[37] This way of presenting the military reality of war is very business-like, an extension of corporate America to the enterprise of war-making, and Franks' task is to devise strategies and mobilize his employees in such a way that they all serve the interests of the company as a whole, in this case the interests of the state.[38]

One cannot help but think that this kind of rhetoric sounds a lot like toeing the "company line." At a time when the Bush administration found itself increasingly questioned by some members of the media and the public (around late 2004 and 2005) who started to doubt the initial explanations given for the war in Iraq,[39] and as the 9/11 Investigating Commission was about to release a damning report on security failures prior to the September 11 attacks,[40] the White House and the Department of Defense needed all the "artillery" they could muster to counter these mounting criticisms, all the more so since Bush was up for re-election. So, if the US Commander in Chief who was in charge of the war campaigns in Afghanistan and Iraq could give credit for the successes of the military campaigns to his own bosses (Defense Secretary Donald Rumsfeld, Deputy Defense Secretary Paul Wolfowitz, Vice-President Dick Cheney, and President Bush primarily), take the blame for some of the failures (which Franks does on several occasions in his book),[41] and reveal who during these necessary military operations was unhelpful and perhaps even a hindrance to achieving America's foreign policy objectives (Richard Clarke is a main target, and Colin Powell, to a lesser extent, does not come across as too useful either),[42] then the Bush administration and re-election campaign could get a beneficial boost. At the same time, though, there appear to be genuine yet symptomatic moments of reflection in Franks' autobiography that indicate an increasing desire to view war as a professional activity. While this understanding of war-making as a professional task by one of its main contemporary protagonists has the effect of presenting war as a normal practice, a business-like transaction to some extent, it also extends a long tradition of military–state relationship whereby the military acts on behalf of and when the institutions of the state need it.

As mentioned above, Hardt and Negri have suggested that, with the contemporary use of the war machine, war has become a "permanent state of exception."[43] As this state of exception is established, the legal and juridical foundations of modern politics are being pushed aside as war now becomes the main basis for the political. Franks' *American Soldier* does not support Hardt and Negri's claim about contemporary warfare as a permanent exception, or at least not directly. For Franks, priority is still to be given to the law (the American constitution, American moral and democratic values) and to those in charge of defending America's sovereignty. Although those in charge – political officers – may not be efficient at preserving the national interest or protecting America's legal sovereignty, or they may have ulterior motives that may take American sovereignty away from its constitutional foundations, it is not up to him, the professional soldier, to decide. Simply, it is not his job. From this perspective that still recognizes and wants to preserve the legal and political bases of the state's sovereignty, the warrior's most professional task is simply to execute his (political) superiors' orders when called upon and, once again, devise plans and strategies to make and win wars in order to defend the United States (from terrorists, rogue leaders, or enemy states).[44] According to this version of sovereignty interestingly reinforced and reasserted by Franks' own war-supporting discourse, the war machine is *not* an exteriority of the state, its always potential and fatal enemy. Rather, it remains *inside* the state, an instrument of the state, and a political and legal one at that, whose purpose is to make sure that America's institutions are still allowed to function well at home since they will be protected from foreign enemies abroad. To some extent, for Franks, there is no American war machine, no monster of war, and 9/11 has not drastically changed the relationship between the American state and its military. If nothing else, there is now a cleaner, leaner, more efficient, more productive, and finally more professional practice of warfare that best serves the liberal democratic interests of modern sovereign nation-states, starting with the United States' own.

This claim about the absence of a war machine post-9/11 and the continuation of business as usual in the relationship between the state and war can of course be self-serving, allowing the military the necessary geopolitical space to conduct its war dealings away from the eyes of the state and its citizenry (as Franks often repeats, the state gives goals and objectives, and the military puts them into motion by going to war). As much as the subordination of the military to the needs of the state creates the image of a political and constitutional continuum,[45] it also establishes a division of labor that, historically, has served both the state and the war machine well. The state remains blind to the deadly violence of its military (which even has its own judicial system, separate from the state's own justice) while the war machine, when given the green light by political leaders, can carry out its missions and conduct war pretty much in any way, shape, or form it likes.[46] Although the war machine is not without responsibility to the state and to international legal standards (since after all its actions are still to be seen as a continuation of the policy-making process through military means), it is still granted the right to have a legal and political space of its own, a space where, once war is politically declared and legally supported, the war machine is given free range (the exactions and tortures by American soldiers on Iraqi prisoners at Abu Ghraib, for example, can perhaps be placed in this context). Moreover, the notion of a continuum from politics to war on behalf of the maintenance of legal sovereignty could also be a not-so-well disguised diplomatic façade, a *trompe l'oeil* of sorts, that affirms the principle of the exception of war when in fact, in political reality, it has already become obvious that war is a permanent state of affairs and law has no valid or useful foundations any more to counter warfare.

From this perspective, what could be better as a fooling device than the use of the most prominent contemporary soldier, the alleged leader of the war machine himself, to clearly assert that war is not limitless, that its inevitable flow does not go against the objectives of the state, and that its terror must be used selectively when political necessities recognized by political leaders call for it? At times, Franks' own narrative has a hard time staying within the bounds of political necessity, and the need to serve a biopolitical objective through war or even the desire to depict war as a heroic activity, as an end in itself, sometimes appear to poke through the General's otherwise well structured, controlled, and largely antiseptic text.[47]

Despite these plausible machinations at work behind Franks' discourse, it is perhaps still plausible to think that war today, particularly as it is being fought by the United States' military, remains a prolongation of American political objectives that have to do with national defense, US national interest, and the preservation of American legal and juridical sovereignty by other means. Traditionally in international relations, realist scholars have been the most ardent supporters of the use of military power on behalf of the national interest.[48] War, realists have claimed, is not necessarily to be averted. Whether realists put the emphasis on human nature or on the idea of anarchy as a structuring principle, the outcome of the realist analysis is not much different. War is to be expected in the relations between states and, depending on the global distribution of power, it may be a proper path of action to the extent that the national interest and the sovereign integrity of the state are at stake. Once again, this classically realist perspective does not automatically see the state and the war machine as antagonistic. For realists, following Machiavelli's advice to the Prince on the proper use of political violence, it is only if war is mobilized for a reason other than to protect the national interest that it can, in fact will, become adverse to the state and its sovereignty. It is striking to note, though, that after 9/11, and in particular since the months that preceded the US invasion of Iraq, most contemporary American realist scholars (most of them tabloid realists, as Chapter 2 explained) collectively disapproved of the use of warfare in this latest American conflict. John Mearsheimer, Kenneth Waltz, John Lewis Gaddis, Joseph Nye, Zbigniew Brzezinski, and to a lesser extent Henry Kissinger, individuals whose views on international affairs and foreign policy shaped the United States' security and defense strategies in prior decades and still tried to do so just before 9/11 as we saw in Chapter 2, opposed the use of war by the American state in Iraq, questioned the motivations behind the decision to attack, and sometimes found fault with the military strategy (which allegedly was supposed to be a continuation of prior American-led diplomatic action vis-à-vis Iraq).[49] Some of these (tabloid) realist critics of the US war in Iraq clearly made the point that the chosen approach did not protect the national interest but instead threatened American national security: "Bad strategists don't know when to make this switch [from war to systemic stabilization]. They become so enamored of shock and awe that it becomes an end in itself. Because they are incapable of providing reassurance, they wind up being system destroyers rather than system builders."[50] Despite these incisive attacks, after 9/11 (as was described in the two previous chapters), realist scholars' views were minimized and often replaced in

US national security and military strategy circles by the opinions of other types of more geopolitically proactive/aggressive intellectuals and pundits (Robert D. Kaplan, Samuel Huntington, Michael Ledeen, David Frum and Richard Perle, and Thomas Barnett among many others) for whom a larger, more encompassing, and more continuous plan for global American war-making needed to be adopted if the United States were to prevail in its war on terror, a war for which these individuals could not foresee any end.[51] As previously indicated, one could see that a transition started to be made from what I called tabloid realism (which seemed to prevail from the mid-1990s to 9/11) to a tabloid imperialistic mode of writing and thinking about geopolitics, culture, and war.

If a tabloid imperialistic justification for America's new wars was indeed deployed, it is doubtful that the modern, legal, and institutional principle of war engagement – war is still the exception, diplomatic relations are the norm – remained valid and meaningful after 9/11. If traditional or even tabloid realist rationalizations for war were no longer pertinent in the aftermath of both the 9/11 attacks and the US war in Iraq, then, as Hardt and Negri suggest, one has to interrogate what making war the new norm means for the legal and juridical concept of state sovereignty and for traditional institutional channels of power. If the warrior is no longer subordinated to the political officer (despite Franks' best efforts to demonstrate otherwise), if the Clausewitzian adage about war and politics has once again been inverted, one must also ask about the relationship between the state and the war machine and about what this revised relationship means for American public culture. Can the war machine remain an instrument of the state, an accomplice of its sovereignty, a means for its defense? Or is it external to the state, always on the brink of betraying it, always about to serve another sovereignty, another modality of power? The next section starts to answer these questions by bringing the specter of total warfare in relation to another form of sovereignty, and to another way of envisioning the political (outside legal foundations), or what might be called biopower.

Act 2: rebuilding national identity

It does not take much of a conceptual effort to go from war as a political strategy deployed to defend the state and its institutions to war as an instrument that guarantees the survival of the nation and, as such, periodically reinforces national unity and identity. As previously indicated, even Franks' discourse at times slides from the need to protect American political institutions to the desire to maintain the unity of the body politic. For example, Franks writes: "the prize we seek in this time in history is a way of life."[52] Maintaining or creating a "way of life" by means of warfare is a much more ambitious project for the military and all those involved in war-making than defending the state. It is an attempt at going to war, using war's destructive force, and mobilizing war's terrifying violence in order to establish a sovereignty that, in a sense, is not just to be found in the presence and development of political and juridical institutions. Waging war to preserve or create life evokes a sovereignty that does not hesitate – if the life of the body politic, of the social compact, is deemed to be threatened – to go beyond the text and the spirit of the laws allegedly to defend them better. This form of war rationale has its roots in a supplementary understanding of sovereignty, a form of sovereignty that is no longer premised upon the laws or other foundational texts and principles of the state, but rather is based upon the exception to those laws. Following the lead of critical thinkers like Michel Foucault, Giorgio Agamben, and Michael Shapiro, this sovereignty is what can be called "biopolitical sovereignty."

Biopolitical sovereignty is concerned with the administration of life. It seeks to manage and regulate life (the life of the body politic in the first place) by devising strategies, policies, and discourses whose main purpose is to determine what modes of existence are to be privileged. By the same token, biopolitical sovereignty is constantly seeking to do away with other modes of life, other collective bodies, whose presence appears to be a danger to the selected, supported, and protected mode of existence. Drawing on Foucault's writing, Shapiro notes that "understanding the biopolitical aspect of state security practices, ranging from the administrative to the violent, requires an approach to sovereignty that treats its non-juridical dimensions, its constructions of worthy versus unworthy human life."[53] In this quest to define, create, and preserve a dominant way of life, biopolitical sovereigns, often modern states, turn to instruments of biopower, tools and techniques whose utility is meant to regulate everyday life (both inside and outside the body politic), and that sovereigns take to be more efficient than existing juridical legislations and other legal and constitutional principles. Once again, it is mostly to Foucault that we owe this insight about the necessity of techniques of biopower. Foucault writes:

> Another consequence of this development of bio-power was the growing importance assumed by the action of the norm, at the expense of the juridical system of the law . . . But a power whose task is to take charge of life needs continuous regulatory and corrective mechanisms. It is no longer a matter of bringing death into play in the field of sovereignty, but of distributing the living in the domain of value and utility. Such a power has to qualify, measure, appraise, and hierarchize, rather than display itself in murderous splendor; it does not have to draw the line that separates the enemies of the sovereign from its obedient subjects.[54]

Agamben comments on Foucault's concept of biopower and remarks that biopolitical sovereignty emerges in modern society "at the point at which the species and the individual as a simple living body become what is at stake in a society's political strategies."[55] According to Foucault, what is at stake for the sovereign is no longer to dispose of human bodies, no longer to do away with individual subjects as he, the sovereign, desires, but rather to maintain life by turning the *subjects* of the sovereign's whimsical power into an ensemble of *objects* of calculation, control, distribution, and technical efficiency. As Foucault repeatedly puts it, individual subjects become docile bodies under regimes of biopower.

Yet, as Agamben suggests, Foucault does not push the analysis of biopower far enough. What Foucault's view on biopower does not perceive is the distinction, but at the same time the continuity, that exists between the inside and the outside of biopolitical sovereignty, and that techniques of biopower help to establish. Although, as Foucault puts it, death is no longer to be brought into play *inside* the domain of the sovereign, this biopolitical sovereign still possesses a "murderous splendor" by displacing violence, destruction, and terror to the *outside* of the body politic. The force of the biopolitical sovereign is thus the result of the sovereign's mastery over the dialectic of inside and outside.[56] By "sitting on the fence," having access to both what is inside the body politic and what forms its outside, and reserving for himself the sole right of determining how expandable the inside can be and how threatening the outside will become, the sovereign constantly recreates a normative order and interprets the laws (and their exception) from this unique standpoint. For Agamben, this positioning of the sovereign at the point of juncture between the internal juridical order (the inside of the body politic) and the external extra-normative (dis)order (outside the national community) empowers the sovereign to make and unmake life, always having the capacity to play with the concept of the law, its limits, and its modes of exception through a series of internal and external, domestic and international techniques of biopower. In this fashion, the prerogative of biopolitical sovereignty is still to manipulate life and death. The life of individual subjects is indeed at stake, as Foucault indicated, but so is its removal and/or suspension by the sovereign and by means of techniques of biopower employed on behalf of the sovereign. Sovereignty thus becomes "the originary structure in which law refers to life and includes it in itself by suspending it."[57]

From this biopolitical perspective, war reveals itself to be a favorite instrument of geopolitical (bio)power to the extent that war's operations necessarily transcend existing laws and institutional orders. War suspends the juridical sovereignty of the warring state and that of other states where the war is being fought in order to better serve the security of the inside, protect the privileged body politic, and take violence and death away from the domestic social order. As Hardt and Negri mention, war is indeed a preferred biopolitical instrument since, at any moment, when the chosen way of life is said (by the sovereign and its agents) to be in jeopardy, the recourse to war can usher in a state of legal and juridical exception. War is furthermore a state of exception that may become a dominant biopolitical practice, a constant state of affairs, since its spatial and temporal limits do not have to be, in fact cannot be, determined in the law, prior to any deployment of this exceptional state. The "limits of war are rendered indeterminate" because this war's success depends upon doing whatever needs to be done, no matter how long it needs to be done, to preserve the body politic, the dominant and privileged social order.[58] According to Hardt and Negri, biopolitical sovereignty does not only justify war by placing the emphasis on the protection of a way of life and by making permanent a state of legal exception. Biopolitical sovereignty also requires absolute war and total warfare because there cannot be any (political) limits to the need to preserve social life. The survival of the social, often national, order is at stake, and the structure of life is made dependent upon not only fighting the war but, more importantly, winning the war. Hardt and Negri call this absolute, biopolitical interpretation of the vital need to have recourse to war "global war." Global war's aim is not only to "bring death but also produce and regulate life."[59] Hardt and Negri further indicate that, in this kind of war, the notion of the defense of the state's sovereignty gives way to the idea of the security of the homeland.[60] As previously mentioned, the idea of the protection of the political institutions also recedes behind the idea of the survival or reinvigorating of the national body politic.[61] Even the concept of population, as a legal abstraction, is no longer useful. Instead, humanity (defined exclusively) is a main motivation for going to war. Shapiro writes that, "[i]n a global context, the most significant post-Cold War change in the model of life upon which sovereignty's approach to peacekeeping/war making is predicated is from a biopolitics of 'population' . . . to a biopolitics of 'humanity'. In this latter conception of life, those who must be defended (as well as those who are criminalized) constitute a new class of bodies to be protected and a new set of threatening ones to confront."[62]

Finally, and as Foucault already intimated, the individual subjects of the sovereign, the citizens, no longer exist and are instead replaced by a vast and indiscriminate amount of docile bodies whose main function is to be disciplined by techniques of biopower, starting with the war machine. The disciplinization, normalization, carceralization, and securitization of such docile bodies are the modalities of biopolitical action that are designed to maintain the integrity of the national social order, both at home and abroad. According to this mode of sovereign operationalization, often as a result of the actions of the war machine, the quest for the good life in the modern state turns into the deployment of techniques aimed at maintaining what Agamben calls "bare life." As "that part of humanity that is excluded from political protection,"[63] as a life that becomes expandable in the designs of biopower, "bare life" becomes a matter of determining "who *may be killed and yet not sacrificed.*"[64] It is often (although not only) in war, when docile bodies are sent outside the limits of the body politic to preserve a way of life by destroying other lives, that bare life finds its most basic expression. Similarly to the way the modern state was seen as the provider and defender of the good life under regimes of juridical sovereignty, the war machine becomes the promoter and enforcer of bare life under regimes of biopolitical sovereignty.

In the months that followed the US military invasion of Iraq, it was not rare to encounter instances of discursive support for the idea of bare life, for techniques of biopower, and for biopolitical sovereignty in tabloid-type geopolitical/international relations/national security literatures that sought to stress the importance for the nation and for its unity of the relationship between the state and war. One such discourse was provided by the contemporary best-selling pundit of statecraft, Samuel Huntington. My objective here is not to describe his tabloid mode of writing and thinking (which I already detailed in Chapter 2). Nonetheless I want to bring up some of his more recent arguments that encourage the idea of using "global warfare" as a way of preserving and reinforcing the American body politic in an era when the "clash of civilizations" seems (to him) to have given way to an absolute war campaign. For Huntington, national identity is at stake, and it is particularly so in the current American war on terror. National identity is the main reason behind current modalities of disciplinization, securitization, and warfare, both inside the US national social order and outside its borders.

In his book, *Who Are We? The Challenges to America's National Identity*,[65] Huntington's focus is no longer political, cultural, and religious confrontations between civilizational blocs, something that was for Huntington a matter of great concern for the United States' foreign policy in the post-Cold War era. Rather, the focus is now placed on domestic American politics, society, and culture, and on the threats of internal dissension and national disorder that, in his view, are likely to proliferate in the twenty-first century. For Huntington, 9/11 was a historic moment, not just because the United States was attacked on its soil, but because the attacks helped to rekindle a sense of national unity and communal identity in American culture that had started to be lost in the last decades of the twentieth century. The events of September 11 particularly mattered for Huntington because they "drastically reduced the salience of these other identities and sent Old Glory back to the top of the national flag pole."[66] Whereas other conservative thinkers (tabloid or not) may have interpreted 9/11 as one of the darkest days in US history,[67] Huntington believes that September 11 and the terrorists who attacked that day provided America with an incredible opportunity: to be one again, to rally around the flag, and finally to start to reorganize itself as a united and cohesive social body, as one unique body politic.

Thus, Osama bin Laden and the terrorists "make us realize that we are Americans," Huntington proclaims.[68] According to Huntington, the main reason why America was left vulnerable and was attacked was that it had become a state without a nation. But the aftermath of 9/11 demonstrated a return to national identity concerns, and Americans seemed to have understood – by collectively coping with the terror, by uniting behind the US troops in the war in Afghanistan – that national unity and a clear sense of American identity were the cornerstones of American sovereignty. In a sense, Huntington continues, Americans after 9/11 gave a mandate to their sovereign, the head of the American state, to take whatever measures were necessary to keep or perhaps make America one again. The American sovereign (the US President according to Huntington) understood that this mandate meant that techniques of biopower, both domestically and internationally, would have to be deployed in order to preserve the American way of life. Among such techniques were an increase in disciplinization and control of Americans' docile bodies at home (through heightened security measures, the passing of the Patriot Act designed to circumvent existing laws protecting some basic individual rights, wiretapping of domestic phone conversations, and incarceration of suspect and potentially disorderly bodies) and the launching of a global war, against Afghanistan first, and later against Iraq, a war outside the limits of the envisioned national community (in this sense, Huntington reprises Kaplan's argument made after 9/11 too). As Huntington intimates, when American national unity is at stake, biopolitical practices and methods must become the main modalities of operation of (bio)power, or, to use Huntington's own words, "[e]ven the most successful societies are at some point threatened by internal disintegration and decay and by more vigorous and ruthless external 'barbarian forces'."[69] When "internal decay" and "external dangers" put the American way of life at risk, American leaders have a sworn duty (a sovereign duty) to "postpone the demise and halt disintegration, by renewing [the] sense of national identity, their national purpose, and the cultural values that [the members of society] have in common."[70] Although there was an obvious attempt to achieve just this in the weeks that followed the attacks of 9/11, Huntington is nonetheless worried that Americans (both the docile bodies and the sovereign leaders) may soon forget about this national survival imperative. And so Huntington's new book is an exhortation to Americans to continue to think in terms of biopolitics and to live according to rules of biopower, to "continue to do this [even] if they are not under attack."[71] One way of continuing to do this is of course to always be under attack, to constantly place the nation under the threat of "ruthless barbarian forces," and to declare an unending war against the enemies of the nation.

War is for Huntington a favorite instrument of biopower. Americans have to realize that war will be in the American nation's future for decades. As Huntington puts it, "[r]ecent history suggests that America is likely to be involved in various sorts of military conflicts with Muslim countries and groups, and possibly others, in the coming years."[72] But not all wars are good for the preservation or reinforcement of national identity. Wars can be waged by the sovereign, but, Huntington asks, "will these wars unite or divide America?"[73] At a time when America's war in Iraq started to become a matter of national controversy (and a potential source of national disunion), Huntington took it upon himself to indicate how and why war – even the one in Iraq – can unite. Huntington creates a matrix to determine which wars are beneficial and which ones are harmful to the nation.[74] Wars that American leaders engage in are a function of a ratio between the "level of perceived threat" to the nation and the "level of mobilization" that the state requires from the nation's "live" human bodies. A high threat level coupled with a high degree of mobilization will create unity, but may later cause disorder (such was the case with World War II, Huntington claims, that later led to the Cold War). A war characterized by high mobilization and low perceived threat is the worst-case scenario for Huntington. With this type of war, it is a sure bet that the body politic will be divided and perhaps irremediably split apart (Huntington uses the Vietnam war as a case in point). A low threat risk and a low mobilization is not much to worry about for Huntington, although this kind of conflict engagement may lead to a slow form of national disunity, particularly if issues regarding national security are not resolved in the course of conflict (Huntington lists the Gulf War in 1991 as an example). Finally, the only war situation that is worthy of being pursued by the state is a war that will mobilize few docile bodies and yet will be characterized by high levels of perceived national threat. This kind of war-making, of which Huntington believes the war on terror is a prototypical case, will create a form of "sustained national unity" and will be put to efficient biopolitical use.[75] The war on terror after September 11 is thus a proper biopolitical war because:

The dramatic images of the planes going into the World Trade Center towers and their collapse embedded in Americans a profound and lasting sense of threat. The Bush administration then maximized national unity and support for the war by not asking people to pay higher taxes, endure shortages, or suffer any except minor inconveniences. With acute political sense, it maintained support for the war by not demanding the sacrifices that some people thought it should demand in order to make the war a "real" war.[76]

By depicting the Bush administration as a "maximizer" of national unity and a protector of American lives, Huntington solidly anchors the American state and its war on terror in the logic of biopolitical sovereignty. In so doing, Huntington has no difficulty perceiving the limitations imposed onto American citizens as "minor inconveniences" because, in order to preserve America's way of life, American lives (not to mention the lives of many non-Americans) will have to be sacrificed. Yet these sacrifices – reduction of individual rights, acceptance of multiple forms of daily societal controls and surveillance, and even death in combat for those placed on the frontlines of the war on terror – are no longer to be seen as extreme or exceptional circumstances, but rather as normal everyday activities and routines in the life of the nation. In fact, Huntington affirms, they are not even to be thought of as sacrifices since, after all, the war, although constant, is still (according to him at least) at a low intensity level. Clearly, Huntington brings the state and its war machine into the domain of bare life. For it is only by thinking about human lives as expendable ("killed but not sacrificed," as Agamben would say) and individual subjects as docile bodies that Huntington can justify the constant mobilization of control and discipline over beings sharing a common national identity and culture on the inside and defend the recourse to the death and destruction of abjected "barbarian" enemies through the operations of a global war on the outside. And should the docile bodies start to harbor some doubt as to the necessity of maintaining this (at once domestic and global) ongoing regime of biopower, Huntington reminds everyone that the war is not about to end. In this Orwellian scheme, future terrorist attacks are inevitable because, if nothing else, these attacks and the war they endlessly prolong are beneficial to the renewed sense of national unity. To quote Huntington: "Recurring terrorist attacks on the United States without substantial mobilization are likely to maintain the salience of national identity and reasonably high levels of national unity."[77]

Thus, from this biopolitical perspective, when "intimately biopower and war are connected in reality and at every level of . . . analysis" as Hardt and Negri assert,[78] war once again cannot have any foreseeable end. Rather, this global war launched by the sovereign across juridical and political boundaries will last as long as the nation needs to be kept united and as long as some agents of the biopolitical state, from pseudo-intellectual (yet tabloid geopolitical) advisors like Huntington to national identity "maximizers" like Bush, find enemies and dangers that are deemed to threaten the body politic and its privileged form of life. War, then, becomes *the* preferred way of life, and the war-crafting and war-organizing institutions of the state have to take over, in both domestic and international politics, as the main employers of the nation's live but disciplined bodies. As we saw at the beginning of this chapter, these war-fighting and homeland security-providing institutions of the sovereign will be able to insert themselves into everyday life, through popular culture, the media, and public tabloid discourses, and they will become the new normalizing instruments of the state. Slowly but surely, as the nation-state increasingly relies upon the war machine for its biopolitical survival, the warriors will start to take control of the well-being of the nation and will incessantly search for, recruit, mobilize, use, and eventually destroy human lives to better maintain and create life.

Act 3: becoming one with war

In a volume titled *Empire of Disorder*, the French war and strategic studies specialist Alain Joxe writes: "The American armed forces and NATO, now the leaders of the global system of repression, have been asking more political questions, either by foundering in a fear of a generalized civil war or by questioning the sacrosanct limit between politics and military strategy."[79] Joxe continues: "It is important to understand that a certain wing of American ideology and, perhaps soon Euro-American, is leading toward a swirling black hole, a destructive fatality, an ideology of absolute superiority of the West over the rest of the world."[80] In these statements, Joxe intimates that a new ideology/story of American national unity, superiority, and triumph has chosen war as its dominant strategy or to achieve its principal objectives. Such a destructive ideology/story (enabled by tabloid media and discourses) has fused the goals of the political (whether they are seen in terms of juridical or biopolitical sovereignty) with those of the war machine. The outcome of this purposeful but fateful strategy can only be experienced along the lines of what Deleuze and Guattari already perceived the war machine would mean for the state form. Called in by the agents of the state, the war machine would launch the state and its subjects (or docile bodies) onto a path of uncontrollable destruction, unpredictable combat, and limitless conquest. Along this unstoppable march, warriors would take over the political and cultural domains, both domestically and internationally (for there is no longer any inside or outside for the war machine), and use war's main logic, or what Joxe calls war's "destructive fatality," to drag humankind into a "swirling back hole" or toward a "hellish descent."[81]

As previously shown, several contemporary American tabloid geopolitical scientists and pundits of statecraft openly exhorted US policy-makers to rely almost exclusively on the military to achieve, post 9/11, so-called American security objectives. Within a year or so of the 9/11 terrorist attacks, many of these tabloid imperialists' arguments started to focus on the need/desire to go to war in Iraq.[82] Whereas attacking the Taliban in Afghanistan and declaring an open war against terrorists after 9/11 could still be conceived in terms of national defense or preservation of national identity, attacking Iraq was not as easily justifiable among those in government and in the military whose task it is (supposedly) to keep America safe. Convincing the bureaucratic and military establishment (not to mention the American public) that the war in Iraq was necessary and inevitable required adopting a different strategy. It required placing the contemporary issues regarding US national security after 9/11 in a context that would make total and absolute war, starting with Iraq, the only possible outcome. Thus, tabloid imperialist pundits and warmongers went to work and, in the course of explaining to the American public why attacking Iraq could not be avoided, opted to relinquish most responsibilities for American sovereignty to the warriors. In order to allow the state to cede its sovereign prerogatives to those in charge of warmaking, a larger-than-life situation had to be constructed in the war narratives. This unprecedented historic situation, prompted by the events of 9/11, was found in the revelation that "evil" had taken over the conduct of everyday international politics and that, consequently, an American-led crusade against "evil" had to be undertaken. As Lawrence Kaplan and William Kristol, two leading American war crusaders, put it: "as the events of 9/11 remind us, evil exists in this world, and it has consequences." They quickly added: "Fortunately, evil can be defeated."[83]

Fighting "evil" is no longer a political strategy, or at least a traditionally recognizable one. A struggle against "evil" no longer appears to respond to clear ideological imperatives either. Rather, as the United States was said to be involved in a final and fatal combat of "good" versus "evil," theological imperatives took over political motivations and means. Put differently, the requirement to fight "evil" became totally removed from any consideration of state sovereignty. In this absolute configuration, the sovereignty of one state, of any state, no longer matters (in fact, it becomes trivial), as a moral battle to the bitter end erases any consideration for a here and a there, an inside and an outside, or good states (friends and allies) and bad states (enemies). As was clearly seen in the preparations for what was truly the first American onslaught of this newly conceived total war against "evil" (against Saddam Hussein's Iraq in 2003), traditional allies, with whom prior pacts to protect and defend each other's sovereignty had been signed and long recognized, could now, at once, become traitors, shadowy figures, and obstructers of the "good." Such was the fate that was reserved by the United States for some ("old") European states, starting with France and Germany, that refused to join the US-built "coalition of the willing" against Iraq in 2003.

While fighting "evil" dissipates any clear sense of state sovereignty (juridical or biopolitical even) and renders common political tactics obsolete, it also shifts the center of command for the strategies that need to be implemented to the war planners and war-makers. The war-makers now hold the keys to the survival, not just of the nation anymore, but also of humanity in general, or more precisely here, of a humanity defined restrictively in terms of those who are willing to join the absolute war and partake of this ultimate moral crusade. The warriors are now in charge. Their mission is to destroy as many sources of "evil" and terror as possible, be they terrorists, states harboring terrorists, states said to be sponsoring terrorists, or any other group or state whose potentiality for "evil" has yet to be manifested. A struggle against "evil" cannot have preset targets since it is precisely through the war that others will reveal themselves as either "good" or "evil." As Kaplan and Kristol indicate, what was truly novel about the Bush doctrine of military preemption announced in the summer of 2002 (and of which the war in Iraq in 2003 was supposed to be a first test-case) was that it transferred the judgment for what is to be considered "evil" in the world (and thus primed for destruction) to the war deciders and fighters. According to the Bush doctrine, the state became but a pale shadow of what the warriors' plans to combat "evil" were. Bush acquiesced that it would be the military from now on that would be required to "take the battle to the enemy, disrupt his plans, and confront the worst threats before they emerge."[84] It would be up to American warriors, those newly envisioned moral crusaders, to "keep military strengths beyond challenge."[85] It would be their job to "concentrate America's military power to devastating effect."[86]

Kaplan and Kristol made it clear that this turn to the war machine was not to be thought as a state of exception. In fact, unlike what was still the case in biopolitical designs, there was no longer any pretense of claiming that war was being used to better restore the sanctity of the law in this fatal and fateful tabloid imperialistic discourse. The only principle that mattered here was the sanctity of the "good" (not the sovereignty of the state and/or nation), a sanctity that got defined and redefined as the warriors' trail of destruction extended to ever new "evil" targets and "evil" lands. As Kaplan and Kristol affirmed, the US war in Iraq was *not* an isolated moment. It would *not* be an aberration in an otherwise traditional policy of national defense or security. Rather, it would announce a "new model for [geo-political] success," a model premised upon what Kaplan and Kristol simply called the "demise of evil regimes."[87] This new war model was America's own model, its future path of action, its "burden" in a sense.[88] In this bellicose and warmongering way of dealing with all sorts of targets (not even others), America and war would inevitably be united as one once again. Recalling Ledeen's own call for abjection presented in Chapter 3, war, this "inescapable reality of American power" after 9/11 and after the war in Iraq, would be the only possible "American idea of itself."[89]

Few recognizable models of sovereignty, if any at all, can come to terms with this newly presented abject and nihilist (tabloid imperialistic) geopolitical reality, with this fusion of America and war in an effort to constantly fight terror and "evil." But perhaps some of Hannah Arendt's writings (and her unique critical sense when it comes to detecting theoretical and discursive sources of violence and human vileness) may come as close as any philosophical and political perspective might in helping us to make sense of this modality of thought/action that fuses the state with the total violence of war, and that seeks to merge the state form and the war machine into one single entity.[90] As Seyla Benhabib has indicated, in *The Human Condition*, Arendt presents two different models of political action: "the first being the agonal or heroic model of politics as the activity of 'performing great and memorable deeds' on the part of a civic republican elite, and the second being the kind of democratic or associative politics that can be engaged in by ordinary citizens who may or may not possess great moral prowess."[91] This second model of action is what Benhabib refers to as Arendt's "narrative model" since politics in this model is "characterized through the 'telling of a story' and 'the weaving of a web of narratives'."[92] Of importance here to help us figure out what new model of sovereignty might be introduced by the US war machine in the post-9/11 era (and by its proponents) is Arendt's first model, her agonal politics. Agonal action is a heroic form of action that takes place in the public domain (to the extent that a public versus private distinction still makes sense) and is conducted by selected public figures who have been endowed with the power to "reveal an antecedent essence" of the political.[93] These powerful figures' heroic deeds enable "a process of discovery" within the public sphere that allows those living in this political domain to realize and respect this finally disclosed great "what is."[94] Although Benhabib adds that, for Arendt, agonal acts are "episodic and rare," since these actions "transcend and in many ways transfigure everyday-ness and our understanding of ourselves," they nonetheless express an extreme passion, a "shining forth," or "an emotion in its quintessential form."[95] Such an unbounded passion unleashes a great force, a violent engagement that defines the political realm. Thus, agonal violence often becomes the mark of this heroic and passionate action undertaken by those whose task it is to reveal what Arendt sometimes calls an "unchangeable identity" though such deeds.[96] The term "ago-nal" (as tied to action, politics, or violence in Arendt's work) is derived from the Greek word *agonia*, which signifies contest, struggle, or combat.

A peculiar form of sovereignty can be derived from Arendt's concept of agonal action. It is a sovereignty that resides in the deeds of those agents whose role it is to express passion, emotion, and heroism and, in so doing, to mobilize force and violence to make manifest the "antecedent essence," whether such an essence is thought of in terms of the republic, the nation, or the "good." Only in the agonal acts of those agents is the chosen essence truly sovereign. Only through those agents' use of force and violence is this essence recognizable. For, while the an-tecedent essence is always assumed to exist, it is not given any actual sovereign meaning and representation until agonal action is performed. Agonal violence is needed to actualize this essence.[97] But for this sovereignty to be actualized, the performance of its agents must also be disconnected from any sort of prior sover-eign attachment. Agonal action must be free roaming, and the violence and force such a performance entails must be free ranging. As Dana Villa has put it, in this model of action, "virtuosity, agonism, and theatricality dominate."[98]

Although it may seem paradoxical to argue that this agonal mode of sover-eignty must be detached from any prior sovereign anchoring in order to be re-vealed, it is nonetheless necessary in order to arrive at a new sovereign essence that can stand on its own. Put differently, only by expulsing any moral, political, legal, or even philosophical dimension from their actions can the agonal agents offer a performance that is truly valued for what it is, for what its deeds actual-ize. As Villa notes, by exposing such a value-free model of action (and possibly sovereignty), Arendt comes close to Nietzsche's attempt at "self-consciously *aestheticizing* action."[99] Agonal action becomes valued because of what it is and because of the sovereignty that reveals itself in the act, in the burst of emotion or passion, in the moment of violence and force. Agonal action is a sovereign action that becomes "immanently valuable in its greatness or beauty."[100] The aesthetics of agonal action do reveal a sought-after "antecedent essence" of the political. Yet, since there cannot be any knowledge or valuation of this sovereign essence prior to the moment when the performance actually takes place, the essence and its sovereign force are inevitably the product of the heroism of the act. Through agonal action, we reach a point at which that which is supposed to be revealed and valued through violence, struggle, and combat – the "good" or to fight "evil," for example – has in fact no value or essence on its own, other than that which is represented and aestheticized every time the heroic agonal agents, the warriors for example, perform their agonal and violent deeds.

It may well be that the "evil" and the terror America fights in its post-9/11 wars are non-existent, meaningless, or, more importantly, non-representable other than in moments of attack, in those instances when American warriors launch yet another offensive. It is in those moments *only* that America is truly sovereign after 9/11. Agonal sovereignty cannot be experienced or revealed outside those episodic (but in many ways endless) bouts of heroism and violent passion. Agonal sovereignty is thus the aesthetic expression of the abject desire to unite America and war as one (and to define America through war). In this uncanny sovereign fashion, through defining acts of agonal violence and sovereignty, the state form has finally actualized the war machine. It has called forth the monster of war. All that remains of political agency and culture in this aesthetic of warfare and in this passion for war is the terrifying and terrorizing majesty of the war machine whose actions are uniquely valued for what they are, that is to say, for the heroic violence made visible every time a new military engagement takes place, every time new enemies are killed, every time new foreign lands are slashed and burned, and every time the warriors' "shock and awe" theatrics (and not just tactics) are on display.

Writing a few months after 9/11, Alain Badiou was perhaps already on to this new form of sovereignty as heroic warfare when he described the US attitude toward war in the following terms: "The particular adversary chosen matters very little in fact and can be entirely disconnected from the initial crime, . . . [but] the pure capacity to destroy this or that will do the job."[101] Badiou concluded that, "in the end, any war is suitable, as long as the *appearance* of victory is overwhelming . . . [and as long as this war is revealed] as the abstract form of a *theatrical* capture."[102] In a sense, revealing too much already, General Franks himself had implied that war was more about "theatrical capture" than about military tactics. Commenting on scenes of US military attack in Afghanistan in late 2001, Franks had declared: "It was as if warriors from the future had been transported to an earlier century. And that image captured this most unusual war: resourceful young troops carrying the world's most advanced military technology onto a battlefield where horse cavalry still prevailed. I was thankful for American technology – and *I was in awe by the performance of these young men.*"[103] Still, despite this rare flourish, Franks was generally subdued about the aestheticization and glorification of the American war machine. But, as we already saw, other post-9/11 American writers of statecraft (and warfare) were not as restrained. For some like Kaplan and Kristol, or even Ledeen (already introduced in Chapter 3), the performance of agonal violence deployed in America's post-9/11 wars was cause for triumphant celebration and jubilation.[104]

According to Ledeen, for example, it was only through war and in war that American values and America's sense of itself could be rediscovered. This, Ledeen claimed, was not new. In fact, this was something the United States had always wanted to practice. If merging America and war was not new (at least as a matter of ideological thinking), if agonal sovereignty had always been what America wanted to be, then it would not be so difficult to continue to justify it today. Again, as previously indicated, unlike biopolitical sovereignty, which always needed to present its recourse to war as a matter of exception (even when it was not the case), agonal sovereignty is never troubled by such a moral or political dilemma. War is the constant. War is American identity. War is national culture. War is the dominant, sovereign performance. Or, to quote Badiou again, "war is unconnected to any law or right, and is indifferent to any project."[105] The American war is indifferent to any project indeed, other than its own performance of course. As was previously found in Kaplan and Kristol's text, it is the warriors who are made into the performers, the agonal agents of this new sovereignty. It is they who will have to "improve our homeland defense, kill or incarcerate the terrorist rank and file, and destroy the regimes that support the new kamikazes."[106] As was already shown at the end of Chapter 3, some tabloid imperialists defined their ideological/moral mission in terms of having to clarify and detail the specific *modus operandi* of this American war machine. They would have to tell us (the American public) who or rather what the war machine should attack, where it should attack, and when it should attack. Constantly being at war was taken for granted by these tabloid warmongers and media prophets of the war machine's terror, and so there was no room in those aggressive tabloid geopolitical analyses for thinking about the reasons why this total war should be needed at all. In fact, despite Ledeen's and Kaplan and Kristol's best efforts, how to go to war was really of lesser relevance in their texts than wanting to affirm that, no matter how it would take place, this war could not and would not be stopped. As Ledeen matter-of-factly declared: "we must destroy them [what he called the terror masters] to advance our historic mission."[107]

Not surprisingly, the heroism of the war machine and the glorified aesthetics of warfare pervade these vicious tabloid geopolitical discourses. These tabloid texts have recourse to abjection in order to redefine national identity not just through war, but *as* war. But, as we now observe, these tabloid imperialists also need to theorize a new mode of sovereignty – an agonal sovereignty – in order to break down all that is political, legal, artistic, cultural, and scientific (both within society and abroad) with the weapons of the war machine.[108] Subsequently, this aggressive tabloid imperialistic and war-producing discourse affirms, the war machine will be able to rebuild all these categories of social and cultural life from its own perspective, with the only form of "agency" or "being" (an abjected being, no doubt) that will be left or remain undestroyed, and thus will be truly sovereign. In these tabloid geopolitical productions that champion the full deployment of the war machine's violence, America's essence can only be to struggle, combat, and (seek to) conquer.

Of course (but sadly), at no point do contemporary tabloid imperialists who proclaim total warfare and the need for absolute destruction pause for a second to wonder whether the American war machine will actually be capable of winning all these wars and battles.[109] At no point do these supporters of agonal sovereignty, violence, and death (heroic as it may be to some) stop to reflect on the possibility that this new belligerent modality of sovereign power/force might some day be matched by the destructive and heroic agony of another war machine, or that the American war machine's own contemporary "creative destruction" (to use one of Ledeen's favorite phrases) might eventually turn not so "creative" any more. In other words, one might wonder, what will be left of this form of sovereign per-formance when the last of its warriors dies? The answer of course is frighteningly clear. Should this be the case, this particular war machine would irretrievably dis-appear in the "swirling black hole" (to borrow Joxe's metaphor) of another war-rior, of the next, more total and destructive yet, war machine. There is indeed, as Ledeen, Kaplan and Kristol, and others (such as, for example, Hanson or Kaplan, also discussed in Chapter 3) intimate, no middle road and no escape strategy in this glorified path toward absolute warfare. As Deleuze and Guattari had argued, once it is brought into the realm of the political, the social, or the cultural by the state form itself, the war machine (for the time being, predominantly American, but for how along?) can never restore the state and its sovereignty to their initial integrity. The war machine cannot even save certain lives/bodies, or a certain way of life (quite the contrary in fact). It is much too late for this biopolitical design. Simply, as some warriors (and, once again, we all become warriors) vanish after having been destroyed in these operations of total warfare, new warriors find a way of taking over and prevailing. Other warriors arrive on the (battle) scene to perform their own agonal, heroic, and nihilistic actions. The war machine never gives way to newly improved state forms. Instead, it passes on the baton to new warriors. The war machine does not die; it merely reshapes itself.[110] And as it does so, the "desert" of political life and everyday culture is further "increased" (to bor-row one of Deleuze and Guattari's metaphors[111]), and perhaps irremediably so.

Coda: dispensing with security, doing away with humanity

In his essay produced a few days after the 9/11 attacks, Baudrillard writes: "[N]obody seems to have understood that Good and Evil climb to power at the same time and in the same move." Baudrillard goes on: "The triumph of the one does not imply the vanquishing of the other . . . At the bottom, Good could only defeat Evil by renouncing its claim to be Good."[112] Turning to final/fatal truths (defeating "evil," protecting the "good," revealing the ultimate "what is," ab-solutely triumphing over despair) and making use of total heroic warfare as a preferred technique to reach such truths is a self-defeating project, Baudrillard intimates. Only by becoming what one never wants to be and what one allegedly abjects can such a prophecy become realized. "Good" can triumph over "evil" only by renouncing its claim to be good, as Baudrillard suggests, and the American state/nation can only defeat terror and terrorism by turning into a terrifying and terrorizing war machine. But, in order to avoid the frightful revelation that, eventually, if "we" do take this path, "we" may be no different from "them" (and that in fact "we" are abject and crave abjection) and, moreover, "our" ideologies and moralities may be just as disruptive and even destructive as "theirs" are said to be,[113] "we" must try to postpone this ultimate realization. In the meantime, to lend credence to the moral superiority (the "good") of our ideologies and policies (and to convince "ourselves" that "we" are different, that "we" are not "evil"), "we" seek to mark the distinction between "us" and "them" through the use of the war machine, through countless instances of agonal violence. Yet, as was the case with abjection, this sovereign agonal violence brings "us" ever closer to being undistinguishable from "them." In these instances of agony that endlessly seek to postpone the fateful realization that "our" so-called better and superior values may themselves, sometimes, be "evil" (at least, to some "others"), the aesthetics of combat and destruction are prized for what they show, that is to say, for the heroism of the deed that they appear to reveal, and nothing else. Foolishly, "we" believe (often because "we" are told that this is so, that it is what "we" need to escape loss and despair) that only in those moments can the claim that "we" are "good" and that "they" are "evil" be demonstrated.

This modality of action that advocates sovereignty, victory, and salvation from "evil" through the glory of war's theatrical brutality is the most insecure and unsafe strategy that could ever be selected. Far from (re)securing the state, the nation, or those who believe or have been told they are "good," it puts us all on a path toward annihilation. The war machine demands ever more blood, ever more battles, and ever more deaths. Since the fateful end can never be accepted or reached (for then, as Baudrillard claims, "we" would have to see that the "good" is indeed not "good" as such, and perhaps not so distinguishable from "evil"), new wars have to be found and must be justified. This is exactly the message that American tabloid imperialistic proponents of agonal violence (and not just statecraft anymore) like Kaplan and Kristol and Ledeen, among others, leave us with. The wars that have been started by the American war machine after 9/11 and championed by these tabloid intellectuals of terror and absolute warfare are just the beginning of things to come. They are part and parcel of an approach to security and sovereignty *ad absurdum*, one that secretly (or unconsciously perhaps) recognizes that the "evil" it fights will never be caught, or else the moment of confrontation between "our good" and "their evil" would take place and reveal not a final triumph of the "good," but rather its possible indistinction from "evil." (Could we perhaps not use this critical insight to make sense of the decision by the United States' war makers in the summer to fall of 2002, when it appeared that they had cornered Bin Laden in some caves in the mountains separating Afghanistan from Pakistan, around an area called Tora Bora, to turn around and start up a plan to invade Iraq instead?).

More pragmatically perhaps, the justifications for these post-9/11 American total wars presented by contemporary tabloid geopolitical pundits of statecraft (redesigned as warfare) reveal that whatever counts as state or national security today has moved away from the spheres in which foreign policy, the national interest, and national identity used to be decided and crafted to the domain where military strategy and war tactics (or theatrics rather) are the only matters that are worth considering and performing. Put differently, the concerns with the sovereignty and security (of the state, of its citizens, of the nation's identity and culture) may have already slipped out of the control of intellectuals of statecraft (tabloid or not), and such considerations may now be in the hands of the warriors themselves. Once again, what passes for sovereignty/security according to the proponents of the war machine is how to win the next battle or how to destroy the next enemy, and not how to make the state, its citizens, or the nation safer. By relinquishing security to the war-makers, the United States and its contemporary tabloid geopolitical intellectuals and pundits have "become suicidal and declared war upon [themselves]" (to quote Baudrillard again).[114]

As the war machine does away with security and with most recognizable forms of state sovereignty, it does not care much about preserving humanity, or at least about providing a new definition of what it means to be human in an age of global terror or of a global crusade against "evil." If my suggestion presented in this chapter is correct that, through the American war on terror since 9/11, we have witnessed the conceptual passage of sovereignty from juridical, to biopolitical, and eventually to agonal, then there is also a parallel movement in the significance of political subjectivity and/or agency. What it means to be or remain human in the era of the war on terror and of sovereign military violence necessarily has to follow suit and adapt to the new geopolitical situation. What concerns me here is the way the notion of the human, of human life, also has to change according to the different modalities of sovereignty and power we have encountered. Whereas the belief that juridical sovereignty matters could leave a place and a role to play for *individual political subjects as citizens*, with rights and prerogatives, within the state (through constitutional guarantees) or outside the state (under international law and human rights treaties in particular), the passage to considerations of biopower and to biopolitical sovereignty left room only for *docile bodies*, for human bodies that "could be killed but never sacrificed" (as Agamben put it). The transfer of human beings from political subjects to docile bodies was probably a key conceptual/cultural moment in contemporary discourses of geopolitical terror and war. It removed any sense of sovereign importance from the idea that individual beings must have juridical personalities and are rational agents (with their corresponding adornments, such as inalienable rights, freedom, and so on). Instead, this passage to bare life introduced the belief that individuals as bodies are eminently replaceable, malleable, and workable. Only those characteristics can give humans their value, their meaningful place in the body politic. Although they can be (must be?) killed through biopolitical designs, their killing is never superfluous, never a vain sacrifice. Their bodies count and matter as bodies, as a quantifiable mass of live, positive, and efficient energies. Every single one of those docile bodies is of importance to the life and being of the larger unit, the nation. Thus, they can never be wasted or sacrificed.

As I suggested above, this version of what it means and why it matters to be human sets the stage for the war machine and its agonal violence. With the war machine's agonal sovereignty, with every new war's burst of destruction, what are now crucially required are not just bodies but rather *body parts*. What passes for human and is valued as such in the moments of war's agony are the parts of the warrior's body that are necessary to hold a gun, launch a grenade, detonate a bomb, cut a throat, and so on. Such bodies are not just replaceable. They have to be interchanged, replaced as needed, wasted, disfigured, and transfigured. The human in agonal violence, in the violence of the war machine, is a matter of flesh, blood, and pulp.[115] The war machine demands that humans (or what is left of them) follow its path and react to its actions as and through (spare) body parts: gut reactions rather than heartfelt sentiments; blind rage rather than reflected choice; a punch in the face or a kick in the crotch rather than an oratorical criticism or a rhetorical invective. Of course, what is just as essential as those body parts are the machinic instruments or appendages that they come equipped with, weapons mostly. What is aesthetic in agonal action is the movement of a limb, a facial expression of joy or pain, bodies colliding, flesh dripping with sweat or blood. The vital and the lifeless, down to their most minute representations, are thus prioritized. And who could be better than the warrior to reveal such an extreme heroic explosion of the flesh?

The war machine's use of the human as body parts or as flesh can be thought of as the ultimate postmodern cultural gesture. After all, as Hardt and Negri have recently argued, the flesh is the most vivid symbol of the breakdown of grand narratives, starting with modern narratives of state-making, creation of social bodies, formation of body politics, and unification of communities.[116] In a sense, the war machine is the most de(con)structive tool there is. It leaves (body) fragments where sovereign structures and discourses want to encompass and systematize. As Deleuze and Guattari once again famously argued, the war machine proliferates smooth space whereas the state form striates and takes control of territories. But Hardt and Negri's apparent postmodern euphoria about the image of the flesh is blind to the way the war machine precisely operates at the level of the human flesh. Hardt and Negri see in the decomposition of the idea of the unity of the social body down to its human flesh a form of resistance, the possibility of a challenge, perhaps the point of departure for the revenge of what they call "the multitude." Hardt and Negri write: "[W]hat we experience [today] is a kind of social flesh, a flesh that is not a body, a flesh that is common, living substance. We need to learn what this flesh can do."[117] They add: "The flesh of the multitude is pure potential, an unformed life force, and in this sense an element of social being, aimed constantly at the fullness of life."[118]

Hardt and Negri's analysis here betrays an astounding naïveté. It reveals a will to believe in the power of docile bodies that, in the end, may be able to reject the way they are controlled, manipulated, or even killed at the hands of the biopolitical sovereign (it is worth recalling that Hardt and Negri never dare to take the analysis of war beyond the confines of biopower and biopolitical sovereignty). This analysis fails to account for the operations of the war machine, a war machine that has swallowed up the state form, the nation, and human beings too. Hardt and Negri's thinking about the flesh – or what amounts to an alternate aestheticization of today's bodies in the age of total war – does nothing to help us better understand and possibly react to what is left of the human (again, the human as interchangeable body parts and bludgeoned flesh) in designs of agonal sovereignty and violence. It does not help us to appreciate the distinct challenges that precarious human lives (both "us" and "them") face in the age of triumphant war machines.[119]

What may instead be a necessary first step in trying to reattach a body – perhaps an agent – to the flesh, the blood, and the pulp that saturate the contemporary war landscape and our cultural/tabloid mediascape is to realize that agonal sovereignty is not just a potentiality that, at any moment, can be actualized by biopolitical sovereigns. The game of power is now a game of war, and the (sovereign) responsibilities have shifted to the warriors. What can be done (if anything at all can be done) to bring back the war machine under the control of the state form before it is far too late *is* the crucial question. Only subsequently, supposing that a reversal can indeed be performed, may Hardt and Negri's hope for the rediscovery of a flesh "constantly aiming at the fullness of life" have a place. In the meantime though, at a more modest level perhaps, human beings or what is left of them (and of their precarious lives, as I will put it in subsequent chapters) need to try to think about ways of fighting to remain human at a time when the war machine constantly aims at a different fullness, that of violence and death. It is toward such preoccupations – different ways of fighting to remain human, or to restore a certain sense of the precariousness of life – that the next chapter and the Conclusion to this book will turn. In the face of absolute and sovereign war machines today, I believe that these are crucial concerns or questions. For, as the Archbishop of Canterbury, Rowan Williams, so rightly put it after reflecting on the consequences of the 9/11 attacks, "If we react [to violence, war, and the war machine] without . . . self-questioning [without realizing where we are or what is left of us, of our so-called humanity, several years now after the terrorist attacks in the United States, but also in Indonesia, Spain, England, and many other places], we change nothing."[120]

5 The sublime spectatorship of the Iraq war

America's tabloid aesthetics of violence and the erasure of the event*

The sublime object must, of course, be frightening.

Friedrich von Schiller[1]

Someone said tragedy is the inevitable working out of things. And the tragedy here is we're savages. We're thrilled to kill each other. We're monsters. And the war is what unmasks us . . . But there's a kind of honor in it too. A kind of grace. I guess if I'm a monster, it's my privilege to be one.

Private Frank "Dim" Dumphy, *Over There*[2]

What makes the event an event is not only that it happens, but that it surprises – and maybe even that it surprises itself.

Jean-Luc Nancy[3]

From NYPD Blue to Abu Ghraib Blues: capturing the sublime

Hollywood executive producer Steven Bochco has done it again. The creator of many pop culturally hip, often violent, and generally profanity-laced American television cop shows like *Hill Street Blues*, *L.A. Law*, or more recently *NYPD Blue* has now turned to the war in Iraq. But the audience-grabbing recipe of the previous cop shows is still the same: to depict in as realistic a way as possible the mundane experiences, interrupted by bouts of extreme tension, brutality, and crisis, of the true heroes out there (whether the heroes are cops on New York city's streets or army privates in the Middle East is just a matter of fate, or bad luck perhaps). Bochco's most recent production, *Over There*, a show about the daily tasks and often ordeals of a US Army unit in Iraq, is eye-catching, traumatizing, perhaps awe-inspiring, and typically exciting to watch. It is drama at its best, or as

* *Millennium: Journal of International Studies.* An earlier version of this chapter appeared in *Millennium*, Vol. 34, No. 3, 2006, and is reproduced with the permission of the publisher.

Bochco boasts: "Without dramatizing the consequences of terrible, violent events, you aren't doing your job."[4] But like Bochco's cop shows before, *Over There* is also a matter-of-factly presented story, with an emphasis placed on daily routines, small details in the everyday life of the soldiers in the midst of war. In a sense, *Over There* can be understood to be displaying a form of tabloid story-telling and tabloid spectacle not unlike those produced by many geopolitical discourses and representations found in the US media (broadly defined) before and after 9/11. Indeed, on the show *Over There*, the dialogues are often banal and non-heroic, and sometimes have very little to do with the war itself. Exchanges between privates over what they did in high school, why they did not go to college, what position they played on the football team, how they got their nicknames, or what their favorite beer is add nothing to the plot of the episodes. Yet these exchanges are crucial to the story and the visuals as Bochco has designed them. They enlist on the part of the audience members a sense of trust, offer them a guarantee that they can feel and understand exactly what these guys on screen are going through. These dialogues make sure that the spectators are indeed experiencing not just yet another Hollywood blockbuster-type fiction, with explosions, fire, and blood everywhere, but rather an existential drama about the "military grunts" out there in Iraq who could easily be any one of them.[5]

At the same time, this apparently mundane and familiar representation of war plays a clever trick on its audience too. Pretending to be culturally positioned beyond any political view about the war and claiming to simply show people back home the daily routines (and often traumas) of "their" troops over there, this television spectacle nonetheless conditions its US spectators to a basic ideological truth. As one commentator has noted, *Over There* is "a way of getting at the truth of war as it is fought by the grunts, whose boots are on the ground."[6] At a time when initial reasons given by the US government to invade Iraq were increasingly placed under suspicion (the show was released in the summer of 2005 in the United States), *Over There* sought to make sure that its audience would understand that there was still a truth to be discovered and fought for in Iraq. Bochco's TV series tried to tell American citizens that it is only in war, in the course of fighting, that this truth can be revealed, thanks to dopey kids who really did not know what they were getting themselves into, but who could nonetheless restore for everybody a basic sense of life, courage, and, most importantly, humanity.

Only war, Bochco intimates, can allow "us" to rediscover the basic truth about who "we" are, how "we" struggle to survive, and where "we" are supposedly headed in an age of growing despair and loss. This is precisely why Bochco suggests in the pilot episode, through Army private Frank "Dim" Dumphy's recorded video email message sent to his wife back home in the United States (and quoted at the opening of this chapter), that the monstrosity of war nonetheless exudes a certain grace and produces honor. Monstrosity – the ugliness of war's violence – is still the inevitable pathway through which being human will be rediscovered. Thus, as the opening quotation taken from the show asserts, it is "Dim" Dumphy's distinct privilege to be a savage or a monster. Being a monster, acting like a savage in America's post-9/11 wars (in Iraq above all), is once again a heroic posture or deed. It is in fact an agonal task (as we saw in Chapter 4) that, Bochco suggests, must be undertaken (by "our" war heroes) and accepted (by all Americans) if America and Americans care to ever be human again. This truth in/of war, popularly and sensationally established through this war show, is also *the* truth about the US invasion and long occupation of Iraq. It is this so-called visually evident truth that explains why this conflict cannot be avoided and why America has a duty to "stay the course."

This basic truth about an American humanity that supposedly can only be found in/through war, and the respect it commands from US spectators/citizens, is very convenient, of course. It absolves "us" of having to attribute political or moral responsibility for the ill-fated military strategies or for the doomsday ideologies that took Americans over there in the first place. It also prevents "us" from worrying about the fate of the tens of thousands of Iraqis (perhaps hundreds of thousands), very few of them soldiers, who have died since the beginning of the US invasion in March 2003 and through the subsequent military occupation. As *Over There* forcefully demonstrates, US soldiers get shot at, are disfigured, and die. Life and death in the struggle for humanity that is war is clearly on America's side only. This is also what this basic truth of the show seeks to tell Americans. Humanity as/in war cannot be shared with the opponent, with the "evil" enemy, whoever s/he is once again. And this point (or "truth") about not being able to share humanity, that it can only be on the side of the US warriors, is where the use of extremely graphic violence, gruesomeness, and brutality on the show comes into play and is at its most ideologically effective. Whenever the sentiments of courage, compassion, honor, or moral conviction that supposedly accompany America's war heroes in Iraq are about to be shared, when for example it looks like a US soldier on screen is about to fall for the belief that "they" might be human too, then everything goes to hell. At this precise juncture in the show's narrative/presentation, very suddenly, the images become "disturbingly horrific," as a commentator has noted.[7] In fact, some of the most visceral and shocking scenes "that series TV has ever done" are abruptly introduced.[8] For example, in the pilot episode, when the soldiers hitch a ride to go to the next town on a beer run and casually chat about normal life back in the United States in the back of a truck, a landmine placed by the enemy on the road blows everything up and leaves young private Bo Rider agonizing with only half of his right thigh bone and flesh still attached to his body. In episode 2, when Private Dumphy realizes that, in a civilian car that he and his mates shot at for refusing to stop at a roadblock, a little Iraqi girl is still alive despite the fact that the back of her skull has been crushed, he ignores the order of his sergeant and rushes to extricate the girl from the car only to be saved by the sound of a cell phone coming from the trunk of the car, and heard by a fellow soldier, that finally indicates to Dumphy that a remotely controlled bomb is about to explode or that someone is hidden in the trunk (it turns out to be both).

Over There constantly plays with the viewer's feelings, with his/her expectations about what s/he will see next. A reviewer wrote that the show is "unsettling,"[9] and indeed the images and dialogues combine to make sure that the spectators can never reach a comfort zone, that they are forced to push further the thinking or believing that comes with watching the images. Put differently, recognizing that America's agonal heroes are rekindling a sense of victory and humanity for all Americans over there is not immediately obvious. It takes some work, some conviction (nonetheless made available by the images) for US spectators to realize what the truth of the show is. This is exactly why imagination can never rest on *Over There*. If imagination is allowed to slow down or settle for a few minutes, it is always haunted by the possibility that everything can go into disarray at any moment, and that some brutally unbearable scenes may soon jump onto the screen. I believe that it is through this display of images and messages that constantly confuse and manipulate emotions (often as a result of unsettling the spectator's imagination) that *Over There* is a particularly effective political, moral, and ideological representation of the war the United States has been fighting in Iraq since 2003. It is a spectacular and largely tabloid representation that finds its place in aesthetic debates and contemporary visual culture as what can be called a *sublime representation* since (as will be explained below) it apparently shakes up some beliefs, thoughts, and sentiments and yet, through this destabilizing of what appears natural or might be taken for granted by the spectator, it also forces the imagination to desperately search for a higher, safer and, in the end, more comfortable truth or idea. What makes *Over There* successful as a tabloid (geo)political spectacle in post-Iraq war American culture is that it manages to capture what Lyotard calls the "pathos of the sublime."[10]

This chapter wishes to use the visual/popular cultural opportunity provided by a television show like *Over There* to engage in a reflection over the meaning and force of the sublime in contemporary American tabloid spectacles of war. Such popular cultural spectacles are commonplace representations that often complement or serve as visual supports for tabloid geopolitical discourses (as we already discovered in Chapter 1). The sublime has been defined as an eventually pleasurable experience achieved through visual representation of a situation that is otherwise normally painful, terrifying, or destabilizing.[11] In many ways, the sublime is a way of capturing an idea of reality, a truth in fact, that is not readily apparent to the spectator/viewer, and thus requires of this spectator or consumer of visual culture a mental or conceptual undertaking that is actually facilitated by the deployment of certain visual strategies. The United States' geopolitics and aesthetics of violence after the invasion of Iraq are grounded in the conceptual and visual experience of the sublime. This experience of the sublime – often relayed by all sorts of media like TV series, news reports, photojournalistic accounts, and tabloid geopolitical literatures and texts too – allows the American public to achieve an aesthetic apprehension and perhaps acceptance of images of violence and terror that are made necessary and sometimes pleasurable not so much because they evince an immediately evident beauty or artistic splendor, but because they require of the public to reach for ideas through and beyond the violent images in order to make sense of and find an eventual satisfaction with what is going on in the world out there. This attraction to the sublime and its pleasure in contemporary tabloid (geopolitical) images and messages is perhaps indicative of a different and changing condition in the American landscape of post-9/11 terror and warfare too. Interestingly indeed, the turn to the sublime image of war violence seems to correspond to an emerging cultural condition according to which political crisis and social instability are more likely to resurface as a result of the lack of readily available images of war success and victory (other than those shown immediately during and after the March–April 2003 US military assault). Thus, I suggest that the turn to the sublime in American tabloid geopolitical representations and discourses of war and terror also seeks to fulfill a desperately re-energizing role in contemporary American culture by forcing US audiences to go far beyond what otherwise would be visually traumatizing and depressing images and realities (dead US soldiers, no apparent end to the conflict, a growing cost measured in terms of domestic social and economic failures, and so on) if it were not for the desire, induced by certain media, pundits, and intellectuals of statecraft, to settle on some visual representations that, even if they are troubling to start with, may be transcended and turn into the confirmation or revelation of some larger-than-everyday-reality sort of truths.

After introducing the concept of the sublime, this chapter turns to another illustration of the way the sublime image of violence has started to operate in America's geopolitical culture of terror, several years after the 9/11 attacks. One such way has consisted of proliferating images of (imprecise and often indiscriminate) "others" in distress or harm's way, or even dead (and often killed by US warriors), in places where America's war on terror is being fought, starting with Iraq. I will turn to some photojournalistic displays of the invasion of Iraq in March–April 2003 reproduced in the United States in many weekly news magazines and often in special commemorative books to interrogate what is being shown, what is being occluded, and what greater idea or concept (as truth once again) must be discovered by the American spectator/viewer beyond what is actually seen in these photographs. How acceptance or even satisfaction can be extracted by US spectators/viewers from photos of dead Iraqi soldiers or tortured prisoners at Abu Ghraib, for example, is a crucial concern that speaks to the power of the sublime and to its ideological uses.

One of the principal operating techniques of the sublime image or spectacle consists of creating a tension between a visual scene and reality (or what is commonly believed) to the point that the spectator's imagination is drawn toward a concept, another belief, or an exercise of reason that finally is able to impose its dominant truth as if it were the prevailing everyday reality. One such concept that has often been captured by contemporary sublime visions of violence and terror in the United States is the idea of the event, or of what an event must be. I am talking here about an announced, anticipated, and controlled event that would have the capacity to elevate American geopolitical and cultural consciousness by bearing witness to the creation of a new humanity that, through the actions of US soldiers in war (as we saw with *Over There*), would be in the process of redefining the moral and political boundaries of Iraq, the Middle East, and much of the world too. In the aftermath of Bush's declaration of the end of the war in Iraq in April 2003 – the famous "Mission Accomplished" slogan – and with the assumption that the United States, through its military victory there, was reshaping the entire Middle East, starting with Iraq, on the basis of a new spirit of democracy, freedom, and moral subjectivity, any situation of surprise in the war on terror, any unexpected revelation, any abrupt image of massacre of US troops (or any insinuation of it with photos of coffins draped in the US flag returning home, for example), or any evidence that Iraq may not be much better off as a society than it was under Saddam Hussein had to be cast away as non-events, as false or unreal representations that cannot be of any strategic or political signification in the US war on terror, in the American crusade to revitalize humanity, and in America's desperate desire to triumph over its post-9/11 despair once and for all. Instead of these so-called unreliable or distorted realities, another more dominant representation of the event, one that would be the sacred holder and firm protector of this new American-made humanity through war, had to take precedence and be given conceptual priority. This is precisely where the turn to the sublime image, both for its tabloid producers and for the spectators/consumers of this spectacle worldwide (but mostly for US audiences), was so crucial.

In the sublime, the event and the (un)reality it announces are rationally discovered and conceptually determined. The event must escape materiality and become the servant of an idea, enslaved by a greater consciousness. In sublime representation, the event is unsurprising and expected once one realizes and rationalizes that it is encapsulated in a superior system of thought or belief. Put differently, the element of surprise of/in the event (already discussed in the Introduction), its quality of "eventness" as Jean-Luc Nancy puts it,[12] is what the sublime image must control by providing visual representations that have to make sense or can be explained by means of a concept, a thought, a reason, and, often ultimately, an ideology. Trapped in the concept and captured by its visually sublime protections and projections, the surprise of the event is conjured away.

Thus, toward the end of this chapter, my choice of situating the problem of the sublime in relation to the production of a certain idea of the event is an attempt to prize open the ideological motivations that are at stake in the sublime and its deployment. The sublime presents itself as a powerful ideological weapon that strives to impose a regime of truth and comes equipped with its arsenal of inclusions and exclusions. It is thus not surprising to find the sublime – this political and ideological weapon, this truth-making and exclusion-producing machine – working on behalf of America's geopolitics of terror and aesthetics of violence after 9/11, and even more so after the US invasion of Iraq. Still, I conclude this chapter by suggesting that a different, resistant, and possibly counter-ideological understanding of the sublime can be envisioned too, one that seeks to restore the quality of surprise to the event and may also be open to differential possibilities for democracy in contemporary geopolitics and international relations. Before arriving at this concluding point, however, a closer examination of how the sublime operates as an image, event, or spectacle that can make war, violence, or terror appear to be necessary, beneficial, and perhaps pleasurable is in order.

The sublime, or how to get satisfaction out of visual unpleasure

The analysis of the sublime provided in this chapter is derived from Kant's aesthetic philosophy and from Lyotard's understanding and revisiting of Kant's theory.[13] But my intention in this chapter is also to go beyond both Kant and Lyotard by interrogating how the experience of the sublime makes possible a certain type of viewership or spectatorship that is more likely to consume, accept, or even appreciate images of violence and war. Rediscovering Kant's thinking on the sublime, Lyotard writes that the sublime is a "strong and equivocal emotion [that] carries with it both pleasure and pain."[14] The sublime, then, is first experienced by spectators of a visual scene or admirers of a work of art as a strong and confusing emotion, as a sensation that is often felt as pain, shock, or incomprehension. Kant explained that such a confusing or destabilizing emotion resulted from the realization that the visual scene present in front of our eyes no longer corresponds to a basic reality, to some obvious, commonplace physical materiality, or to what Kant often simply equated with the idea of nature.[15] With human imagination thus stumped or shaken (since it loses all sense of any readily available correspondence with what is thought to be known or taken for granted), a strong sense of unpleasure or bewilderment followed. Yet, such unpleasure, Kant continued, was not an emotional end in itself. It was supposedly always in search or need of some closure or conclusion. Consequently, the second part of this equivocal emotion was for the image, the visual scene, or the artistic object to transcend the initial shock or trauma it first seemed to introduce by pushing us, the viewers or spectators, toward the presence of something not yet realized or materialized that would nonetheless, and finally, make sense of it all (and thus provide a convenient closure). This "greater something," for Kant, was the certainty of the presence of a concept, an idea, or a rationality that the sublime image would eventually evoke or approximate. As Lyotard clarified: "We have the Idea of the world (the totality of what it is), but we do not have the capacity to show an example of it."[16]

With the passage from the beautiful (that is to say, an image or object that faithfully represents reality or nature as it is, or as people are conventionally used to seeing it) to the sublime, Kant argued that the task of artistic imagination and aesthetic production (and, as Lyotard would add, of media representation too) was to present the unpresentable. This passage to the sublime and to the contradictory emotions it creates has important consequences for the process of spectatorship. Among other things, spectatorship in the sublime is constantly (supposed to be) played with. The spectator of the sublime image is placed in an expectative emotional state whereby s/he must desperately wait for a subsequent explanation or justification in order to surmount the initial traumatic and unbearable scene. Moreover, the sublime spectator's initial shock or incomprehension is a way of capturing the senses of the viewing subject too, of grabbing his/her attention by awakening in this subject sentiments s/he may never have felt before. Still, this awakening of an apparently individualized (and highly emotional) spectatorship in the sublime is also a trick that better prepares the individual viewer or spectator to be receptive to the "greater" explanatory power and truth value of an idea, a concept, or ultimately reason. As Kant mentioned in passing and Lyotard tried to further elaborate by tying the sublime to the spirit of the avant-garde,[17] the sublime experience (and its contradiction of feelings) only offers a semblance of being personal or intimate, of producing an individual subjectivity, one that allegedly would be capable of mastering its human destiny or staying in control of its identity. In actuality, the sublime is a controlled experience with – and sometimes manipulation of – a visual scene or artistic object with a view to benefiting a greater idea, concept, or mode of rationalization. Indeed, in the passage from the representation of what supposedly is to the presentation of the unpresentable, rationalism and ideality gain full force over empirical knowledge since the sublime imagination "imparts no knowledge about reality."[18] In the scheme of the sublime, everyday materiality no longer governs the conditions of appearance of the image. Furthermore, despite an initial impression of providing emotional autonomy to the spectator, individual sensations are not really afforded either as ideality and the dictates of a larger-than-life rationality (or a greater cause) are now fully in charge.

Thus, by steering spectatorship toward expectative stances and toward an evocation of ideational/rational constructs, the sublime is a controlled emotion provided by images or objects that, at first glance, shock or do not make sense. This is precisely why cultural studies scholars have turned to the notion of the sublime in their many analyses of film, media events, photography, artistic objects, or everyday culture in general. For them, the sublime is understood as "moments of intense and surprising visual power" provided to spectators, viewers, or consumers by means of technological media, artists claiming to be endowed with superior vision or a greater intellect, or social, economic, and political institutions in search of clarification or imposition of cultural meaning.[19] What cultural studies scholars using the notion of the sublime intimate is that the controlled emotion or experience of the sublime image is crucial to the establishment and propagation of certain ideas and ideological beliefs in society and culture. The steering of apparently individualized emotions (of fear, terror, shock, or incomprehension) toward some ideas that supposedly can provide solace, understanding, and ultimately pleasure to the spectator by evoking unpresentable (but highly desirable) justifications or rationalizations is a powerful ideological operation that needs to be recognized as such. Indeed, as the next section explains, it is often by means of the sublime image (of war and terror in particular) that dominant and violent ideologies take hold of our contemporary global cultural and political landscape.

The sublime spectatorship of war

The task of aesthetic philosophers interested in theorizing the sublime (from Kant to Lyotard) was to explain how presenting the unpresentable is necessary to give effect to larger-than-life concepts and ideas. But to understand the power of sublime images and of some tabloid media that produce/represent them, what we need is not just another critical philosophy of the sublime, but rather a critique of the ideology of the sublime, that is to say, of the ideological operations involved in the deployment of the sublime image. Whereas the dominant (Kantian) philosophy of the sublime image was primarily concerned with the production of images that call for greater concepts and ideas, an ideology of the sublime needs to place the analytical focus on the reception and experience of the sublime image, on its spectatorship.

As we saw with the show *Over There*, from the perspective of the consumer of tabloid spectacles of war, the sublime often presents itself as a picture (still or moving) that leaves one shocked, taken aback, in pain, and possibly speechless. In the modern (Kantian) philosophy of the sublime, this is the point where one encounters the initial unpleasure, later to be transcended through the realization of a greater idea or concept. In this fashion, the sublime image often emerges as what visual studies theorist Nathan Stormer has called an *apostrophe*. An apostrophe is a particular mode of visual address that requires one, when faced with shocking or apparently nonsensical images, to "turn away or break off" from the narratives or representations that one was used to experience, consume, rely upon, or enjoy.[20] But the apostrophe of the sublime is not just a rupture from previous modes of representation, from the experience of the beautiful for example, as Kant himself had intimated. Rather, this apostrophe is a mode of arrest, a deviation or rerouting of visual perception that appears to call into being a new subject position, and seeks to direct a new identification toward something that, at first, does not make sense and yet must be expected or accepted. As Stormer suggests, around the corner, past the visual turn, "another entity" is there waiting for us, waiting to capture our "eye/I."[21]

Thus, the apostrophic shock of the sublime invokes, announces, and creates a new and particular kind of subjectivity (sometimes an "abjected subjectivity," as I suggested in Chapter 3) through the presentation of the unpresentable or the shocking. This is precisely where the ideology of the sublime emerges and starts to be operative, the point where ideology takes advantage of the viewing subject's sense of incomprehension, loss, and possibly fear. A new ideologically induced subjectivity, created through shock and pain, first appears as a highly personalized, almost intimate, form of identification or consciousness. Yet, this apparently novel consciousness or identity is actually common, communal, and collective. Stormer prefers to refer to this seemingly individualized but in reality communal subjectivity as a "mass subjectivity."[22] This mass subjectivity is constructed on the basis of the unquestioned assumption that, in order to finally reach some comfort or to gain pleasure out of what are otherwise painful visual scenes, the viewer of this sublime, often tabloid, spectacle must accept a new collective ideology or belief system, a new "humanity" as Stormer puts it, along with the truth values that inevitably come with it and that finally can give meaning to what has been seen. Stormer clarifies: "Addressing a mass subject through sublime scenes forms a commonplace about humanity by constituting a relationship between the spectator as a certain kind of human being and the sublime object as greater than human." Stormer adds: "The sublime scene does not represent a specific identity; it embodies a relationship in a mode of address."[23]

The relationship between the viewing "subject" and the greater evoked idea is ideological. What gives the so-called human subject his/her (semblance of) subjectivity is the connection to an idea that must prevail and determine thought and possibly action. The subject is indeed a mass in the sublime because every individual being who witnesses the same sublime scene or image and is called away by its apostrophe is made to respond to and is united by a single ideological belief. Although the apostrophe is individualized, the relationship to the idea it conveys is about producing a "commonplace" concept of humanity. Stormer's apostrophic sublime is not without recalling Louis Althusser's notion of interpellation.[24] Like Althusser's ideological hailing, the apostrophe of the sublime image appears to personalize the emotion and its experience. Yet it creates what Stormer, turning to Arendt's thought, calls a "space of appearance" in which one can "become a recognizable self in a public sense" only.[25] What I called above a common or collective subject, readied for public needs, tasks, ideas, and actions, is thus produced and possibly put to ideological and political uses. By means of what seemed to be an initial paradox of having to search for pleasure through visual unpleasure and shock, the spectator of the sublime is not just primed to receive and perhaps enjoy tabloid spectacles of war (like *Over There*, for example). The sublime spectator is also primed for specific political ideologies. And, as Stormer suggests, this ideology is often concerned with finding ways of establishing a commonplace discourse of and about humanity in times when the chaos or trauma of the images has put the apparent naturalness of human values in question.

The photography scholar Bernd Hüppauf has noted that scenes of destruction and war are often "likely to revitalize the discourse of the sublime."[26] In the tabloid geopolitical and cultural context of the US war on terror, a show like *Over There* mixing mundane and brutal images and messages about the invasion of Iraq and its aftermath of military occupation and guerrilla fighting is still very much an exception, at least in the United States (and the show was actually pulled off after only one season, supposedly because of lower than expected ratings). Most of the images of the Iraq war that have come into the United States and have been made available to the public have been either short video sequences filmed by Western TV crews or still photographic shots captured by photojournalists and reproduced in newspapers, magazines, or online. These Western news or photographic agencies' visual displays, even if they are still or freeze-frame pictures, are some of the most powerful sublime representations of the war in Iraq provided to American spectators. What is sublime about these war photos is not just the shock or horror that they sometimes depict, but also the fact that they appear to demand a higher degree of attention on the part of the viewer, a concentrated gaze that arrests, disturbs, but soon rechannels the initial sense of surprise or incomprehension toward an understanding that an important mission, supportive of a greater cause, is taking place.

In this post-Iraq war media and representational context, the volume *Witness*

Iraq: A War Journal, February–April 2003 is particularly revealing. This volume is a commemorative work that gathers many of the pictures that were taken by Western photojournalists, and later appeared in most Western newspapers and news magazines and on the internet, during the months that followed the US invasion of Iraq.[27] In its conception and design, this volume also recalls some of the post-9/11 photojournals that sought to keep alive the terror and trauma provoked in New York and Washington, DC, by the terrorist attacks.[28] Interestingly, 9/11 seems to have rekindled among American audiences/spectators a curiosity, if not a craving, for documentary photography, this older medium of war coverage/representation that some thought had been rendered obsolete by the impact of new media like television, film, or the internet.[29] Undoubtedly, there is a tabloid quality to many of those commemorative photojournalistic displays and volumes that resurfaced in the United States after the 9/11 attacks. The eye-catching, attention-grabbing, purposefully disturbing, generally sensationalistic images found in these volumes, and the overall moralizing tone of the accompanying narratives (when there are some), aim at mobilizing the public's attention by means of visual shock. But they also seek to provide simplistic explanations and ready-made truths (as truth-effects once again) about the geopolitical realities of everyday life after 9/11. This particular photographic collection about the war in Iraq is no different. It is also worthwhile to note that *Witness Iraq*, even though it was released in late 2003/early 2004, stops right after the fall of Saddam's regime in April 2003, just before George W. Bush is about to proclaim the famous "Mission Accomplished" slogan. The images in the volume are virtually all war scenes: battlefields, storming US and British troops, ravaged buildings and villages, and of course dead and blood-soaked bodies everywhere. Still, even though the photos gathered in this visual journal represent mostly "our" agonal heroes (US warriors) in action, none of these soldiers is ever shown dead, disfigured, or even hurt or wounded. By contrast, the volume is filled with images of Iraqis – soldiers *and* civilians – in distress, in pain, humiliated, massacred, and often lying lifeless right there in front of the US spectator's eyes.

From the perspective of the sublime image, several photos in this commemorative volume are particularly arresting. One photograph, taken by Paolo Pellegrin for the Magnum agency on April 7, 2003, in Basra,[30] displays close-ups of the dead, blood-speckled faces of two pro-Saddam militia fighters. Both have their eyes open. One is partially covered by the Iraqi flag, while the other has his mouth open and some dried-up blood seems to have dripped from the back of his head to his nose. Both bodies also have white stickers on their foreheads, possibly indicating who they are or, more than likely, where and when they were killed. These stickers on the forehead suggest – and the accompanying caption confirms it – that the photo is taken in a makeshift morgue, and that these are fresh kills. The photo has a tabloid, sensationalistic, and shocking quality because people are shown dead, lying on a cement floor, looking almost like freshly slaughtered cattle. Humanity seems to have been taken out of them and this is reflected in their death. Like dead animal carcasses, unworthy of human life, dispossessed of a soul, they are awaiting burial, as the caption intimates.

Another photo, shot by Faleh Kheiber, a photographer contracted by Reuters, is the famous apostrophic image, published in most weekly news magazines in the West in the spring of 2003, of young Ali Ismail Abbas who lost both his arms and suffered extensive burns on much of his body when a US missile fell on his house in early April 2003.[31] His entire family died in the explosion. This photo, and many others of Ali like this one, would later be used as the postcard shot of Western, and mostly American, good intentions, compassion, and humanitarianism vis-à-vis the Iraqi population during the war offensive. A US-led international campaign would subsequently be launched to fly young Ali to the West where he would undergo treatment for his many wounds. With this photo, graphically displaying poor Ali's mutilated body, the young Iraqi boy becomes quite literally the poster child of the US military's alleged good will and humanity. The initial horror and lack of understanding caused by this disgusting image for the (Western) spectator later turns into comfort, comprehension, and acceptance once it is made clear that this boy, and the people of Iraq along with him, will be saved, taken out of their misery, by the West and the United States mostly.

Yet another picture, taken by French Associated Press/Wide World Photos agency photojournalist Jean-Marc Bouju in Najaf on March 31, 2003,[32] is supplemented with a caption that reads "[a]n Iraqi man comforts his 4-year-old son at a regroupment center for POWs of the 101st Airborne Division. The man was seized with his son, and the US military did not want to separate them." This photograph contains many devices that are likely to elicit shock and pain once again. The adult figure, dressed in a white robe and with only sandals on his feet, has his head covered in the typically dark-green plastic hood that US troops put on Iraqi prisoners (this hood/head-bag would later be made infamous with the release of the Abu Ghraib photos). He is cradling and trying to console a visibly upset young boy who is wearing military pants and a jacket, but remains barefoot. Both figures, the adult and the child (the father and the son, the caption tells us), are sitting on the ground, with nothing but sand and dirt around them. Interestingly, they are shown to us from behind a thick barbed wire that reinforces the idea that they – or rather, he, the boy, who is crying in his father's arms – are indeed trapped. The father's actions, we are made to deplore, led to where both of them are now and left the child with no dignified, honorable, or even pleasurable future. Yet, because the child's face is not covered, he enjoys a visual, perhaps symbolic, distance and difference. He might be redeemed (he is only a child), he may be saved (by US troops), and he may even be able to enjoy a worthy future.

These three photos have an apostrophic quality about them that interpellates the "I/eye" and demands of the viewer that s/he turn away from other, cleaner and safer representations of the war in Iraq (often provided by Western TV news crews) showing US or British troops in combat action (to which much of the *Witness Iraq* volume is dedicated). At first glance, these three images are troubling and destabilizing. They depict death, suffering, and humiliation in a most graphic manner whereas "we," audience members/spectators in the West, were told, by other media, often tabloid, sources (including the cleansed images of war technology dispatched by television journalists embedded with US troops), that the military operations had been clean, surgical, efficient, and to the point. Yet, all of a sudden, some different pictures are now coming at "us" that reveal an apparently gruesome reality, a reality that at first glance seems to be well beyond our capacity of understanding. These photos, US audiences first believe, do not make sense, all the more so since the rest of the images they are bombarded with demonstrate military victory and political success and since, moreover, the overall discourse in the tabloid media is intent on confirming the idea of the obvious military triumph. These horrendous photos are confusing and clearly unpleasant to watch. In fact, how could US spectators have been shown such images in the first place?

But these types of photos actually make perfect sense. They correspond to a logic of sublime spectatorship, and they condition US viewers to get used to looking at, accepting, understanding, and perhaps enjoying such images of war, destruction, and death that are part of the heroic American struggle in the war on terror.[33] They prepare the US public to accept the violence and the terror of the American war machine, as was explained in Chapter 4. These three photos demand that their initial apostrophic unpleasure be surmounted. As indicated above, they already come equipped, in the image or in the accompanying caption, with devices that allow people watching them to appreciate why they had to be taken. More importantly, in their very presentation, these photos point to a greater idea, to a larger-than-life rationality that can only be experienced by going through the ordeal of the gruesome image of war destruction. This larger-than-life (or larger than death) rationalization is of course placed at the service of post-9/11 and post-Iraq invasion American ideological purposes. Thus, I disagree with Gregory's reading of some of the photos coming from Iraq (including the image of young Ali, which Gregory analyzes too). Gregory argues that those horrendous photos, when they become available to the American public, come to be interpreted as unfortunate instances of collateral damage and thus further point to the irrelevance of the Iraqi people in the conflict (other than as some objects of compassion at times). Behind the blatant sight of young Ali's maimed body, the violence of America's warriors is still ignored.[34] This is, of course, partially true, but this analysis is far too literal. Those extreme images of war brutality do matter, but not just as exceptional visual scenes of violence that demand to be explained by means of collateral damage or compassion. Rather, they matter because of the normative, ideational, and ideological dimensions contained in them, or at least made available through the transcendental exercise of horror and incomprehension that they enable. Thus, they are not unusual or atypical images that have managed to escape the flow of sanitized visual representations coming out of Iraq. They are part and parcel of the same representational norm that seeks to condition by using both visual banality (coming from Western television crews' video reports, for example) and visual sublimity (coming from still photographic shots that initially shock and destabilize).

Among the greater ideas or concepts that these sublime images of war evoke is the belief that there are no real American or Western casualties (not even US troops), that only the "abject other," who probably needs to suffer and repent in the first place, indeed does suffer. The life of this absolute and indiscriminate "other," this "evil" enemy, is not worthy of humanity, of living. It is animal-like and must die as such. Even when the dead "other" is a fighter, he (or it, rather) cannot be compared to "our" own fighters, "our" agonal heroes. Thus, there is really no humiliation or indignity to be felt by the American public if some images of captured, injured, or killed Iraqi soldiers are shown. The life they represent (if it is even worthy of being a life) is so lowly that images of their brutal annihilation are not to be seen as shocking after all, not even from the perspective of the Geneva Conventions that strictly prohibit the visual display of captured or fallen prisoners.[35] Not all Iraqi lives are worthless, however, and not every represented "other" must be abjected. American ideology in/as war (in Iraq and against terror) is still affirmed to be human and humanitarian (again, as we saw in Chapter 4, this war against "evil" is about saving and redefining all of humanity). The basic sense of humanity – even if it is a redefined humanity that cannot so easily be disentangled from (visual) monstrosity or savagery – can be extended to a few Iraqi "others" who were the innocent victims of Saddam's regime and to some "others" throughout the Middle East who are prisoners of terrorism and "evil." For those who are not completely "other" to us (not quite like "us," but getting closer to "us" as they accept to be saved by "us"), redemption, compassion, and some dignity can then be afforded. This is how, I believe, the enjoyment derived (among Western/US spectators) from the sight of the otherwise unbearable image of poor young Ali's mangled and burnt body is to be understood. The obscene reproduction of this horrific photo throughout Western, and again mostly American, media and tabloid channels and networks, and the multiplication of many other pictures like this one, is not just a matter of the United States and its citizens trying to assuage their sense of guilt (if any at all). It is also more than a basic sadistic display of suffering in the midst of war. It is rather, more cynically and purposefully, a matter of reaching beyond this painful image toward sentiments, thoughts, and beliefs about a new humanity through/as war, about what it means to be free, democratic, saved, safe, and finally sound as a human being in the era of the war on terror, that only America and Americans *as* soldiers can provide.[36] Once again, as Private Dumphy in *Over There* put it, it is about the privilege of partaking of an ideology (of humanity as war and war-making) that allows one to be human and monstrous at the same time. In fact, this is precisely how Marcel Saba, the editor of the *Witness Iraq* volume, urges spectators/viewers to look at the photos in this collection. "Through the eyes of some of the world's most renowned photographers working today," Saba writes, "through powerful images of conflict, you will see not only the horrors of war, *but humanity at its best.*"[37]

Images of war that not only shock but, moreover, initially appear to disempower or undermine violent/military actions, like the photo of young Ali or more recently the images of tortured Iraqi prisoners at Abu Ghraib, do have a place and a purpose in the ideological mobilization of the sublime. These particularly troubling war images reveal in an extremely intense fashion the amount of pain, the struggles, the higher degrees of unpleasure that are needed and must be accepted by the American public in order to transcend the image and finally arrive at the key idea or concept that only a superior reason or mode of rationality can present.[38] From this perspective, the sight of the Abu Ghraib photos, for example, is *not* meant to shake our belief in the humanity of the US warriors and war-makers, as might have been thought at first. These photos do *not* reveal a monstrosity or savagery of soldiers that would be beyond human redemption. Rather, and all the more so after those "few" soldiers who made these "mistakes" were punished, what these images show is the frailty, fragility, or "illness" that is a normal, expected part of what it means to be human, particularly when being human is defined through extreme experiences like war (as *Over There* intimated).[39] This fragility or "illness" can take place only if one is human. And so these images of war torture require of all of us who have seen them to push our minds further and force our reasons harder toward those important and superior ideas, beliefs, and final truths that will prevent us from straying away from the path of human dignity. As Stormer had noted: "The curative to this illness is of course a restoration of the self."[40] But this so-called self who witnesses and consumes the sublime images of war can only be restored (granted a new human consciousness) through what Stormer calls a "humanist rhetoric of rebirth" that makes him/her realize that failure or monstrosity (as long as it remains temporary) is still part of the overall purpose or plan.[41]

The apparent excess or failure of the image of war's terror – the sublime image in excess of itself – is a strong and crucial instrument of mobilization of certain ideologies, ideas, and ideals. It is no excess or failure at all. It is simply the sublime at work. The sublime image of war, war destruction, and war torture makes sure that, through the painful task of seeking to overcome what does not make sense, a more docile or compliant mass subjectivity is achieved. One could say that such an ideology (here, in the case of *Over There*, the *Witness Iraq* volume, and the Abu Ghraib photos, the ideology of a globally supreme and unchallenged American humanity in/as war and war-making) simply puts to efficient use what was always one of the key traits of the aesthetic of the sublime as Kant theorized it. Indeed, Kant thought that the sublime feeling was at its most intense when it was capable of producing in the human subject an attitude that he called "subreption." Subreption, for Kant, was "a favor obtained at the price of an abuse," a privilege that the subject is granted at the cost of accepting "an abuse of authority."[42] Thus, as Kant already argued and as the photos from the invasion/occupation of Iraq have demonstrated, the sublime spectacle seems to produce a new collective consciousness or subjectivity. It invents a mass or communal "subject" who expects and becomes accustomed to abuses of authority, and who in fact best defines himself/herself through such abuses (we rediscover here the theme of the abject developed in Chapter 3). Normalizing a situation whereby individuals (actors or spectators) come to accept and in fact demand abuses of power is no doubt the acme of the ideology and politics of the sublime. The next section pursues this investigation further, but it also starts to wonder what happens when an image or event stubbornly appears to resist the ideological impositions often enabled by the use of the sublime.

The sublime (un)representation of violent events to come

What passes for an event today is often the image of a spectacular situation or phenomenon that has been deemed, generally by the media (tabloid or not), to be of importance, to be worthy of public interest, in other words to be newsworthy. The event today becomes that which produces the spectacle and the spectacular. The event is what makes a spectacle of itself. To the extent that some events are described as violent, destructive, or warlike today, it is because they are presented to us, the spectators, as images that capture scenes of violence, destruction, and war. Put simply, what constitutes a violent event today is often the ability to mobilize a sublime image that shocks and destabilizes, but also can rechannel people's thinking and feeling toward a greater idea or concept, toward some ideational or ideological purpose.

Thus, often at a very practical level, the aim of any ideology that seeks to make use of the sublime image is to gain control over the event, to decide its fate and public presentation. The ideology of the sublime is successful when it can produce visual events that, by playing with the viewer's sense of shock and search for a pleasurable solution to the apparent trauma, reveal or reinforce what is already given, assured, and established ideologically. In the US war in Iraq, the event is an image that first catches us unaware but soon comforts us by gradually making us realize that there is a greater force at work behind the pictures, that those photos are to be seen for a reason, and that once again a larger-than-life and most salutary ideal is operating behind these apparently atrocious scenes and endows them with true meaning. The event in Iraq is Bush's slogan that the "mission has been accomplished." The event is that the US military has won the war, that the United States has not just won the war in fact, but that it has also won the hearts and minds of the people of the Middle East. The event is the belief that Americans – soldiers over there or proponents and supporters of the war at home – are the true heroes because they have brought democracy, freedom, and the "good" to Iraq and that it has worked. And finally the event is that America in action, particularly if the action is war, has been redefining humanity, what it means to be human, one (dead or alive) enemy/terrorist at a time, for all of the world to see. From such an ideological perspective that has already decided what the event will be and what it will look like, any image appears to do the trick, even or particularly a violent image that at first might have seemed more difficult to use politically, like a scene of torture from Abu Ghraib or the sight of young Ali's own maimed body as discussed above.

From this ideological point of view, to remain under control and to be kept in check, the event must pass through the filter of the sublime, through the ordeal of a negative, shocking, and perhaps destabilizing visual representation. Thus, the ideology that the advent of an already determined event guarantees must hope that the sublime operates as it is supposed to, that the initial shock indeed will be overcome, and that spectators will find the rational will, the emotional courage, or simply the desire to continue to search for pleasure through the visibly unpleasurable. A certain will-to-believe no doubt accompanies those who have discovered and championed the ideational and ideological possibilities offered by the aesthetic of the sublime (from Kant to the tabloid media and ideologues of the US war in Iraq). Such a will-to-believe, however, also prevents one having to question and worry about whether the sublime is indeed so powerful, so hermetic, or so demanding that the individual subject (even if s/he is abjected) unequivocally accepts to identify with a mass subjectivity that desires or accepts to be abused by authority.

Slavoj Zizek has suggested that the struggle for pleasure of the sublime allegedly found in the search for (and belief in) superior concepts or ideas may actually not be able to yield any of the desired or anticipated results for the spectator (and, by extension, for the purveyor of the ideology to be accessed by way of the sublime image). From the perspective of viewership, Zizek argues that the sublime may never be able to surmount the apparent initial failure or excess of the first shocking image. The sublime may be a failed quest for a desirable idea and such an idea may well be totally un(re)presentable, or endlessly unattainable. Zizek agrees with Kant's basic premise, with the belief that the sublime presents itself as an attempt at surpassing material reality or the representation of the beautiful. But, beyond what Zizek calls "phenomenality," there may actually be nothing to be found. Zizek writes: "We overcome phenomenality not by reaching beyond it, but by the experience of how there is nothing beyond it – how its beyond is precisely this Nothing of absolute negativity, of the utmost inadequacy of the appearance to its notion."[43] If there is nothing beyond the representation of things, beyond the image, except for lack itself, then the concept or idea is never visible. It cannot even be approximated. Its existence might also be doubted. Or, as Zizek prefers to see it, the concept may have to be experienced as lack or loss. Zizek concludes by suggesting that the sublime "is no longer an (empirical) object [or artistic/aesthetic image] indicating through its very inadequacy the dimension of the transcendent Thing-in-itself (Idea) but an object which occupies the place, replaces, fills out the empty space of the Thing as the void . . . [In the sublime object/image], we are dealing with a miserable 'little piece of the Real,' . . . some miserable, radically contingent corporeal leftover."[44] Zizek's reading critically undermines the aesthetic and ideological purposes of the sublime image. It also challenges the so-called greater ideational enterprises such an image is supposed to serve. For Zizek, the sublime image can never overcome its representational negativity, its initial shock. The sublime image does exist for Zizek. But it exists and matters as a haunting mark, a scarring piece of reality that denotes something that refuses to hide the gaping wound left by the initially terrifying sight. According to this differential and radical conceptual configuration of the sublime, the visible fragility of the initial image (to be surmounted by means of a greater idea) is in fact the weakness or outright absence of the concept itself, a concept that has no pertinent mode of presentation and thus is even lacking to itself. This critical reappraisal of the sublime image introduced by Zizek also recalls Friedrich von Schiller's own way of describing the sublime as that representation that "supposes comprehension of some kind of awesome, destructive power," as some sort of malevolence.[45] This different approach to the problem of the sublime now presents the concept (and its image) to us not so much as an ordeal to be transcended in order to arrive at desirable and larger-than-life realizations and rationalizations, but rather as a haunting force, as a malevolent power indeed, that refuses to let the image fall prey to any ideological order. It is a visual presence (or absence) that also prevents the event from unfolding as something already planned, announced, or decided.

Jean-Luc Nancy's attempt at retrieving what he calls the "eventness" of the event, at returning to the surprise that is the event,[46] is also a resistance against a certain idea and usage of the sublime. It is also a challenge to the belief that the sublime image must have a greater meaning than itself and that its negativity must be transcended so that certain regimes of truth can finally prevail. In a manner reminiscent of Zizek's analysis and of Schiller's incantation of the sublime as some malevolent force, Nancy's event and its surprise (or *as* a surprise) are always already to come. They never arrive, are never programmed, and yet they do take place. It is only thus that the event and the sublime can retain a haunting presence. Similarly to Zizek's sublime that marks its own void and never reaches beyond its traumatic image, Nancy's event-as-surprise postpones and disseminates the ideational impositions that could/should be achieved by means of a certain, often dominant, aesthetic and ideology of the sublime.[47] Instead of the event as a spectacle (the event presented as a sublime image of violence or destruction that must make sense of the unpresentable and whose meaning has already been determined), the event-as-surprise offers itself as a negativity of the image, as an image that is both in excess of itself (it continues to haunt human comprehension whereas it should start to evoke ideas were it to function properly) and short of meaning and substance (it is not able to make one realize what the ideological designs are). Nancy claims that the event is "the visibility of nothing as a condition for the possibility of any visibility of something."[48] Thus, one can agree with literary critic Florian Tréguer's interpretation of Nancy's "sublime event." Tréguer argues that the event-as-surprise is the point where "representation collapses onto itself."[49] It is the unanticipated, yet perhaps not so unusual, moment when we, as spectators of or witnesses to this image-event that we cannot understand and shocks us, start "to feel the foreboding sentiment that the overall connectivity of the world," that this ideational connection that is supposedly far greater than us and our life even, will in fact "never be able to be made intelligible to us."[50]

Jacques Derrida has usefully supplemented Nancy's reading of the event, and he has chosen to polemicize about the importance, for what he calls a "democracy to come," of maintaining the event as the mark of something that is always impossible, undecidable, and unconditional. Derrida writes that the event, similar to "all the figures I place under the title of the *im-possible*," can be opposed "to the order of the 'I can,' ipseity, the theoretical, the descriptive, the constative, and the performative (inasmuch as this latter still implies a power for some 'I' guaranteed by conventions that neutralize the pure eventfulness of the event, and inasmuch as the eventfulness of the to-come exceeds this sphere of the performative)."[51] For both Derrida and Nancy, reclaiming the event (away from ideological impositions and their modalities of spectatorship), demanding its return and recognition, is also establishing a presence. It is the presence of a political injunction, an act of resistance to ideological and ideational designs. Nancy's sublime event and Derrida's (democratic) event to come, far from being prophecies, are the mark/presence of a politics that cannot be planned ahead of time and that comes as/when the event comes, if it is to come at all. In deconstructive language, one could say that the event is the necessary aporia of the political, the aporetic (non-)precondition of a democratic politics that seeks to offer a thinking and practice of freedom that is precisely political and democratic when/as it calls into question the thinking and practice of freedom as ideological force.[52] As Nancy claims, refusing to succumb to the constraints of past representations or to the requirements of a future idea/ideal, this political/democratic event to come interrupts the progression of time[53] and seizes a place that is, as Derrida adds, "without horizon, un-masterable by any . . . conventional and thus consensual performativity," and "whose irruption should not and cannot be limited by any conditional hospitality on the borders of a policed nation-state."[54]

Nancy and Derrida imply that the conditions of possibility for thinking the political and democracy today, in the margins of the dominant ideologies of abusive and hyper-powerful sovereign (perhaps imperial) states and their war machines, depend upon events to come, surprises as events. A different politics of the event depends upon a differential apprehension of the sublime and its image, upon a different political use of the image. Indeed, this democratic politics to come may also be reliant upon a certain image of violence, upon an image that does violence to itself and to its designs that are supposedly to be found beyond its representational limits. Derrida writes, in passing, that the (sublime) event is "always monstrous," that it has an "unpresentable character, demonstrable [only] *as* unmonstrable."[55] For the immediate analytical purposes of this chapter, the question becomes whether the monstrosity of the sublime image of violence, the visual demonstration of war monsters in television shows like *Over There* or in photojournalistic displays like those captured in the *Witness Iraq* volume for example, can be (re)thought as being in excess of itself. Beyond ideological appropriations and political plans, can violent and negative images of war become events to come? Can they be the mark of a different sort of presence, the unexpected sight of a surreptitious real that, in opposition to the imposed American ideology of a new humanity in/as war, seeks to rethink democracy and freedom when and where both democracy and freedom are already given, often by force and through abuses of sovereign authority and agonal terror? Is the sublime image of the sublime event a shock that, as some sort of malevolent force, some other haunting violence, can indeed manage to shock us, mass subjects of the spectacular and tabloid ideological sublime, but into reaction, into resistance this time?

Instead of returning to the images of war presented above to ask if they are not also the mark/presence of events to come, of different events, whose meanings cannot be laid to rest, I prefer at this point to turn towards other images or situations than those discussed in the previous sections of this chapter. I do so, not so much to extend the conceptual/visual range of the present analysis, but rather to shift the emphasis on the violence of the image away from the sublime image of war, a violent, often tabloid, sight that generally has to be one of soldiers fighting over there in Iraq. Indeed, I want to suggest that, in the midst of today's geopolitical tabloid discourses and representations on the American war, events-as-surprises sometimes do take place in the global media spectacle, even if they are unannounced, do not last long, go unnoticed to many (at least for now), and, since their plan or purpose is not the one imposed by the dominant war ideology, are often "incalculable and aleatory" (as Derrida suggests).[56] Such resistant events also have no guarantee of political or democratic success. They may be captured, co-opted, or forcefully erased by violent sovereigns and their war machines. Still, their happening, their presence, and their surprise may nonetheless actualize a critique of the global war ideology and of tabloid geopolitical representations/discourses and, as such, may force an opening (or aporia as I put it above) in American popular/public culture for a different freedom to come.

Here, I want to propose another event, unexpected by those in power and by their tabloid scribes, as a candidate for such a resistance or haunting presence. This was provoked by the initial irruption of Cindy Sheehan, the mother of a US Marine who was killed in Iraq, outside Bush's private ranch in Crawford, Texas in August 2005.[57] As is now well known, Sheehan decided to set camp outside the ranch while Bush was vacationing there, hoping that, on one of Bush's outings, he might be able to stop by to talk to her and explain to her, face to face, why it had to be that her son was sent to Iraq to die. Sheehan's unannounced and unwelcome visit – and Bush's stubborn refusal to stop and talk to her – led other American mothers whose sons and daughters had died in Iraq and Afghanistan to join her, and before long a spontaneous camp of tents was erected in a field across from Bush's ranch. Later, the mothers would install white crosses representing their dead children along the road that leads to the ranch.[58]

Sheehan's and the other mothers' initial encampment in the path of the Commander in Chief who spearheaded the war in Iraq and continues to claim that the United States' warriors are succeeding in their efforts to bring democracy, freedom, morality, and humanity to the Iraqis is an act of resistance, a moment of interruption. It is an event that is far from spectacular, and only becomes so after the US media start to dispatch their broadcasting arsenals there, once the media, their pundits, and their tabloid geopolitical experts decide that the event is worthy of news coverage. But it is nonetheless an event that commands a presence, that does not want to be ignored (in fact, that is its main point), and that brings a haunting reality back in the face of those who promote and champion a higher idea, ideal, and ideology. The Sheehan irruptive event is an abrupt mark, possibly without future and hope (although, it must be noted, the event would later be co-opted by a burgeoning anti-war movement, and Sheehan herself would later be turned into an ideological symbol by this movement), a demand to speak, a demand to ask questions, a request to those who revel in the abuse of authority and think they know better (who believe that American warriors have to "stay the course" in Iraq) to question freedom and democracy, to open up the idea of humanity. It is an event that is sublime both in its arresting mode of address (it demands that the visual attention be moved away from the images of the Iraq war) and in its conceptual negativity (it questions whether there is indeed such a thing as a globally triumphant American humanity that is fighting and winning the war). Yet, it is very simple, mundane, modest, and commonplace. The event, and that is also what is so surprising, is not about US troops killing Iraqi "others" or themselves being slaughtered by some unknown terrorists or "evil others" over there. It is about someone, a mother, right here at home, in the heartland of America, asking to meet the President, wanting to talk to him, wishing to establish a human contact with him, not so much because she hopes this encounter will change things, but rather so that she (and indirectly we) can try to envision another humanity, one that deals with others differently.[59]

There is no obvious violent image attached to this event (at least, not yet),[60] and still it is perhaps the bearer of another violence to come, one that encourages against all hope a different image, a different sublimity, and a different political and democratic eventness. By happening, as a surprise, this kind of event tries to make possible a (re)turn to another reality, to a daily and ordinary reality where individuals die violent deaths as a result of the American agony of war. Tréguer uses the term "trivial sublime" to refer to this kind of anodyne, almost uneventful, and yet symbolically and critically violent event.[61] Claiming a presence in a reality without conceptual horizon or ideological depth, the "trivial sublime event" manages to do violence to already programmed ideas and concepts by no longer providing a linkage to them, by opening onto nothing.[62]

Toward a different apprehension of the sublime in contemporary international politics

At a time when the practice and idea of international relations, particularly in the United States, are increasingly seduced by the tabloid geopolitics and aesthetics of violence justified by and placed at the service of the American war machine's terror, the chances of success of what I have called a different violence, of a violence that, following the model of the trivial sublime event, may cause damage to already announced or programmed ideas, ideals, and ideologies, can never be guaranteed. The power of this different sublime event, this surprise of the event, is as unpredictable and unconditional as its emergence is. Unlike some other critical theorists of war, terror, and politics (introduced earlier in this book) who, faced with the advent of the imperial sovereignty of contemporary war machines, would rather incant the arrival of a new democratic spirit and movement in the shape of a so-called multitude and, in the process, seek to position themselves as the prophets of a new collectivist spirit,[63] the proponents of a democracy to come have no hope for democracy as a project. In fact, it is precisely because democracy is currently presented as an inevitable plan by contemporary ideologues of statecraft, empire, and war that critical thinkers of the sublime event suggest that the democracy to come can only be actualized as a mode of questioning regarding what democracy is or means.

People who think about international/domestic politics and the effects of contemporary global policies and ideologies on everyday public culture today, several years after 9/11 and after the US invasion of Iraq, can take advantage of opportunities presented here and there in the global polity to actualize a certain sublime event. This, I believe, is the democratic task to come, a political intervention that cannot be planned or forecast, and yet needs to take place lest culture and life become the undisputed conceptual and geopolitical terrains of an imperial ideology of war and war-making as "our" new humanity. The critical task to come is on the lookout for other, dominant, and allegedly sublime usages of democracy, for mobilizations of a democracy always already doomed because it has been surrendered from the get-go to larger-than-life ideas or ideals. The critical or radical sublime today, as a political irruption, can be on the lookout for and identify attempts at abusing the name of democracy in contemporary American military operations in Iraq or elsewhere, and in their visual, generally spectacular, and often tabloid representations on television, in films, in news magazines, or in treatises and pamphlets by contemporary intellectuals of statecraft and warfare. But the critical sublime also needs to keep an eye on less obvious but no less ideologically abusive manifestations of a desire to put democracy to the service of today's American imperial and agonal ideas such as when photos of tortured Iraqi prisoners or of maimed Iraqi civilians are released to the American public, for example. As we saw above, the shock or trauma of such images may not be so destabilizing after all if indeed the sublime spectacle – particularly in its invocation of a fragile but redeemable humanity as/through war – functions as it is intended to.

The sublime event to come and its radicalization of the image of war and violence in contemporary American culture has much critical work to accomplish. And it must be said that this work is often not facilitated by the intervention of some allegedly democracy-loving and human rights defending liberal intellectuals (often American too) who, despite their stated intentions, do contribute to contemporary hegemonic and abusive visions of international relations by advancing concepts that, these so-called soft intellectuals of statecraft argue, are "necessary evils" justified by the need to protect democratic politics from the agonal violence of the American war machine.[64] In an era when some of these self-proclaimed champions of global democracy and rights do not (want to) think twice about selling off democracy (and the questions it ought to raise) to those who abuse, dehumanize, and torture in the hope that they too, like their more conservative tabloid imperialistic counterparts, may find a way of earning the trust of those who currently steer American foreign policy towards war, an interruption in democratic thinking, in what democracy can be or mean, can only be welcome. As we saw in previous chapters, contemporary tabloid geopolitical discourses of war and terror have a way of colonizing the American popular cultural and political landscape. This too is part of the "colonial present" Gregory speaks of. These discourses and representations have also found a way of influencing supposedly more sedate and moderate academic discussions and debates about the post-9/11 American wars and their uses and meanings. Yet, once again, such a democratic interruption, although dearly needed, cannot be planned or even organized, and its course must remain aleatory.[65] The discursive and representational rupture is to come, to happen. Only the open gift or unpredictable opportunity offered by this surprise of the event, by a sublime event that shocks and destabilizes but without providing answers and without bringing in new hopes, can achieve this critical and radical democratic challenge (democracy as a challenge, not as a certainty). Perhaps it is time for international relations/geopolitics, for global democratic politics, to be without hope.

Conclusion
Tabloid terror and precarious lives

[D]ominant forms of representation can and must be disrupted for something about
the precariousness of life to be apprehended.

Judith Butler[1]

In [the eyes of the war protestors], the U.S.A. should engage with other nations of
the world – no matter how corrupt or tyrannical – in a "collegial" fashion. What's
wrong with that? Simple. That philosophy does not look out for you, the everyday
American . . . [A]s we all learned the hard way on 9/11 and in the run-up to the
Iraq War, some foreign countries do not seem to have the welfare and security of
Americans on top of their dance card.

Bill O'Reilly[2]

The O'Reilly fear factor

Since 9/11, the conservative, populist, and loud-mouthed Fox News network talk-
show host and pundit Bill O'Reilly has taken it upon himself to represent and
protect American lives. His show, *The O'Reilly Factor*, is an hour-long infotainment, current events, and topical issues daily review that is really more of an
opportunity for O'Reilly to voice his opinion on social and political matters than
anything else. The *O'Reilly Factor* has been at the forefront of American tabloid
news media and popular culture since the late 1990s. This program regularly tops
television ratings in the United States, and not just among cable TV networks.
Moreover, many of O'Reilly's books, as spin-offs of his TV show, have been national bestsellers. Like it or not, O'Reilly's opinion on the world out there and on
culture and politics in here seems to matter to many Americans. I would suggest,
however, that his opinion matters as much for its content (a politically, culturally,
and morally conservative, pro-government, and pro-US military content) as for
the format that is used to present it. The *O'Reilly Factor* and O'Reilly's infiltration through other media channels (popular books, the internet, op-ed pieces
in newspapers, interviews on late-night TV comedy programs, radio talk-shows,
and so on) are intent on producing the impression of news reporting, information

providing, facts revealing, and truth declaring to millions of Americans when, quite often, all that O'Reilly really wants to achieve is convince his audience of the moral superiority and greater commonsensical value of his punditry. O'Reilly's punditry is made up of a set of populist beliefs and views that are generally based on nothing more than his own experiences or rather ideological preferences (or those of some chosen guests on his show whom he deems worthy of sharing or representing his views), but that are nonetheless presented as objective, factual, and true. The shock-value of O'Reilly's interventions (or interpretations) is aimed at garnering popular support or triggering public scandal by unleashing waves after waves of fear among his audience members. Presenting Americans with daily doses of problems or crises generally caused or further aggravated by selected scapegoat figures – the left, what O'Reilly calls the "mainstream media" (anything but the Fox network), academics, those who protest the war on terror, foreign countries like France, Germany, Russia, or China that were hesitant to back the Bush administration over Iraq, and of course the terrorists and those in the Middle East who support them – O'Reilly imposes himself to his American public as the only one capable of providing answers, solutions, comfort, and, of course, the "truth."[3] As O'Reilly puts it in one of his books, "your humble correspondent" simply writes or talks "for everyday Americans who are fighting the good fight."[4] By producing and manipulating anxiety on his show and depicting a dangerous and often terrifying world out there that leaves very little comprehension for American "people who do not have much control or authority over the pace or the content" of what is happening,[5] O'Reilly has put himself in the position of the number one tabloid pundit of statecraft in the United States today.[6]

Tabloid geopolitics is the bread and butter of O'Reilly's sensationalistic and opinion-driven media productions and interventions, and tabloid terror is generally the outcome of such presentations. The popular and populist medium that the O'Reilly phenomenon has become ("O'Reilly" is a label in the tabloid media universe that ranges from television and radio to the internet and journalistic writing[7]) is one of the flashiest tabloid geopolitical productions found in the United States in the first decade of the new millennium. The reason why I choose to conclude this book with a brief reflection on O'Reilly, his fear factor, and his production of tabloid terror is because, in many ways, the O'Reilly cultural/political phenomenon and its representational strategies reveal in a condensed fashion many of the techniques, ideas, ideologies, and sometimes practical outcomes of tabloid geopolitics in American culture since the late 1990s.

The *O'Reilly Factor* started as a news show with a different kind of format in the late 1990s (1996–97 season). It would be a show that would duplicate the genre of reporting already made available in several news-as-entertainment programs like *Inside Edition* (which O'Reilly himself hosted for a while) or *Entertainment Tonight*, programs for which the style of presentation (short, vivid, attention-grabbing) mattered more than the story that was depicted (which often had to be spectacular, popular, and trash). As O'Reilly proudly boasts, the *O'Reilly Factor* was the show that put Fox News on many people's radar screens in the United States at about the turn of the millennium. And Fox News, like O'Reilly's show, liked "to focus on traditional things that are either being challenged or celebrated."[8] With O'Reilly as its number one success story in the late 1990s, Fox News became "the flag-waving network that looks to America's past for perspective."[9] Openly embracing the tabloid populist format, O'Reilly added: "Of course, we also cover everyday news, but usually with an eye on how it affects the working-class American."[10] At the time, this newly conceived tabloid news network and O'Reilly's show were conservative, defensive, protective, and "unabashedly patriotic."[11] Thus, dangers or risks, particularly those found in the international domain, outside US borders, were crucial topics of discussion and fear production on *The O'Reilly Factor*. These topics were also the opportunity for O'Reilly to lambaste the Clinton administration, which, in his view, was bringing the United States and its people closer and closer to the catastrophe (whether it was Y2K or cyberterrorism, as we saw in Chapter 1, letting too many immigrants into the country, or not properly addressing geopolitical threats like China, Iraq, or Iran). Unsurprisingly, a generally tabloid realist style and tone of argumentation were deployed both on *The O'Reilly Factor* and in many other Fox News programs (such as the one I described in Chapter 1) to try to redirect the focus of foreign policy makers and of the population in general toward national defense, domestic security, and military build-up. Many of these tabloid realist themes developed by O'Reilly in the late 1990s are still part of the O'Reilly mediascape today, but they have also been filtered now through an aggressive, retribution-seeking, and often outright imperialistic and expansionist discourse and presentation.

What is also interesting from the perspective of the tabloid geopolitical terror theorized in this book is that, after 9/11, O'Reilly (and Fox News in general) became more than ever before *the* media figure for the defense, protection, and preservation of the American nation. After the attacks of September 11, and even more so after the invasion of Iraq in 2003, O'Reilly's style and content turned to tabloid geopolitics in a more forceful, sustained, and strategic manner. His show warmly embraced tabloid imperialism. O'Reilly's message and medium were now mainly about supporting the American wars and telling audience members the "truth" about such wars. In O'Reilly's "no spin zone" (the motto about his style of "reporting"), war would not be excused. War would not be avoided. And war would often need no justification other than simply uttering the phrase "September 11" (a rhetorical strategy used, if not crafted, by the Bush administration too). War, in the O'Reilly tabloid phenomenon, was first and foremost about boosting and supporting the troops (or so O'Reilly claimed), the American true heroes of the post-9/11 tabloid mediascape (after the victims of the 9/11 attacks, for whom O'Reilly often made himself the spokesperson in the first few months after the terrorist events – no matter whether the victims' families wished for O'Reilly to do so or not – but whom he later started to de-emphasize and even criticize as several among them chose to voice their opposition to the war in Iraq).[12] According to O'Reilly's growing tabloid imperialistic discourse, supporting America's war heroes demanded that American citizens at home adopt a moral posture appropriate to the situation. Americans at home had to emulate the moral vigor and certainty of America's warriors over there. To quote O'Reilly: "The brutal truth is that the only people who possessed absolute moral certainty in this conflict were the ones who died for their country."[13] O'Reilly went on: "The military heroes and heroines alone [hold] the high moral ground, and nobody should forget it."[14] Telling the truth about America's war heroes also meant that the truth had to be revealed about the enemies, those "our" heroes were killing in Afghanistan and Iraq. And here, Americans could not be left with any doubt as to the moral standing of those who attacked on 9/11 and that "our" troops were now combating. They, whoever or whatever they were, had to be without any moral ground in this tabloid geopolitical discourse. America's morality and humanity could not be shared with others, with those that American warriors were fighting, but also with others who wanted to slow down the United States' military campaigns in the Middle East. Here, O'Reilly claimed, emotion had to be thrown out of the picture, and the O'Reilly tabloid reporting made sure to tell its American public that it was all about "examining the facts," and only the facts.[15] The "facts" (and their "truth") were that the "philosophy of internationalist sympathy" (O'Reilly's phrase) did "not look out for you, the everyday American."[16] Consequently (and that too was a "fact," O'Reilly stated), Americans should be worried about "very powerful people . . . who give moral equivalencies to foreign countries and even to organizations and philosophies that are bent on harming the U.S.A."[17]

But covering war for O'Reilly's now openly tabloid imperialistic discourse was also about championing the policies and tactics of the war-makers as wartime required that dissension and critique in the public be cast aside. As O'Reilly put it: "As a journalist I want to be fair, but I also want President Bush to put the protection of Americans above the economic and political concerns of other countries . . . your family's security is more to me than Gerhard Schroeder's political career."[18] In this tabloid imperialistic discourse, an administration (all the more so if it was politically conservative) had to be praised if it did not back down and, instead, opted to let the military run the show. Thus, after 9/11, Bush rightly "personalized the attack so that America's reply was swift and strong."[19] O'Reilly was clear that "that was exactly the reaction our country needed . . . Bush rose to the occasion and was looking out for us by aggressively bringing out the fight to our enemies."[20]

As the war in Iraq dragged on and no outcome other than more war, terror, and destruction became more and more obvious, *The O'Reilly Factor*, like many other contemporary tabloid imperialistic and aggressive geopolitical discourses in the United States, soldiered on. Images in Abu Ghraib and other revelations that no weapons of mass destruction existed or that there was never any link between Al Qaeda and Saddam Hussein had to be ignored in the tabloid geopolitical discourses and representations. Or better yet, these "findings" had to be transcended, sublimated. With the focus still placed on the agonal heroes, America's warriors, valiantly fighting an endless conflict in Iraq (a conflict that had to be won no matter what, it was argued), other larger-than-life and greater-than-reality reasons or ideas had to be mobilized (despite the brutal images, or rather, along with those images) to continue to explain the "truth" about the war to American audiences. Humanity was still on America's side, it was said, and humanity was really the reason, a grander and nobler reason in fact, why the Bush administration had sent US troops to invade Iraq in the first place. The fate of humankind, this now desperate (but just as vicious) tabloid imperialistic geopolitical discourse argued, was dependent upon the military victory of US warriors "over there." Thus, *The O'Reilly Factor* explained, the United States had a moral duty toward humankind (measured by the standard of the American population), toward the preservation of the "good," to dislodge Saddam Hussein's sympathizers and to continue to fight the extremist elements found in Iraq. As O'Reilly put it, "with fanatical Muslims dedicated to using any and all methods in order to kill American civilians, it would have been irresponsible for an American president to allow the United Nations to permit Saddam . . . to continue his rule. What did our people die for in 1991?"[21]

If the fate of humanity was at stake in the heroic actions of "our" soldiers in Iraq, doubting the motivations for the war, being suspicious of the connection between the war in Iraq and 9/11, or simply wanting the troops to come home could not be tolerated either in this tabloid imperialism happily relayed and/or produced by O'Reilly and his multi-media arsenal. Thus, on *The O'Reilly Factor* as in other American tabloid/media discourses of the war in Iraq, those American citizens who chose to question the invasion and its aftermath had to be branded as traitors to the nation, as betrayers of the memory of those "everyday Americans" who died on 9/11 or, afterwards, perished for "our" security and protection in Afghanistan and Iraq. The protestors' voices had to be silenced by O'Reilly and other pundits of statecraft who, like him, did their best through their tabloid spectacles or writings to eviscerate these critical views. As I put it in Chapter 5, the eventness of such critiques or resistant moments (along with their possibly democratic potential) had to be cast away, reduced to meaninglessness by other, still more dominant, louder (in voice and in style), and more populist representations like those propagated by O'Reilly throughout the media.

In the summer of 2005, for example, O'Reilly launched multiple verbal attacks against Cindy Sheehan, using his media channels to discredit her initial event (her camping outside Bush's ranch) and, just as importantly, to place her irruption in the American post-9/11 political and cultural landscape in a larger geopolitical and ideological discourse of attacks of the "internationalist left" against America, its president, its warriors, and its citizens. On one of his shows, O'Reilly declared: "I think Mrs. Sheehan bears some responsibility for this [the resurgence of a leftist, anti-war critique against the Bush administration], and also for the responsibility of other American families who have lost their sons and daughters in Iraq, who feel that this kind of behavior borders on treasonous."[22] In a rant-driven, ideologically motivated narrative that was not so well disguised by the appearance of "fact revelation" and "truth promotion" that he claimed his show was all about,[23] O'Reilly went on to link Sheehan to larger concepts and ideas (9/11, the war on terror, the US campaign against "horror" in the world) that trapped her challenge to the war inside a larger ideological battle of rightist conservative moral responsibility (which O'Reilly sought to embody) versus left-wing surrendering and betrayal of the nation's values (which Sheehan's actions were deemed to represent). Quickly, almost effortlessly, and perhaps invisibly to many viewers, O'Reilly's tabloid geopolitical discourse/presentation managed to make Sheehan appear like a post-9/11 Benedict Arnold, an ally of the terrorists, and an instigator of social dissension inside US society.[24] As O'Reilly forcefully concluded: "There is no question that she has thrown in with the most radical elements in this country . . . now, it happened before. Some of the 9/11 families also took this road, you'll remember . . . And, you know, there are some people who hate this government, hate their country right now, and are blaming Bush for all the terrorism and all the horror in the world."[25]

As we have seen in this book, tabloid geopolitical images and discourses (like O'Reilly's and many others' in contemporary American popular/political culture) excel at convincing their audiences that the American nation is constantly in danger, that American people are about to be attacked and perhaps destroyed and, ultimately, that war is the most common, normal, almost natural response to these tabloid media-induced fears.[26] As I suggested throughout this book, O'Reilly's claim to provide a value-free "no spin" zone inside which facts about the world out there and the United States' role and place in it can be presented and truths can finally be revealed is not unique. It is not so novel either (except for technological gimmicks that make such tabloid displays more spectacular and entertaining to watch, listen to, or read). O'Reilly is not even a model for such tabloid geopolitical productions of fear, terror, and war. Simply, O'Reilly and his tabloid media panoply are symptoms of what has become of American public culture and informed political discussion and debate in an age when a war on terror has grafted itself onto the reality-making and truth-producing operations of the media.

Tabloid geopolitics and the control of the public sphere

Judith Butler has argued that public debate in the United States in the aftermath of 9/11 has been characterized by an exclusion of dissent. Political and media discourses, Butler goes on to remark, have been driven by the desire to produce labels (traitor, terrorist-sympathizer, leftist, internationalist, postmodernist, and so on) that support ready-made explanations aimed at creating a "climate of fear in which to voice a certain view is to risk being branded and shamed with a heinous appellation."[27] Inside the contemporary spaces of alleged debate or dialogue of the global mediascape, critical reflection is rendered obsolete, useless, and possibly threatening to the nation and its people. Thus, Henry Giroux adds that, "[j]ust as violence is staged as a global spectacle, language, sound, and image lose their critical functions as they are turned into weapons to combat an enemy that is ubiquitous and to glorify a politics mobilized around an unrelenting campaign of fear."[28] Butler's and Giroux's insights are perspicacious commentaries on the discursive politics of popular shows like *The O'Reilly Factor* and many other seemingly open and free-flowing public debates about the future of the United States and its people in an age of global terror. But these commentaries are also lucid recognitions of the powerful and dreadful consequences of the ideological work of imposition, control, and domination of tabloid geopolitics as a discourse of fear, terror, and war. As I have shown in the previous chapters, tabloid geopolitics (in its different instantiations as tabloid realism before 9/11, as tabloid idealism or imperialism after 9/11, and perhaps as a more defensive and desperate – but also more vicious – tabloid imperialistic and aggressive narrative after the debacle of the war in Iraq) is a set of discursive and/or visual representations that seek to take over the American cultural landscape in order to determine what can or cannot be said in the public domain in the new millennium. By dictating what will be legitimately uttered or not, tabloid geopolitical discourses and representations also decide who will count as valued speaking subjects, as subjects capable of pronouncing "truths." In addition, the tabloid texts, sights, and sounds also reveal to their readers/viewers/listeners what or who is not worthy of interest or, worse yet, what or who needs to be abjected, dehumanized, and eventually killed. Thus, this tabloid discursive and representational production constantly threatens speaking subjects – whoever they are, and whatever they may want to say – with a potentially "uninhabitable identification" (as Butler puts it).[29] Speaking subjects ("us" and "them"), if and when they dare to speak, are interpellated into compliance with the dominant narratives and images and into acceptance of not being allowed to voice doubt or questioning. As Giroux clarifies, "in this cold new world, the language of politics is increasingly mediated through a spectacle of terrorism in which fear and violence become central modalities through which to grasp the meaning of self in society."[30]

As I argued in the Introduction to this book, tabloid geopolitics needs to be understood as a discursive formation. Foucault indicated that a discursive formation is ultimately a disciplinary exercise, a normative operation whose objective is precisely to control discourse or language, to decide what can be said and how it can be said. A discursive formation is concerned with both the content of the utterance and its conditions of production. Tabloid geopolitics, as a fully functioning and disciplining discursive formation in American politics and culture since the late 1990s in particular, has developed tools and techniques that can control both the substance and the form of the (geo)political message. Once again, it has done so with a view toward regulating and shaping the public sphere, a public sphere whose occupants must accept that, in an age of global terror, war and war-making are the main modalities of political existence and meaning. Still, in an era when reality is saturated with all sorts of media constructions, discursive formations intent on taking over and shaping the public sphere must also devise disciplinary and normalizing strategies that necessarily account not just for what is said, but also for what *appears* to be said. As we saw in Chapter 5, what is seen and how it is meant to be seen become just as crucial to the control of meaning as what might be said. Butler's analysis of the post-9/11 political cultural domain concurs with this view. Butler writes: "The public sphere is constituted in part by what can appear, and the regulation of the sphere of appearance is one way to establish what will count as reality, and what will not."[31]

Thus, as I showed in this study, at the turn of the millennium tabloid geopolitics embarked upon the regulation of the public sphere of appearance by deploying a discourse (on the internet, in books) and representations (TV programs, maps, and so on) provided by intellectuals of statecraft, pseudo-academic experts in technological security matters, and media pundits. This discourse made use of a language and imagery of inevitable danger, incalculable risk, and growing waves of terror (such as Y2K computer collapses, cyberterrorist attacks on the internet, widening fault-lines between civilizations, or decaying former geopolitical empires like the old Soviet Union) to produce an American public culture of fear. Still, after some of the dangers or risks enumerated above actually took place (in a fashion not directly anticipated by the former fear-driven tabloid realist scenarios though), when fear did materialize in US culture after 9/11, and once reality appeared to catch up with the previously simulated tabloid models, different techniques or tactics had to be mobilized by the tabloid geopolitical discursive formation. Often the same intellectuals or pundits of statecraft (Robert D. Kaplan or Samuel Huntington, for example) had to readjust their discourses and their modalities of appearance of danger, fear, and insecurity. At this point, tabloid realists turned into or gave way to tabloid imperialists,[32] and the American public sphere became one where representations of terror and war were encouraged to dominate democratic debates.

At the same time, though, the passage from tabloid realism to tabloid imperialism was more than mere technical fine-tuning (although the tabloid style of the discourse and representations certainly made it look as if it was a continuation of what had been initiated in the late 1990s). Unlike tabloid realism, tabloid imperialism as a discursive/representational construct was no longer about proliferating simulated scenarios or models (World War III, an electronic or digital Pearl Harbor, holographic maps, and so forth). Rather, tabloid imperialism became a matter of deploying vivid, gruesome, or "factual" situations and so-called events, and more importantly of attaching those real or imagined phenomena to larger-than-life and ideationally superior reasons, rationalizations, and ideologies, so that Americans could not just fear or panic, but also could openly hate, abject, dehumanize, and agonize over life and death. The new tabloid imperialistic scenarios provided by intellectuals and pundits of statecraft and war (and their media, government, and military supports and supporters) were not concerned with simulation any more. They were now interested in recapturing good old representation, and in excavating from it images, symbols, or messages that could help to better produce meaning, reality, and truth by idealizing, rationalizing, and (conveniently also) glossing over those that "we," Americans, had to demonize, bestialize, or kill through "our" heroic actions. Whereas simulation was a crucial technique for tabloid (hyper-)realists, tabloid imperialists openly embraced transcendence and sublimation instead as their main discursive, representational and, finally, ideational strategies. After 9/11, the buffering effect offered by simulation models was no longer potent. A new Pearl Harbor (although not electronic or digital) was said to have taken place. As many in the media had noted, the reality of the terrorist attacks made Hollywood-type *trompe l'oeil* fictions look obsolete. And tabloid geopolitical scientists no longer had to craft virtual dangers in order to encourage American citizens to be afraid, seek revenge, assault others, and support an unending war on and of terror.

But, with tabloid imperialism, the public domain of appearances was just as saturated, controlled, and put to efficient uses as it was before 9/11 with the tabloid realists. In fact, tabloid imperialism, also making itself the discursive echo chamber of many Bush administration policies both at home and abroad, intensified the demands on the public sphere and on what could be said or seen. As intellectuals and pundits of statecraft became apologists for the war machine and its agonal agents, the popular and political tabloid requirement was now to affirm realities, facts, and truths (never to be doubted, never to be challenged, never to be questioned about their possible lack of objectivity) that could evoke ideas and ideologies capable of surmounting or vanquishing terrorizing sights, sounds, words, voices, thoughts, or events. Among the tabloid imperialistic demands now imposed onto American political and popular culture was the obligation to see the war in Iraq and the actions of US soldiers "over there" as the making of morality and humanity in the Middle East, perhaps in the entire world too. As a blatant ideological instrument, tabloid geopolitics as tabloid imperialism in the aftermath of the US invasion of Iraq turned into not just any discourse that tried to regulate what could be said/seen or not said/not seen in American political culture. It became a rhetorical and visual censor that sought to keep control over the field of appearances by repressing haphazard events and spontaneous critiques that were not allowed to count as events (and thus could not be apprehended by the public in any way).

In the face of such a terrorizing discursive and representational modality of control/production of political/ideological meaning, what can critical geopolitical, international relations, and cultural/social studies scholars do? As I intimated in Chapter 5, other events, events about others perhaps, need to find a way of inserting themselves into the dominant sphere of tabloid geopolitics if the public domain of appearances is to be democratic or open again. I agree with Badiou's claim that a reopening of the contemporary public domain depends upon a certain form of democratic challenge, one that, like the lines of resistance introduced by Nancy and Derrida (discussed in Chapter 5), strives to demonstrate "how the space of the possible is larger than the one assigned – that something else is possible, but not everything is possible."[33] I also subscribe to Butler's view that it is at the level of representation that the challenge to tabloid geopolitics must be met. Butler argues that "representation must not only fail, but it must *show* its failure."[34] Only by blatantly displaying its failure (instead of endlessly trying to sublimate it) can tabloid geopolitics become something other, some other possibility, than what it presently is or looks like.

Tabloid geopolitics in one form or another is unlikely to disappear any time soon. Once again, the tabloid genre of presentation of reality and of story-telling is part of the fabric of today's American popular/public culture. After 2005, the surge of a more critical popular geopolitical literature about the US war in Iraq, but also about many of the Bush administration leadership and policy failures in the fight against terrorism, in the economy, in the handling of the hurricane Katrina catastrophe in New Orleans, and so forth, has revealed that, in fact, neither the "conservative right" nor the "progressive left" holds the privilege of mastering and propagating tabloid (geo)political discourses and representations.[35] A blatant example of the durability but also instability and elusiveness of tabloid geopolitics as a narrative and/or media genre was the ability of the popular documentary film-maker and leftist pundit Michael Moore to use some of the same tabloid recipes (in both style and content) employed by so-called conservative tabloid realists and tabloid imperialists. Since after 9/11 in particular, Moore – perhaps as a counterpoint on the left to the O'Reilly media phenomenon on the right – decided to flood bookstores' and newsstands' shelves, radio airwaves, and the televisual and cinematographic mediascapes with his own anti-war, anti-Bush, and anti-conservatism blend of popular and populist (geo)political narratives and images.[36] Although Moore was certainly not unique as a critic of the Bush administration's campaign of terror since 9/11, his own mode of tabloid geopolitical presentation of so-called facts, truths, and everyday realities culminated with the release of his film *Fahrenheit 9/11* in the summer of 2004.[37] But the point I wish to make here – and that I have sought to make throughout this book – is that tabloid geopolitics, and the emergence within tabloid geopolitics of specific discursive and ideological modalities such as tabloid realism or tabloid imperialism in particular, is not to be seen as the prerogative of the "conservative right" in the United States as opposed to a "progressive left" that, for example, would not partake of this genre at all. Such a facile, and inaccurate, categorical division is far too convenient, and it is as incorrect as some of the beliefs held by certain contemporary critical social and geopolitical theorists who, in the hope that a leftist materialist critique might be resurrected, are far too eager to attach all the post-9/11 ideological constructs and formations and their often disastrous consequences (of war, destruction, and death) to neo-conservatism only.[38] To be clear, tabloid geopolitics – as tabloid realism and tabloid imperialism in particular – is broader, deeper, and possibly more lasting than American neo-conservatism, even if it is undeniable that key neo-conservative figures have played a crucial role in the deployment and subsequent expansion of tabloid geopolitical discourses, after 9/11 above all. As such, and to repeat, tabloid geopolitics – and the use or replication of tabloid or trash culture for certain political and cultural uses – also goes beyond a simplistic "right versus left" divide (whatever those terms or categories are supposed to mean).

Tabloid media culture *is* our trash popular/political culture. It is like a second or third nature to most of us, and it is an undeniable presence in our daily lives (and probably not only in the United States). But if tabloid culture sticks around, if it is all around us, this does not mean that inevitably it has to fall prey to discourses and representations whose main objectives are to dehumanize and destroy. In other words, the target is not, should not be, tabloid culture, but rather certain geopolitical and ideological appropriations of it, particularly by those texts and images of war and terror that have been showcased in the United States since the mid- to late 1990s. In order for the geopolitics of (tabloid) terror that prevails in the American public sphere in the first decade of the new millennium to change or disappear, a certain violence on representation or discourse, as Butler intimates, has to take place. Representational or discursive ruptures in the form of events that cannot be presented, that cannot yet be shown, or that may be possible (to use

Badiou's language), perhaps need to happen. Put succinctly, what Butler calls "the media's evacuation of the human through the image" has to end.[39] But how?

A call to achieve a representational or discursive rupture in presently dominant tabloid geopolitical narratives or visions of terror (and, moreover, a demand for an interruption that cannot be planned ahead of time) is easier to proclaim than to actualize. I want to end this concluding chapter with a possible alternative, or rather an attempt at formulating one, in order to encourage the deployment of such representational/discursive ruptures inside public culture. The attempt at a resistant, critical, and possibly democratic way out that I propose below is derived from Butler's own suggestion (itself borrowed from Emmanuel Levinas' ethical thought). But it is also revised and reworked through my own analysis and critique of the contemporary status of the American public sphere, a critical reading that benefits from both Nancy's and Derrida's call for a democracy to come, as we saw at the end of the previous chapter.

As always when critical challenges are introduced, a note of caution is necessary. Indeed, it bears remembering that contemporary dominant tabloid geopolitical discourses of war, terror, and violence are robust. Far more than the policies, institutions, or agents that they empower and whose fateful actions they authorize, these geopolitical discourses are strong, persistent, and long-lasting because, once again, they are seated in everyday culture, in the politics of the mundane or the ordinary, in our most commonsensical mythological significations, as Barthes famously argued,[40] or in the sort of ideological/cultural operations that "go without saying."[41] They also have ways of capturing, recombining, or even reinventing popular beliefs that defy seemingly evident trends. For example, despite the growing backlash since 2005 against the war in Iraq, the intensity of the tabloid imperialist discourse of global expansion of/through war and of limitless utilization of the war machine has not abated (at least, as of the writing of this chapter). In fact, tabloid imperialism of late has started to turn its attention towards possible new targets such as Iran, North Korea, or even (as some pundits of statecraft have argued) "radical Islam" in its entirety.[42] Thus, the failure or collapse of the contemporary tabloid geopolitical discursive formations of terror cannot be anticipated, wished for, or taken for granted just because public opinion appears to swing in a different direction (as seemed to be the case with the overwhelming anti-Bush and anti-Republican party returns of the 2006 midterm elections in the United States).[43]

As tabloid geopolitical discourses of terror seek to spread their narrative tentacles to ever more zones of intervention (perhaps Iran, perhaps North Korea, perhaps a global "Islamo-fascism"), the so-called "we" that tabloid geopolitical experts in the United States claim they wish to protect are not left with too many political and cultural options to live "our" lives. As we saw in Chapter 3, abjecting others inevitably means abjecting "us" too. In the war on terror and in its dominant tabloid productions, it is after all not just others who are left with an "uninhabitable identification," as Butler would have it. "We," the supposedly protected and cared-for ones, also have such an unlivable identity ultimately imposed on us since, as a result of these discourses and representations of boundless violence and terror, "we" actually end up more vulnerable than ever. Once again, "we" too are docile bodies (or body parts) that at any moment can be mobilized for the next war or terror campaign. But this vulnerability or docility is never one that allows "us" to open up to others, or that permits "us" to apprehend a fragility or precariousness of being that might rescue everyone, "us" and "them," from agonal destruction. A few critical thinkers have recognized that, as the tabloid production and control of war and terror in the public domain of appearances has become "a major organizing principle of all aspects of ['our'] daily life, it is all the more imperative for educators, artists, parents, students, and others to develop a language of critique and possibility capable of expressing what is new and different in the constantly shifting interface of politics and culture."[44] This kind of plea to come up with a different critical language or posture suggests that, although fighting off tabloid geopolitical impositions may be fruitless in the end, it is still worth the fight. Perhaps a democracy-to-come will reveal itself as "a language of critique and possibility" in the course of the struggle. Or perhaps, if nothing else, it is worth trying to oppose today's tabloid imperialism and its terrorizing discourses and representations in order to (try to) remain human, in order to (try to) discover what it might mean for human lives, "us" and "them," to be precarious again. Thus, it is by offering a brief reflection on the precariousness of life as a possible motif of resistance to dominant tabloid geopolitical constructs that I wish to conclude this book.

Can precarious lives be saved?

After 9/11, Butler found it necessary to turn to Emmanuel Levinas' ethics, and his notion of the demand made upon us by the "face of the other," to recover a sense of human dignity in political life. With the help of Levinas, she called for a return to the precariousness of life, of every human's life. The face of the other, Butler explains, makes a demand upon me or us (the first person, singular or plural) that is imperative but not immediately obvious. Levinas clarifies what this demand is: "The face is the most basic mode of responsibility . . . [It is] the other who asks me not to let him die alone, as if to do so were to become an accomplice in his death."[45] Levinas adds: "Thus the face says to me: you shall not kill."[46] Levinas' ethics of the face is steeped in the Judeo-Christian moral tradition. Yet it is far more complex than the classical Judeo-Christian call to altruism that, at some level, this demand from the other and his/her face appears to be. Butler indicates that the demand made upon me/us by the face of the other is a plea to recognize the fragility or precariousness of the other. But the understanding of the precariousness of the other, of his/her dying, is also the revelation of my/our own fragility, of the vulnerability and finality of my/our own life/lives.

Still, the recognition of the first person subject's own precariousness of life is more than an apprehension of the other as an alter ego, as another self, or as a brother or sister whom I am obligated (morally, altruistically) to keep and protect. My own precariousness, Levinas intimates and Butler theorizes, is the result of the fact that the evident fragility of the other and his/her face is actually, for me, a temptation to kill. Thus, Butler continues, the precariousness of the face of the other brings to me a double contradictory request. On the one hand, I am commanded to protect and preserve this vulnerable other as I would my self. On the other hand, the other tempts me with the desire to kill, to annihilate, and to turn the vulnerability that is facing me into murder. Butler argues that the full complexity of the Levinasian ethical demand through the face of the other is embodied in this precariousness of life that depends upon maintaining intact, in suspense, this double possibility and moral tension. As she puts it: "The non-violence that Levinas seems to promote does not come from a peaceful place [or peaceful ethic, or purely altruistic moral command], but rather from a constant tension between the fear of undergoing violence and the fear of inflicting violence."[47] Indeed, the moral tension created by the precariousness of the other's face appears to me, and is translated by me in everyday life, as a dual anxiety that ought to govern my actions and, ultimately, my recourse to violence and destruction. The fear of doing harm to the other, of hurting his/her face, or of defacing him/her is constantly confronted (or faced) with the fear of my own death, my own disappearance, and my own survival that is at stake if I do not take advantage of the other's vulnerability and kill him/her. This tension must remain though. It is a tension between "two impulses at war with each other."[48] But, Butler suggests, "they are at war with each other in order *not* to be at war."[49] The ethical tension brought up by the other and his/her face is salutary for Levinas, as it maintains the wars and destructive actions that I or we might undertake inside me/us, and it prevents me/us from taking the agony outside myself or ourselves, toward others whom I/we would have to kill.

At the same time, as already mentioned above, Levinas implies that this tension or precariousness must always remain a demand or an imperative placed above us, superior to us, one that we must live with (and presumably struggle with), and never seek to translate or even put into words (in order to better rationalize it, for example). As Butler puts it, the speech that comes from the face of the other, if it can be called a speech, is one "that does not come from a mouth" or "has no ultimate origin or meaning there."[50] It seems to emanate from "a figure [that] cannot be named."[51] The tension that dictates both the precariousness of life and the continuation of non-violent actions is thus dependent upon a certain representational silence (or violence of meaning), or at least upon words that are not meant to be explained or deciphered. The language of the face of the other must remain an enigma to me/us. By contrast, seeking to translate this speech, wanting to make sense of the tension, and coming up with a discourse that claims to know the answer to the riddle and now decides that it understands how the "you shall not kill" command is to be interpreted is a sure path toward destruction, agony, and death. To kill the other (and myself in the other too) requires, Levinas and Butler intimate, the intervention of a language/discourse that severs the connection and tension between the two fears or impulses described above. With such a discourse, consequentialist intentions, justifications, and rationalizations are now advanced in order to explain how and why a decision to break the suspense has to be made. Often, as a result, decisions are made in favor of externalizing the war, and of doing so on behalf of a so-called righteous cause (that often passes for ethics, morality, and justice) that has no choice but to take advantage of the vulnerability of others and kill them.

I suggest that, in our contemporary times, tabloid geopolitics is precisely such a discourse of "both consequentialist and deontological justifications that [gives me/us] many opportunities to inflict violence righteously."[52] Tabloid geopolitics is a language of clarification and rationalization that has sought to take control of or produce the public sphere and to explain to many people, in the United States above all, that it is better to take the war (between both impulses and both fears) to the outside, to others as mortal enemies, rather than to live with the tension, with precariousness inside (both inside the body politic and inside American selves), after 9/11 in particular. Before 9/11 in fact, tabloid geopolitical discourses and representations of terror started to "name and classify" (as Jameson puts it[53]) for Americans – for people like "us" who need to be differentiated from others whom "we" have to know how to abject – which fear was going to be more valuable and valued. As we have seen throughout this book, the fear that was translated, produced, and prioritized by contemporary tabloid intellectuals and pundits of statecraft was an anxiety about "our" own vulnerability (often still revealed through others, like those who attacked us on 9/11, for example), but an anxiety that supposedly commanded us to dehumanize, destroy, and murder even more others.

The return to non-violence and non-destruction in this apparently unending era of the war on terror – if there is to be such an eventual or eventful return, such a returning event – thus requires a double, complementary movement. It requires that a tense but salutary balancing act be restored between our fear of the other (which, ultimately for Levinas, is the fear of our own fragility and death) and our fear of causing harm to the other. Internal or personal psychoses and traumas, impossibilities of deciding, undecidabilities (disarming as all these may be) may well be better, and may leave us better off (as safe/saved human bodies), than turning our fears into vengeance, retribution, and war. But accepting to live with those psychoses and traumas, with incomprehension after 9/11, also requires that the therapies and feel-good remedies readily prescribed by our contemporary public comforters and media counselors be constantly challenged, as these tabloid pathologists' discourses, intent on finding the "truth" about the trauma in the form of others to be abjected and killed, often cause far more harm than good. Among the therapies that must be questioned and probably rejected are all those media representations – used as supports for a message of fear about one's survival rather than one of fear for one's life that also recognizes the anxiety about terminating other lives – that placard faces of others that are never meant to reveal a precariousness of life. Images of faces of others we have killed (those of dead Iraqi soldiers seen in Chapter 5, for example), of others we have tortured (the Abu Ghraib pictures), of others we have abjected (Saddam's portrait, the 9/11 terrorists' mug-shots), and of others we have been saving (young Ali and his maimed body as we saw in Chapter 5) also deface the face of the other and, like the tabloid geopolitical discourses that they reinforce, help us to resolve the ethical tension that might otherwise keep war and agony at bay.[54]

Butler is right when she writes that all these representations, discourses and images of and about America at war "seem to suspend the precariousness of life."[55] As I suggested above, any attempt at restoring the balance or tension between the apparently contradictory impulses to kill and to fear to kill require some representational violence, some discursive rupture, some interruption of the sublime image. Butler's and Levinas' call for a return to the precariousness of life through a rediscovery of the face of the other (and of the ethical tensions this face allegorizes) is a fine and justified undertaking. But it still relies upon a form of hope (the hope that Americans will start to fear as much about killing others as they do about being killed) rather than on what might be done for events, surprises as events, to happen, without the hope or expectation that they will happen.[56] As I argued at the end of Chapter 5, it is time to be without hope. It is also time to stop placing all our hopes in the person or figure of the other, even if the other presents himself or herself to us as a face that asks us not to kill or not to die alone. Restoring the precariousness of life (of our lives and of others') may demand a certain politics of resistance, one that is neither active nor passive, but that seeks to take advantage of opportunities presented here and there in everyday American popular and political culture for representational ruptures. An image that shocks, that destabilizes, that arrests does not have to make sense, does not have to be recuperated by meaning, and does not have to be transcended. A geopolitical discourse of imperialism, agonal sovereignty, or surrender of society, law, and culture to the terror of the war machine does not have to be accepted as yet another piece of defensive or protective American ideology in times of war, for example. Rather, such images and discourses need to be confronted (when they happen and as they happen) with a silence, a meaninglessness, a gaping wound in the field of vision, an unprepared spontaneous reaction perhaps, an unexpected and aleatory defiance, in other words, with anything that can prolong the moment of incomprehension and undecidability of meaning, with any tool or technique that can postpone the rationalizations and justifications that the media and other dominant actors of the public sphere are likely to want to impose. Our precariousness of life may be dependent upon being on the lookout for events (other sublime events that surprise) or primal scenes (that shock, as I put it in the Introduction) that do not terrorize by means of an overwhelmingly vigilantist discourse or by naming or labeling but, instead, that put us face to face with the incommensurability of the to-come, of a future not decided beforehand, of an eventness beyond representation (because it cannot even be imagined). Precarious lives may be saved if we – and others – make the space and take the time to resist having to make sense of discourses and representations that are far too eager to make sense and far too quick to produce meaning whereas, upon closer examination, and if we were afforded the space and time to reflect upon them, it would become obvious that they make no sense at all and that their so-called meaning is nothing but a succession of carefully crafted mediatized or tabloidized truth-effects. In the end, if we care to rescue our fear of killing others, if we care to retrieve some possibly democratic questioning, and if we care to save ourselves, this is perhaps what the event and its to-come have to look like: open spaces and temporal gaps of non-sense and incommensurate meaning that actually allow us to think, and especially to think about what we are doing when we melancholically long for the past or when we apprehensively project a supposedly better, safer, and less "evil" future. Perhaps Levinas should be given the final word. Levinas writes: "The relationship with the other will never be the feat of grasping a possibility . . . [and] the future is [also] what is in no way grasped . . . [The future is] absolutely surprising."[57] Levinas adds: "The other is the future. The very relationship with the other is the relationship with the future."[58] For our sake and for the sake of the other, may the future be more precarious than it presently is.

Notes

Introduction

1 Blaise Pascal, *Pensées: The Provincial Letters*, trans. W.F. Trotter (New York: Random House, 1941), p. 103.
2 Fredric Jameson, "The Dialectics of Disaster," in Stanley Hauerwas and Frank Lentricchia (eds.), *Dissent from the Homeland: Essays after September 11*, Special Issue of *The South Atlantic Quarterly*, Vol. 101, No. 2 (2002), p. 299.
3 The objectives of this mission are summarized in John L. Hirsch and Robert B. Oakley, *Somalia and Operation Restore Hope: Reflections on Peacemaking and Peacekeeping* (Washington, DC: US Institute of Peace Press, 1995).
4 François Debrix, *Re-Envisioning Peacekeeping: The United Nations and the Mobilization of Ideology* (Minneapolis: University of Minnesota Press, 1999), pp. 97–134.
5 Sidney Blumenthal, "Why Are We in Somalia?" *The New Yorker*, October 25, 1993, p. 50.
6 Ibid., p. 51.
7 See Warren Strobel, *Late-Breaking Foreign Policy: The News Media's Influence on Peace Operations* (Washington, DC: US Institute of Peace Press, 1997), pp. 176–7.
8 See, for example, L.M. Katz, "Graphic Photos from Somalia Gave 'Urgency'," *USA Today*, October 13, 1993, p. 8A, or James Sharkey, "When is a Picture too Graphic to Run?" *American Journalism Review*, December 1993, p. 188. See also the cover of *Time* magazine on October 18, 1993, which showed the tortured and bloodied face of the helicopter pilot taken hostage by the Somali mob.
9 Debrix, *Re-Envisioning Peacekeeping*, pp. 126–34.
10 See, for example, Carol Banks, a travel agent from Los Angeles, who recounts: "The phone rang. It was a coworker, crying her eyes out. She told me to turn on the TV. I put on the news and I started sobbing." Or, again, Sue Levytsky, a freelance copywriter from Michigan, who explains: "I was watching TV in Michigan and when the towers went down I felt like the core of my being was ripped out." See TV Guide Staff, "We Watched and Wept: Americans Express Shock, Anger and Sorrow over the Events They Witnessed on Television," *The TV Guide: Terror Hits Home Special Edition*, Vol. 49, No. 39 (2001), pp. 17–18.
11 On the incomprehension of the journalists immediately after the attacks, see "Ground Zero: For the Dedicated TV Newspeople Covering a Day of Infamy, There Was Unexpected Danger and Overwhelming Sadness," *The TV Guide: Terror Hits Home Special Edition*, Vol. 49, No. 39 (2001), pp. 12–16 and pp. 38–42. Fox News Network's anchor Shepard Smith recalls: "We decided to set up our cameras on the roof of the Fox News building. Fighter jets were buzzing over our heads. We couldn't process it, and everybody was breaking down. People were vomiting. It was impossible to be a dispassionate journalist . . . I lost it repeatedly during the show." Ibid., p. 38.

12 James Der Derian, "The War of Networks," *Theory and Event*, Vol. 4, No. 4 (2002), paragraph 9, no page given; available at http://muse.jhu.edu/journals/theory_and_event/.

13 On the replay/return of time as a consequence of the September 11 events, see also David Campbell, "Time is Broken: The Return of the Past in the Response to September 11," *Theory and Event*, Vol. 4, No. 4 (2002), no pages given; available at http://muse.jhu.edu/journals/theory_and_event/.

14 Marshall Berman, *All that is Solid Melts into Air: The Experience of Modernity* (New York: Penguin, 1988), pp. 131–71.

15 The phrase "a repressed reality creaks through" is Berman's expression. Ibid., p. 152.

16 Jean-François Lyotard, *The Postmodern Condition: A Report on Knowledge*, trans. Geoff Bennington and Brian Massumi (Minneapolis: University of Minnesota Press, 1984).

17 Kevin Glynn, *Tabloid Culture: Trash Taste, Popular Power, and the Transformation of American Television* (Durham, NC: Duke University Press, 2000), p. 2.

18 The notion of "discursive formation" is derived from Foucault's work on language and knowledge. See Michel Foucault, *The Archeology of Knowledge*, trans. A.M. Sheridan Smith (New York: Pantheon Books, 1972).

19 Lyotard, *The Postmodern Condition*, p. 76.

20 Richard Keller Simon, *Trash Culture: Popular Culture and the Great Tradition* (Berkeley: University of California Press, 1999), p. 2.

21 See S. Elizabeth Bird, *For Enquiring Minds: A Cultural Study of Supermarket Tabloids* (Knoxville: University of Tennessee Press, 1992).

22 Jean Baudrillard, *Simulations* (New York: Semiotext(e), 1983).

23 Glynn, *Tabloid Culture*, p. 3.

24 Ibid., p. 3.

25 As John Fiske has noted, tabloid culture is rarely interested in completely public matters. For the tabloid story to catch the attention of the public and stir strong emotions, it must often relate issues that are "close to home," that audience members, in some private capacity, can readily recognize as theirs, as potentially happening to them. Thus, Fiske writes that tabloid culture's "subject matter is generally that produced at the intersection between public and private life; its style is sensational, sometimes skeptical, sometimes morally earnest; its tone is populist; its modality fluidly denies any stylistic difference between fiction and documentary, between news and entertainment." See John Fiske, "Popularity and the Politics of Information," in Peter Dahlgren and Colin Sparks (eds.), *Journalism and Popular Culture* (London: Sage, 1992), p. 48. See also Fiske's study of American television in a tabloid context in the 1990s: John Fiske, *Media Matters: Race and Gender in US Politics*, revised edition (Minneapolis: University of Minnesota Press, 1999).

26 Edelman understands politics principally as the making or constructing of social or political "problems" or "crises." See Murray Edelman, *Constructing the Political Spectacle* (Chicago: University of Chicago Press, 1988).

27 John Agnew, *Geopolitics: Re-Visioning World Politics*, second edition (New York: Routledge, 2003), p. 5.

28 See Halford Mackinder, "On the Scope and Methods of Geography," in John Agnew, David Livingstone, and Alisdair Rogers (eds.), *Human Geography: An Essential Anthology* (Oxford: Blackwell, 1996), pp. 155–72. On Friedrich Ratzel's geopolitical thought, see Gearóid Ó Tuathail, *Critical Geopolitics: The Politics of Writing Global Space* (Minneapolis: University of Minnesota Press, 1996), pp. 36–8.

29 For example, Schulten notes that, in the American context, geopolitics – and geography in general – "works to create and entrench particular ideas about the world and the place of the United States within it." See Susan Schulten, *The Geographical Imagination in America, 1880–1950* (Chicago: University of Chicago Press, 2001), p. 14.

30 Agnew, *Geopolitics*, p. 1.
31 Ibid., p. 3.
32 Ibid., p. 6.
33 Schulten, *The Geographical Imaginary*, p. 44.
34 Ibid., p. 44.
35 Simon Dalby, *Environmental Security* (Minneapolis: University of Minnesota Press, 2002), p. xxiv.
36 Ó Tuathail, *Critical Geopolitics*, pp. 15–16.
37 Ibid., p. 17.
38 David Campbell, *Writing Security: United States Foreign Policy and the Politics of Identity*, revised edition (Minneapolis: University of Minnesota Press, 1998), p. 23.
39 See Michael J. Shapiro, *Violent Cartographies: Mapping Cultures of War* (Minneapolis: University of Minnesota Press, 1997). But perhaps even more emblematic of this trend is Michael J. Shapiro, *Methods and Nations: Cultural Governance and the Indigenous Subject* (New York: Routledge, 2003).
40 See, in particular, Joanne Sharp, *Condensing the Cold War: Reader's Digest and American Identity* (Minneapolis: University of Minnesota Press, 2000). See also François Debrix, "Tabloid Realism and the Revival of American Security Culture," *Geopolitics*, Vol. 8, No. 3 (2003), pp. 151–90.
41 Sharp, *Condensing the Cold War*, p. 35.
42 Ibid., p. x.
43 See, once again, Foucault, *The Archeology of Knowledge*.
44 For more on this lack of distinction between language and discourse in Foucault's work, see François Debrix, "Language, Nonfoundationalism, International Relations," in François Debrix (ed.), *Language, Agency, and Politics in a Constructed World* (Armonk, NY: M.E. Sharpe, 2003), pp. 3–25.
45 Foucault, *The Archeology of Knowledge*, pp. 21–39. On Foucault's discursive formations, see also Jon Simons, *Foucault and the Political* (New York: Routledge, 1995), pp. 23–7.
46 On this idea of "intervention" at the level of language/discourse, Foucault notes: "[I]n every society the production of discourse is at once controlled, selected, organized and redistributed according to a certain number of procedures, whose role is to avert its powers and its dangers, to cope with chance events, to evade its ponderous, awesome materiality." See Michel Foucault, "The Discourse on Language," in Foucault, *The Archeology of Knowledge*, p. 216.
47 Texts by Kaplan, Huntington, Hanson, and other American tabloid geopolitical intellectuals of statecraft like them are analyzed in the following chapters (especially Chapters 2 and 3).
48 For an extensive study of neo-conservatism in American politics, and in US foreign policy circles above all, see Irwin Stelzer (ed.), *The Neocon Reader* (New York: Grove Press, 2005). For an application of neo-conservative thinking to US foreign policy prior to 9/11, see Robert Kagan and William Kristol (eds.), *Present Dangers: Crisis and Opportunity in American Foreign and Defense Policy* (New York: Encounter Books, 2000).
49 It should be noted, however, that this book is not predominantly concerned with analyzing the place and meaning of public intellectuals – and public intellectuals as pundits in particular – in contemporary foreign policy debates. For a detailed account of the phenomenon of public intellectualism today, see Richard Posner, *Public Intellectuals: A Study of Decline* (Cambridge, MA: Harvard University Press, 2003). Additionally, and to be clear, the book does not wish to replicate or prove the fashionable, yet narrow and often short-sighted, belief that, quite simply, the media, its pundits, and neo-conservative spin-doctors are manipulating the public (although there is no doubt a dimension of manipulation in these actors' designs) and controlling people's minds and actions (by manufacturing public consent, for example). Many studies – most of them superficial and indeed tabloid – have been published

of late and have made this specific argument. But these studies have not pushed the analysis very far and instead have been mainly interested in sensationalizing and in fact leaving untouched the dominant media-spins. Thus, these contemporary studies have been of little critical scholarly value. See, for example, Norman Solomon, *War Made Easy: How Presidents and Pundits Keep Spinning Us to Death* (New York: Wiley & Sons, 2005), or Howard Kurtz, *Spin Cycle: How the White House and the Media Manipulate the News* (New York: Free Press, 1998). These volumes are mostly show-and-tell presentations of the contemporary media in the United States, and they basically try to make a single point about the attitude of the media (that the media's message shapes the masses' beliefs) that they indirectly derive from the argument (which they also over-simplify and de-politicize) made by Herman and Chomsky, more than a decade ago now, in their famous *Manufacturing Consent*. See Edward Herman and Noam Chomsky, *Manufacturing Consent: The Political Economy of the Mass Media* (New York: Pantheon, 2002). For a more carefully crafted introspective and analytical approach to the topic of media manipulation, control, and spin, one is better served to turn to Todd Gitlin, *Media Unlimited: How the Torrent of Images and Sounds Overwhelms Our Lives* (New York: Owl Books, 2003).

50 See, for example, Charles Kegley, "The Neoidealist Moment in International Studies? Realist Myths and the New International Realities," *International Studies Quarterly*, Vol. 37 (1993), pp. 131–46. For a critical reading of Kegley's argument about the alleged end of realism, see Cynthia Weber, *International Relations Theory: A Critical Introduction* (New York: Routledge, 2001), pp. 35–57.

51 See Julia Kristeva, *Powers of Horror: An Essay on Abjection* (New York: Columbia University Press, 1982).

52 On the contribution of Kristeva's theory of the abject to the philosophical and cultural motif of disgust, see Winfried Menninghaus, *Disgust: Theory and History of a Strong Sensation* (Albany, NY: SUNY Press, 2003), pp. 365–401.

53 Rey Chow, *The Age of the World Target: Self-Referentiality in War, Theory, and Comparative Work* (Durham, NC: Duke University Press, 2006).

54 Judith Butler, *Precarious Life: The Powers of Mourning and Violence* (New York: Verso, 2004).

55 Once again, inside these texts and images of tabloid terror, violence and destruction shape the contours of public discourse. Or, as Gregory eloquently puts it, "the power to narrate is vested in a particular constellation of power and knowledge in the United States" that actually imprisons millions of people throughout the world inside a global geopolitical domain defined by violence, terror, and war. See Derek Gregory, *The Colonial Present: Afghanistan, Palestine, Iraq* (Oxford: Blackwell, 2004), p. 16.

1 Cyberterror and media-induced fears

1 Written on DM Building, Florida International University, Miami.

2 Quoted in *Cybercrime, Cyberterrorism, Cyberwarfare: Averting an Electronic Waterloo*, A Global Organized Crime Project (Washington, DC: Center for Strategic and International Studies, 1998), p. 15.

3 J.G. Ballard, *War Fever* (New York: Farrar, Straus and Giroux, 1990), pp. 23–32.

4 Brian Massumi, "Everywhere You Want to Be: Introduction to Fear," in Brian Massumi (ed.), *The Politics of Everyday Fear* (Minneapolis: University of Minnesota Press, 1993), p. 11.

5 Marshall McLuhan, *Understanding Media: The Extensions of Man* (Cambridge, MA: MIT Press, 1994), p. 9.

6 Ibid., p. 57.

7 For example, McLuhan thought that the media technique that best represented late modernity was the radio. More than television, radio was described by McLuhan as a "hot medium" to the extent that it "excludes." As a hot medium, radio exacerbates

the degree of alienation of the human subject from his/her social environment. By contrast, TV was for McLuhan a "cool medium" that "includes," brings audiences together through its stimulation of knowledge. Obviously, McLuhan had not had the opportunity to witness the power of television in the age of global TV consortia, cable communication, CNN international, or Fox News. Still, it was somewhat naïve of McLuhan not to foresee that TV would one day "be filled with data" (like other "hot media") and, instead, to claim that it would remain a (democratic) guarantee for social participation. See McLuhan, ibid., pp. 22–32.

8 For more on the ideology of the media, see Mark Taylor and Esa Saarinen, *Imagologies: Media Philosophy* (New York: Routledge, 1994).

9 In this sense, McLuhan's approach stands in contrast to Noam Chomsky's view about "manufacturing consent" as a result of media manipulations. See Edward Herman and Noam Chomsky, *Manufacturing Consent: The Political Economy of the Mass Media* (New York: Pantheon, 1988).

10 Jean Baudrillard, *The System of Objects* (New York: Verso, 1996).

11 Baudrillard writes: "The masses are no longer a referent because they no longer belong to the order of representation. They don't express themselves, they are surveyed. They don't reflect upon themselves, they are tested. The referendum (and the media are a constant referendum of directed questions and answers) has been substituted for the political referent." See Jean Baudrillard, *In the Shadow of the Silent Majorities* (New York: Semiotext(e), 1983), p. 20.

12 Baudrillard explains: "The real is produced from miniaturized units, from matrices, memory banks and command models – and with these it can be reproduced an indefinite number of times. It no longer has to be rational since it is no longer measured against some ideal . . . It is hyperreal: the product of an irradiating synthesis of combinatory models." See Jean Baudrillard, *Simulations* (New York: Semiotext(e), 1983), p. 3.

13 Jean-François Lyotard, *The Postmodern Condition: A Report on Knowledge* (Minneapolis: University of Minnesota Press, 1984), p. 5.

14 A paradigmatic model of modern fear was the system of political government/authority imagined by Thomas Hobbes. Hobbes' system consisted of imposing Leviathan, his supreme ruler, as an authority capable of bringing order by centralizing fear. Individual subjects no longer had to be fearful about their everyday existences because, under Leviathan, they knew exactly where the fear came from. Only the fear of the sovereign – capable of "keeping them all in awe" – was what they had to worry about. See Thomas Hobbes, *Leviathan*, ed. C.B. MacPherson (London: Penguin, [1651] 1985).

15 For a good example of such a Y2K media-induced frenzy, see Edward Yardeni, "Y2K: An Alarmist View," *The Wall Street Journal*, May 4, 1998, p. A22.

16 All subsequent quotes are directly drawn from the script of the program (Fox News Network, Fall 1999).

17 McLuhan wrote: "Concern with *effect* rather than *meaning* is a basic change of our electric time, for effect involves the total situation." See McLuhan, *Understanding Media*, p. 26.

18 Taxonomy is generally understood to be an organization of knowledge that relies upon classificatory schemes and typological designations.

19 Barry Collin, "The Future of Cyber Terrorism: Where the Physical and Virtual Worlds Converge," remarks prepared for the Institute for Security and Intelligence (Chicago: Office of International Criminal Justice, University of Illinois-Chicago, 1999), available at http://oicj.acsp.uic.edu/spearmint/public/pubs/, no page given.

20 Barry Collin, ibid., no page given.

21 See "What is Information Warfare," available on the Infowar Website at http://tangle.seas.gwu.edu/.

22 To use Laqueur's term. See Walter Laqueur, "Postmodern Terrorism," *Foreign Affairs,* Vol. 75, No. 5 (1996), pp. 24–36.
23 To use Klare's terminology. See Michael Klare, *Rogue States and Nuclear Outlaws: America's Search for a New Foreign Policy* (New York: Hill & Wang, 1995).
24 John Arquilla, David Ronfeldt and Michele Zanini, "Networks, Netwar and Information-Age Terrorism," in I.O. Lesser, B. Hoffman, J. Arquilla, D. Ronfeldt, and M. Zanini (eds.), *Countering the New Terrorism* (Washington, DC: Rand Corporation, 1999), p. 47.
25 Ibid., p. 47.
26 Ibid., p. 49.
27 See *Cybercrime, Cyberterrorism, Cyberwarfare*, p. 11.
28 Ibid., p. 10.
29 Ibid., pp. 12–13. See also "Examples of Available (or Possible) IW Weapons" on the Infowar Website, available at http://tangle.seas.gwu.edu/.
30 This division of the body is reminiscent of Negroponte's suggested dualism between atoms and bits in a digital age. See Nicholas Negroponte, *Being Digital* (New York: Vintage Books, 1995).
31 Manuel Castells, *The Rise of the Network Society*, Volume 1 of *The Information Age: Economy, Society and Culture* (Malden, MA: Blackwell, 1996).
32 See Graeme Browning, "Infowar," *The Daily Fed*, April 21, 1997, available at www.goexec.com/dailyfed/, no page given.
33 Matthew Devost, Brian Houghton and Neal Pollard, "Information Terrorism: Can You Trust Your Toaster?" The Terrorism Research Center, available at www.terrorism.com/, no date or page given.
34 See "NIPC Cyber Threat Assessment," Statement for the Record of Michael Vatis, Director of the National Infrastructure Protection Center, FBI, before the Senate Judiciary Committee and Subcommittee on Technology and Terrorism (Washington, DC), October 6, 1999, available at www.fbi.gov/pressrm/congress/, no page given. The National Infrastructure Protection Center (NIPC) is an interagency center located at the FBI. It was created in 1998 pursuant to Presidential Decision Directive-63 to serve as the US government's main response structure against cyberintrusions. Its role is in the domain of warning, investigation, and response systems. After 2003, the NIPC was integrated into the newly created Information Analysis and Infrastructure Protection Directorate of the Department of Homeland Security.
35 Katherine N. Hayles, *How We Became Posthuman: Virtual Bodies in Cybernetics, Literature, and Informatics* (Chicago: University of Chicago Press, 1999).
36 Ibid., p. 3.
37 On the problematic of the body as/through cybernetic organisms, see Donna Haraway, *Simians, Cyborgs, and Women: The Reinvention of Nature* (New York: Routledge, 1991).
38 Browning, "Infowar," no page given.
39 Carol Cohn, "Sex and Death in the Rational World of Defense Intellectuals," in John Vasquez (ed.), *Classics of International Relations*, third edition (Upper Saddle River, NJ: Prentice Hall, 1996), pp. 327–39.
40 Arthur Kroker, Marilouise Kroker, and David Cook, *The Panic Encyclopedia* (New York: St. Martin's Press, 1989), p. 13.
41 Thomas L. Dumm, "Telefear: Watching War News," in Brian Massumi (ed.), *The Politics of Everyday Fear*, p. 313.
42 On the role of the new media (such as the internet) and the politics and spectacle of terror, see Henry Giroux, *Beyond the Spectacle of Terrorism: Global Uncertainty and the Challenge of the New Media* (Boulder, CO: Paradigm Publishers, 2006). See also Jay David Bolter and Richard Grusin, *Remediation: Understanding New Media* (Cambridge, MA: MIT Press, 2000).
43 Jennifer Ruth Fosket and Jennifer Fishman, "Constructing the Millennium Bug: Trust,

Risk, and Technological Uncertainty," *C-Theory: Theory, Technology and Culture*, Vol. 22, No. 3 (1999), Event-Scene 82, no page given.

2 Tabloid realism and the reconstruction of American security culture before 9/11

1 Robert D. Kaplan, *The Coming Anarchy: Shattering the Dreams of the Post-Cold War* (New York: Random House, 2000), p. 24.
2 Joshua Gamson, *Freaks Talk Back: Tabloid Talk Shows and Sexual Nonconformity* (Chicago: University of Chicago Press, 1998), p. 224.
3 Initially, the term "tabloid" referred to the half-broadsheet format of the paper on which the stories were printed. See S. Elizabeth Bird, *For Enquiring Minds: A Cultural Study of Supermarket Tabloids* (Knoxville: University of Tennessee Press, 1992), p. 8.
4 Jane Shattuc, *The Talking Cure: TV Talk Shows and Women* (New York: Routledge, 1997), pp. 17–18.
5 According to Hinerman, tabloid literature's goal is to sensationalize reality while keeping it at the level of people's experience. To provide a basic moralizing discourse centered on everyday's petty injustices, the tabloid text must maintain an appearance of authenticity. Even when it showcases the lives of popular stars, the tabloid story must make sure that the scandals are about individuals who are currently part of everyday American culture. See Stephen Hinerman, "(Don't) Leave Me Alone: Tabloid Narrative and the Michael Jackson Child-Abuse Scandal," in James Lull and Stephen Hinerman (eds.), *Media Scandals: Morality and Desire in the Popular Culture Marketplace* (New York: Columbia University Press, 1997), pp. 143–63.
6 See Kevin Glynn, *Tabloid Culture: Trash Taste, Popular Power, and the Transformation of American Television* (Durham, NC: Duke University Press, 2000), pp. 18–19.
7 Ibid., pp. 17–18.
8 Ibid., p. 18.
9 As was mentioned in the Introduction, the phrase "trash culture" is often used today as a synonym for tabloid culture. While tabloid culture makes reference to a larger tradition of tabloid journalism and reporting, trash culture more specifically denotes the commodified objects and signs of contemporary (tele)visual entertainment. Additionally, trash culture is often defined in opposition to the so-called "great tradition" of literary works. Again, see Keller Simon, *Trash Culture: Popular Culture and the Great Tradition*.
10 See Tom Engelhardt, *The End of Victory Culture: Cold War America and the Disillusioning of a Generation* (New York: Basic Books, 1995).
11 Ibid., p. 23.
12 Ibid., p. 23.
13 Ibid., p. 27.
14 Virginie Mamadouh, "11 September and Popular Geopolitics: A Study of Websites Run for and by Dutch Moroccans," *Geopolitics*, Vol. 8, No. 3 (2003), p. 192.
15 Joanne P. Sharp, *Condensing the Cold War: Reader's Digest and American Identity* (Minneapolis: University of Minnesota Press, 2000), p. 35.
16 David Campbell, *Writing Security: United States Foreign Policy and the Politics of Identity*, revised edition (Minneapolis: University of Minnesota Press, 1998), p. 23.
17 Sharp, *Condensing the Cold War*, p. 35.
18 Ibid., p. 36.
19 Susan Schulten, *The Geographical Imagination in America, 1880–1950* (Chicago: University of Chicago Press, 2001), p. 7.
20 Ibid., p. 7.
21 Engelhardt, *The End of Victory Culture*, p. 113.
22 Ibid., p. 113.

23 Derek Gregory, *The Colonial Present: Afghanistan, Palestine, Iraq* (Oxford: Blackwell, 2004), p. 248.
24 Sharp, *Condensing the Cold War*, pp. 13–14.
25 This point is reminiscent of Neil Smith's argument about the contrast in the United States today (and through most of the twentieth century) between the mobilization of geographical knowledge – often for intelligence purposes – by government authorities and what he calls the "popular geographical illiteracy" of the vast majority of the US public. See Neil Smith, *American Empire: Roosevelt's Geographer and the Prelude to Globalization* (Berkeley: University of California Press, 2003), p. 3.
26 Gregory, *The Colonial Present*, pp. 197–214.
27 See, for example, James Rosenau, *Turbulence in World Politics: A Theory of Change and Continuity* (Princeton, NJ: Princeton University Press, 1990).
28 For a reflection on the effects of postmodernity and postmodern phenomena on international relations and geopolitics, see Paul Virilio, *Speed and Politics: An Essay on Dromology* (New York: Semiotext(e), 1986); Edward Soja, *Postmodern Geographies: The Reassertion of Space in Critical Social Theory* (New York: Verso, 1989); James Der Derian, *Antidiplomacy: Spies, Terror, Speed and War* (Cambridge, MA: Blackwell, 1992); Timothy W. Luke, "Discourses of Disintegration, Texts of Transformation: Re-reading Realism in the New World Order," *Alternatives*, Vol. 18, No. 2 (1993), pp. 229–58; John Agnew and Stuart Corbridge, *Mastering Space: Hegemony, Territory and International Political Economy* (New York: Routledge, 1995).
29 See, for example, Benjamin Barber, *Jihad versus McWorld: How Globalism and Tribalism Are Reshaping the World* (New York: Ballantine Books, 1995); Zbigniew Brzezinski, *Out of Control: Global Turmoil on the Eve of the Twenty-First Century* (New York: Maxwell Macmillan, 1993) and *The Grand Chessboard: American Primacy and Its Geostrategic Imperatives* (New York: Basic Books, 1997); Samuel Huntington, *The Clash of Civilizations and the Remaking of World Order* (New York: Touchstone, 1996); Robert D. Kaplan, *The Coming Anarchy: Shattering the Dreams of the Post-Cold War* (New York: Random House, 2000); Michael Klare, *Rogue States and Nuclear Outlaws: America's Search for a New Foreign Policy* (New York: Hill and Wang, 1995) and *Resource Wars: The New Landscape of Global Conflict* (New York: Metropolitan Books, 2001); John Mearsheimer, "Why We Will Soon Miss the Cold War," *The Atlantic*, Vol. 266, No. 2 (1990), pp. 35–50; Max Singer and Aaron Wildavsky, *The Real World Order: Zones of Peace/Zones of Turmoil* (Chatham, NJ: Chatham House, 1996). But even some traditionally non-realist scholars have attempted to partake of this literary genre. See, in particular, Francis Fukuyama, *The Great Disruption: Human Nature and the Reconstitution of Social Order* (New York: Touchstone, 1999); or Stanley Hoffmann, *World Disorders: Troubled Peace in the Post-Cold War Era* (Lanham, MD: Rowman and Littlefield, 1998).
30 Michel Foucault, *The Archeology of Knowledge* (New York: Pantheon Books, 1972), pp. 31–9.
31 As Mirzoeff has argued, postmodern culture is a predominantly visual and interfacial culture. Thus, it is best captured from the perspective of visual analyses and media. See Nicholas Mirzoeff, *An Introduction to Visual Culture* (New York: Routledge, 1999), pp. 3–8.
32 Kaplan, *The Coming Anarchy*.
33 "Dromography" can be loosely defined as the recording, writing, or graphing of movements and motion in and across space. Dromography is characteristic of the collapsing of space and time by means of speed. On this topic, see Paul Virilio, *Speed and Politics* (New York: Semiotext(e), 1986).
34 Kaplan, *The Coming Anarchy*, p. 50.
35 Ibid., p. 50.
36 Ibid., p. 54.

37 In this book, *An Empire Wilderness*, Kaplan laments: "But now we face the loss of the protection that geography once provided. Because the United States has been so overwhelmingly a creature of geography, in the twenty-first century shrinking distances will affect us more than they will our competitors, whose economic development never depended on continental isolation [unlike the United States' path of development]." See Robert D. Kaplan, *An Empire Wilderness: Travels into America's Future* (New York: Vintage Books, 1998), p. 15; my insert. For a critical reading of this reinvented "regional geography" (and of Kaplan's vision of a newly forming "Cascadian entity" in particular), see Matthew Sparke, *In the Space of Theory: Postfoundational Geographies of the Nation-State* (Minneapolis: University of Minnesota Press, 2005), pp. 111–12.

38 Kaplan, *The Coming Anarchy*, p. 54.

39 Ibid., p. 55.

40 Simon Dalby, "Reading Robert Kaplan's 'Coming Anarchy'," in Gearóid Ó Tuathail, Simon Dalby and Paul Routledge (eds.), *The Geopolitics Reader* (New York: Routledge, 1998), p. 199.

41 As Smith has noted, the need to treat maps and representations of global space in general "with a simplicity and absolutism that is continuous with 19th century Europe" and its Realpolitikally understood strategies and relations between sovereign nation-states is a typical realist trait. See Smith, *American Empire*, p. 8.

42 Dalby, "Reading Robert Kaplan's 'Coming Anarchy'," p. 199.

43 See, for example, Kaplan's panic about what he fears is the porous fragility of the US–Mexican border. See Kaplan, *An Empire Wilderness*, pp. 142–5.

44 To quote Baudrillard's famous slogan about postmodernity as an age of simulated reality. See Jean Baudrillard, *Simulations* (New York: Semiotext(e), 1983).

45 As some of his detractors are often tempted to do. See, for example, Christopher Hitchens, "Africa Adrift," *The Nation*, Minority Report, May 27, 1996; online version, available at http://past.thenation.com/.

46 Brian Jarvis, *Postmodern Cartographies: The Geographical Imagination in Contemporary American Culture* (New York: St. Martin's Press, 1998), p. 188.

47 Ibid., p. 188.

48 Samuel Huntington, *Political Order in Changing Societies* (New Haven, CT: Yale University Press, 1968).

49 Samuel Huntington, *The Third Wave: Democratization in the Late Twentieth Century* (Norman: University of Oklahoma Press, 1991).

50 An article by Robert Kaplan on the meaning of Huntington's work in the aftermath of the September 11 attacks sought to explain (and at the same time champion) Huntington's conservative perspective on politics and order. Kaplan argued that Huntington's vision of conservatism "recognizes the primacy of power in international affairs; it accepts existing institutions; and its goals are limited. It eschews grand designs, because it has no universal value system that it seeks to impose on others." See Robert D. Kaplan, "Looking the World in the Eye," *The Atlantic Monthly*, Vol. 288, No. 5 (2001), pp. 68–82. Huntington's conservatism has also been noted by David Campbell, who reminds us that, in the 1960s, Huntington warned against the danger of social justice programs. Huntington believed that such programs "could not be met by a fiscally constrained state" but that rising expectations would create a "disjunction between the extent of governmental activity and its authority." This "excess of democratic measures" (Huntington's terms) would thus be American democracy's greatest threat, Huntington claimed. See Campbell, *Writing Security*, p. 163.

51 See, for example, Samuel Huntington, *The Common Defense: Strategic Programs in National Politics* (New York: Columbia University Press, 1961); and Zbigniew Brzezinski and Samuel Huntington, *Political Power: USA/USSR* (New York: Viking Press, 1964).

52 Huntington, *The Clash of Civilizations*. Similarly to Kaplan's, Huntington's book was an extension of the essay "The Clash of Civilizations" that he had previously published in the journal *Foreign Affairs*.

53 See also Lawrence Harrison and Samuel Huntington (eds.), *Culture Matters: How Values Shape Human Progress* (New York: Basic Books, 2000).

54 Huntington, *The Clash of Civilizations*, pp. 30–1.

55 Ibid., p. 135.

56 Ibid., p. 136.

57 Ibid., p. 137.

58 Ibid., p. 138.

59 Michael J. Shapiro, *Violent Cartographies: Mapping Cultures of War* (Minneapolis: University of Minnesota Press, 1997), p. 30.

60 Ibid., p. 30.

61 Of course, Huntington's readers were not asked to actively cast away this picture of disorder. What they were mainly asked to do was to follow Huntington's own lessons and conclusions to their bitter end. After all, he already had the answer to the problem. Again, typically with the tabloid genre, adherence to the model offered was mainly what was demanded of the reading subject.

62 Gearóid Ó Tuathail, *Critical Geopolitics: The Politics of Writing Global Space* (Minneapolis, University of Minnesota Press, 1996), p. 246.

63 Ibid., p. 244.

64 Huntington, *The Clash of Civilizations*, p. 302; my emphasis.

65 Ibid., p. 307.

66 Ibid., p. 306.

67 The *Boston Globe* journalist Patrick Healy noted that, in the aftermath of the terrorist attacks on 9/11, Simon and Schuster, the publishers of Huntington's *Clash,* had rushed 20,000 new copies into print. Asked by the journalist how he felt knowing that his predictions had apparently come true, Huntington replied: "Events are showing it [his book] to have a certain amount of validity. I wish it were otherwise." Still, it is hard to believe that Huntington may really have wished for his predictions about civilizational clashes to be wrong or inaccurate. In fact, he concluded this interview by adding: "I fear that while Sept. 11 united the West, the response to Sept. 11 will unite the Muslim world." Far from reconsidering his earlier prophesies in the wake of the attacks, Huntington was actually hammering them in further. See Patrick Healy, "Harvard Scholar's 96 Book Becomes the Word on War," *The Boston Globe*, November 6, 2001, p. A1.

68 Huntington, *The Clash of Civilizations*, p. 311; author's emphasis.

69 Brzezinski, *Out of Control.*

70 Brzezinski, *The Grand Chessboard.*

71 It is in this sense that Huntington wrote that Brzezinski's *The Grand Chessboard* "is the book we have been waiting for." See Huntington, praise for *The Grand Chessboard*, back cover.

72 Zbigniew Brzezinski, *The Grand Failure: The Birth and Death of Communism in the 20th Century* (New York: Scribner, 1989).

73 Brzezinski, *Out of Control*, p. 210. Note in passing that Brzezinski pandered to popular sentiments by identifying the new threats as Muslim (or "Moslem" as he preferred to spell it).

74 After all, Soviet communism was "the most costly human failure in all of history," Brzezinski asserted. Ibid., p. 17.

75 Zbigniew Brzezinski, "A Post-Divided Europe: Principles and Precepts for American Foreign Policy," Lecture given at the Woodrow Wilson Center for Scholars, July 19, 2000, available at http://wwics.si.edu/.

76 It is the core of what Brzezinski later renamed (in one of his many pamphlets) the "Geostrategic Triad." The Geostrategic Triad – Europe, Russia and China – are now

the three main pieces of this geopolitical puzzle. See Zbigniew Brzezinski, *The Geo-strategic Triad: Living with China, Europe, and Russia* (Washington, DC: Center for Strategic and International Studies, 2001).

77 Brzezinski, *The Grand Chessboard*, pp. 34–5.
78 Ibid., p. 34.
79 Ibid., p. 30.
80 Ibid., p. 37.
81 Ibid., p. 37.
82 See, once again, Gregory, *The Colonial Present*, p. 4.
83 My understanding of orientalism is derived from Edward Said's seminal work on the subject. For Said, orientalism is not only "a Western style for dominating, restructuring, and having authority over the Orient." It is also a way according to which "European culture gained in strength and identity by setting itself off against the Orient as a sort of surrogate and even underground self." Edward Said, *Orientalism* (New York: Vintage Books, 1979), p. 3.
84 For another tabloid and orientalist vision of global politics, see Barber, *Jihad versus McWorld*. Although for Barber the term Jihad was supposed to refer to more than a Muslim holy war (against the West mostly), the very choice of the term denoted a stereotypical orientalist posture on the part of this author.
85 Thus, Brzezinski appears to be one of those realists that, in the Cold War US tradition of foreign policy making, do not hesitate to mix power politics (and American hegemony) with claims to global moral superiority. On the moral dimension of Cold War American political realism, see Keith Shimko, "Realism, Neorealism, and American Liberalism," *Review of Politics*, Vol. 54 (1992), pp. 281–301. Some orthodox realists would undoubtedly consider such a position to be a failure of understanding and application of basic realist premises. On this kind of critique, see in particular Hans Morgenthau, *Politics among Nations: The Struggle for Power*, sixth edition (New York: McGraw Hill, 1985), p. 13.
86 Brzezinski, *Out of Control*, p. xii.
87 Ibid., p. xiii.
88 Baudrillard, *Simulations*, p. 32; author's emphasis.
89 Gamson, *Freaks Talk Back*, p. 96.
90 Ibid., p. 168.
91 In the aftermath of 9/11, many political chroniclers, pundits, and intellectuals did not hesitate to equate the terrorist attacks with postmodernism. See, for example, Edward Rothstein, "Attacks on US Challenge the Perspective of Postmodern True Believers," *The New York Times*, September 22, 2001, p. A17, available at www.nytimes.com/2001/. More will be said on this in the next chapter.
92 "The Prophet" was the December 2001 *Atlantic Monthly*'s headline advertising Robert Kaplan's piece on the life and work of Samuel Huntington.
93 To borrow Gregory's terminology. See Gregory, *The Colonial Present*.

3 Discourses of war, geographies of abjection

1 Quoted in TV Guide Staff, "We Watched and Wept: Americans Express Shock, Anger and Sorrow over the Events They Witnessed on Television," *The TV Guide: Terror Hits Home Special Edition*, Vol. 49, No. 39 (2001), p. 19.
2 Robert N. Bellah, "Seventy-Five Years," in Stanley Hauerwas and Frank Lentricchia (eds.), *Dissent from the Homeland: Essays after September 11*, Special Issue of *The South Atlantic Quarterly*, Vol. 101, No. 2 (2002), pp. 258–9.
3 Julia Kristeva, *Powers of Horror: An Essay on Abjection* (New York: Columbia University Press, 1982), pp. 1–2.
4 See Tom Engelhardt, *The End of Victory Culture*.
5 Englehardt, *The End of Victory Culture*, p. 15.

6   Badiou writes that the linguistic, symbolic, and representational pairing of "terrorism" and "America" after the 9/11 attacks inevitably "determines a sequence – the entire current sequence is from now on considered as 'the war against terrorism.' We are warned that it will be a long war, an entire epoch. In short, the 'war against Islamic terrorism' takes over from the Cold (and Hot: Korea, Vietnam, Cuba . . .) War against communism." See Alain Badiou, *Infinite Thought* (London: Continuum, 2003), p. 107.

7   Ibid., p. 116.

8   Ibid., p. 116.

9   See Neil Smith, *American Empire*, p. xii.

10 Ibid., p. xiii.

11 Derek Gregory, *The Colonial Present*, p. 48.

12 Ibid., p. 49.

13 Engelhardt, *The End of Victory Culture*, p. 21.

14 Unlike recent critical geopolitical studies such as those described above, I do believe that those discourses of war, those geopolitics of security, those policies of violence, and those theories of national identity are new. They are new in the sense that they shape America's post-9/11 war story around the theme of abjection, and they take the US desperate search for new forms of triumphalism beyond simply building another set of us/them dichotomies.

15 Kristeva, *Powers of Horror*, pp. 1–2.

16 Ibid., p. 1.

17 Ibid., p. 1.

18 Ibid., p. 2.

19 Winfried Menninghaus, *Disgust: Theory and History of a Strong Sensation* (Albany, NY: SUNY Press, 2003), p. 369; my inserts.

20 Kristeva, *Powers of Horror*, p. 22.

21 Menninghaus, *Disgust*, p. 370.

22 Ibid., p. 370.

23 Kristeva, *Powers of Horror*, p. 10.

24 While no longer useful in explaining quests for identity, "us" and "them," "self" and "other" are still struggling to define themselves, to be meaningful as "subject positions" now performed through the abject. Thus, the abject can also provide us with critical opportunities to "rethink who we are, who they are, and what the relationships between us and them might be," as Weber puts it. See Cynthia Weber, *Imagining America at War: Morality, Politics, and Film* (New York: Routledge, 2006), p. 2.

25 Kristeva, *Powers of Horror*, p. 3; emphasis in original.

26 Ibid., p. 3.

27 Ibid., p. 2.

28 In this chapter, I often use the term "America" instead of the more common "the United States," or "the United States of America," because it is the preferred denomination used by many of the scholars/pundits whose tabloid works and ideologies I engage here. In these works, the term "America" seems to evoke a certain geopolitical imaginary, a sense of nationhood, a collective entity, or a republican idea around which a specific group of people rally.

29 Or, perhaps, we could call them "tabloid colonialist," if we are to follow more closely Gregory's line of analysis about what he calls the "colonial present" of US militarism and imperialism. See, once again, Gregory, *The Colonial Present*.

30 See Simon Dalby, "The Pentagon's New Imperial Cartography: Tabloid Realism and the War on Terror," in Derek Gregory and Allan Pred (eds.), *Violent Geographies: Fear, Terror, and Political Violence* (New York: Routledge, 2006), pp. 460–72. Dalby's analysis is based upon a critical reading of tabloid intellectual of statecraft Thomas Barnett's book, *The Pentagon's New Map: War and Peace in the Twenty-First Century* (New York: G.P. Putnam's Sons, 2004). Like Kaplan, Hanson, or Ledeen,

whose writings and thoughts I feature in this chapter, Barnett can be seen as another emblematic figure of post-9/11 US tabloid imperialism. Another critical geopolitics scholar, Matthew Sparke, also comes close to labeling such discourses (by Kaplan, Ledeen, Hanson, Barnett, and others) tabloid imperialist when he remarks that these types of narrative productions consist of presenting "a much rougher-edged national-imperial geopolitics, an imagined geography of uneven and occupied space associated with ideas of an assertive and unilateralist American empire." See Sparke, *In the Space of Theory*, p. 245. In Sparke's opinion, it makes sense to call these representations/discourses imperialist or even idealist since they are characteristically so in another sense as well. Indeed, like most historical imperial or colonial projects and utopias, American (tabloid) imperialist geopolitics after 9/11 assumes the presence of a universalizing, evenly applied, all-encompassing, and univocal force or authority over multiple spaces or places. This, of course, is a fiction that imperialist totalizing projects must keep alive whereas, in reality, imperial geographies have traditionally been built upon diffuse, inconsistent, uneven, complex, and often discontinuous spatial usages and mobilizations of (representational and physical) violence.

31 Kristeva, *Powers of Horror*, p. 8.
32 Robert D. Kaplan, *Warrior Politics: Why Leadership Demands a Pagan Ethos* (New York: Random House, 2002).
33 Victor Davis Hanson, *An Autumn of War: What America Learned from September 11 and the War on Terrorism* (New York: Anchor Books, 2002).
34 Michael Ledeen, *The War Against the Terror Masters: Why It Happened, Where We Are Now, How We'll Win* (New York: St. Martin's Press, 2002).
35 I place the pronouns "we," "us," or "our" (as well as "they," "them," or "their") in quotation marks to indicate the fact that these are mostly Kaplan's, Hanson's, and Ledeen's own versions and interpretations of what America and Americans ("we") are supposed to be.
36 Kaplan, *Warrior Politics*, p. 113.
37 Ibid., p. 51.
38 Ibid., p. 61.
39 Ibid., p. 36.
40 Ibid., p. 50.
41 See on this topic, once again, Simon Dalby, "Reading Robert Kaplan's 'Coming Anarchy'," in Gearoid Ó Tuathail, Simon Dalby, and Paul Routledge (eds.), *The Geopolitics Reader* (New York: Routledge, 1998), pp. 197–203; See also the argument developed above in Chapter 2.
42 Kaplan, *Warrior Politics*, p. 119.
43 Ibid., p. 119.
44 Ibid., p. 119.
45 Ibid., p. 121.
46 Ibid., p. 146.
47 Ibid., p. 14.
48 Hanson, *An Autumn of War*, back cover.
49 See, once again, Dalby, "The Pentagon's New Imperial Cartography."
50 Ibid., p. xx.
51 Ibid, pp. 75–8.
52 Ibid., p. 110. Hanson, a Professor of History at California State University in Fresno, apparently wishes to distance himself from his "leftist" colleagues in American academia. Yet, interestingly enough, and despite having participated in several pro-Bush administration meetings and conferences, Hanson describes himself as a democrat and a populist. In American conservative circles, there has been a growing backlash against the so-called "leftist curriculum" since George W. Bush was elected President. See, for example, many of conservative chronicler John Leo's weekly interventions in the American magazine *US News and World Report*.

53 Ibid., p. 78.
54 Ibid., p. 71.
55 Ibid., p. 72.
56 Ibid., p. xiv.
57 Ibid., p. xiv.
58 Ibid., pp. xv–xvi.
59 Ibid., pp. xvi–xvii.
60 Ibid., p. xviii.
61 Ibid., p. 73.
62 Since the publication of his book, Hanson has appeared in many American print, audio, and visual media, and he has been the object of several biographical portraits in some of these media outlets. See, for example, Andrew Curry, "Arms and the Man: Portrait, Victor Davis Hanson," *US News and World Report*, March 17, 2003, pp. 38–9.
63 Hanson, *An Autumn of War*, p. 194; my emphases.
64 Ledeen, *The War against the Terror Masters*, p. 211.
65 Ibid., p. xxii.
66 Ibid., p. 213.
67 Ibid., p. xxi.
68 Ibid., p. 215.
69 Ibid., p. xxiii.
70 Ibid., pp. 113–14. One should note in passing that George W. Bush – perhaps heeding Ledeen's plea – has done his fair share of "rehiring" of some former Iran–Contra key individuals.
71 Ibid., p. 78.
72 Ibid., p. 74.
73 Ibid., p. 159.
74 Ibid., p. 169.
75 Ibid., p. 185. The aftermath of the war in Iraq has demonstrated that this belief was far from the reality.
76 Ibid., pp. 188–9.
77 Ibid., p. 195.
78 Ibid., p. 206.
79 Ibid., p. 206.
80 Ibid., p.150.
81 Ibid., pp. 150–1.
82 Ibid., p. 155.
83 Similarly to Hanson's, Ledeen's *truth* is so self-evident that his writing does not require much in terms of citation. Ledeen does not need to cite or quote sources for the information he provides because, as he puts it, "once I decide that the information is reliable, I simply claim it as my own" (ibid., p. 240). Additionally, Ledeen explains that he often does not cite his sources on purpose because "many of the best informed people will only be helpful if they are not identified, and I have respected their desire for anonymity" (ibid., p. 239). Needless to say, this is extremely convenient. It helps Ledeen to claim to his readers that he is indeed the only one who knows, the only one with the *truth*.
84 Ibid., p. 213.
85 Ibid., p. 212.
86 Ibid., p. 213; my emphasis.
87 Kristeva, *Powers of Horror*, p. 18.
88 For a theoretical analysis of the inversion of Clausewitz's famous adage, see Michel Foucault, *"Society Must Be Defended": Lectures at the College de France, 1975–76* (New York: Picador Press, 2003).
89 Karl von Clausewitz, *On War* (Princeton, NJ: Princeton University Press, 1976).

4 The United States and the war machine

1 George W. Bush, press conference, quoted in the film *Fahrenheit 9/11* (director Michael Moore).
2 Gilles Deleuze and Felix Guattari, *Nomadology: The War Machine*, trans. Brian Massumi (New York: Semiotext(e), 1986), p. 7.
3 In 2004, the Army even decided to become the main sponsor for one of NASCAR's professional car racing teams. NASCAR is a popular sport among younger working-class American males, a perfect target group for Army recruiters.
4 See, for example, Pauline Jelinek, "Billions of Dollars Spent on Iraq: How Much was Wasted, How Much more Needed?" *The Associated Press*, press report, July 23, 2004, no page given.
5 Roland Barthes, *Mythologies*, trans. Annette Lavers (New York: Noonday Press, 1972).
6 To my knowledge, it is Foucault who first brought up the possibility of the reversal of Clausewitz's principle. See, once again, Michel Foucault, *'Society Must Be Defended': Lectures at the Collège de France, 1975–76* (New York: Picador, 2003), pp. 15–19 and pp. 47–8.
7 Gilles Deleuze and Felix Guattari, *A Thousand Plateaus: Capitalism and Schizophrenia*, trans. Brian Massumi (Minneapolis: University of Minnesota Press, 1987).
8 Deleuze and Guattari, *Nomadology*, p. 3. The book, *Nomadology: The War Machine*, is based on excerpts from *A Thousand Plateaus*.
9 Ibid., p. 5.
10 Ibid., p. 8.
11 Ibid., p. 7.
12 They ascribe somewhat arbitrary dates to the different levels of writing or "plateaus" they introduce in *A Thousand Plateaus*. Thus, for example, the date for their "Treatise on Nomadology – The War Machine" plateau is 1227. But such dates are not to be seen as indicating that the writing is time or period specific.
13 See Karl von Clausewitz, *On War* (Princeton, NJ: Princeton University Press, 1976).
14 Deleuze and Guattari refer to this as the need to develop thoughts and practices of resistance to state "capture." See Paul Patton, *Deleuze and the Political* (New York: Routledge, 2000), p. 110.
15 Ibid., p. 113; my inserts.
16 Ibid., p. 113.
17 Ibid., p. 114.
18 Ibid., p. 115; my inserts.
19 See, for example, Julian Reid, "Deleuze's War Machine: Nomadism against the State," *Millennium: Journal of International Studies*, Vol. 32, No. 1 (2003), pp. 57–85.
20 Michael Hardt and Antonio Negri, *Multitude: War and Democracy in the Age of Empire* (New York: Penguin Press, 2004), pp. 10–11.
21 Ibid., p. 4.
22 Ibid., p. 4.
23 Ibid., p. 7.
24 Ibid., p. 7.
25 Ibid., p. 13.
26 Ibid., p. 14.
27 Ibid., p. 14.
28 Ibid., p. 12.
29 Ibid., p. 13.
30 In this sense, I agree with Butler's analysis of the "new" configurations of power post 9/11. Butler suggests that the "new configuration of power requires a new theoretical framework or, at least, a revision of the models for thinking power that we already have at our disposal." See Judith Butler, *Precarious Life: The Powers of Mourning and Violence* (New York: Verso, 2004), p. 92.

31 More, of course, has been said about this in Chapter 2.
32 General Tommy Franks, *American Soldier*, written with Malcolm McConnell (New York: Regan Books, 2004).
33 For example, upon being asked by Defense Secretary Rumsfeld to prepare a plan of action for Iraq in 2001, Franks simply writes: "New work to be done." See ibid., p. 315. Or again, when describing the task ahead in Afghanistan: "As my dad would have said, 'lots of work to do, . . . and not long to do it'." Ibid., p. 252.
34 Thus, Franks always makes it a point to clarify for whom he is working and to indicate the risks associated with letting the military run the show. Talking to Rumsfeld and recalling an argument among commanders in chief, Franks states: "I work for you and for the President, not for the Service Chiefs [the commanders of the four American military forces, the Navy, the Air Force, the Army, and the Marines]. They were fighting for turf yesterday. If this continues, our troops – and the country – will suffer. We should not allow narrow-minded four-stars to advance their share of the budget at the expense of the mission." Ibid., pp. 277–8; my inserts.
35 One of the most telling statements in Franks' book that supports this view is the following one, describing his position regarding his newly assigned task as Commander in Chief of Central Command: "[I]n the coming months, I would be called upon to practice both statecraft and diplomacy . . . I had read about both war and peace: the accumulated wisdom of Sun Tzu and Clausewitz, Bertram [*sic*] Russell and Gandhi. And what had gradually come clear in my mind was that war involved a continuum of interaction between nations, factions, and tribes. Across the breadth of this continuum, I perceived five distinct states of interaction – states I categorized as the five Cs. At one end of the spectrum was *Conflict*, in which the armed forces of two nations or more engaged in combat. That usually arose from a *Crisis*, a state of angry tension between opponents. *Co-existence* was one step removed: Potentially hostile countries or tribes overcame their antagonisms to live side-by-side. *Collaboration* was an endeavor in which parties worked toward their mutual benefit. Finally, active *Cooperation* was the most positive relationship: open borders, joint commercial and governmental enterprises, harmony and progress . . . At virtually every point in the region lying below that hazy Mediterranean horizon, nations were gripped in conflict or crisis – or, at best, co-existence. My responsibility would be to help move these states as far along the Five C continuum as possible – from conflict to crisis to co-existence and beyond." Ibid., pp. 203–4.
36 About the "Shock and Awe" tactic, Franks writes: "This is a campaign unlike any other in history, . . . a campaign characterized by shock, by surprise, by flexibility, by the employment of precise munitions on a scale never before seen, and by the application of overwhelming force." Ibid., p. 484.
37 Ibid., p. 330.
38 Or, as Franks once again claims, his job as "manager" of the US troops is to "find innovative solutions to difficult problems." Ibid., p. 184.
39 See, for example, Richard Clarke, *Against All Enemies: Inside America's War on Terror* (New York: Free Press, 2004) and Joseph Wilson, *The Politics of Truth: Inside the Lies that Led to War and Betrayed My Wife's CIA Identity* (New York: Carroll and Graf, 2004). See also Michael Moore's documentary/essay film, *Fahrenheit 9/11*, released in 2004 too.
40 See the National Commission on Terrorist Attacks, *The 9/11 Commission Report: Final Report of the National Commission on Terrorist Attacks Upon the United States* (New York: Norton, 2004).
41 Franks takes part of the blame for the US claim that Iraq did indeed possess weapons of mass destruction, the main reason advanced by the Bush administration to justify the war against Iraq at the United Nations in January–February 2003. See Franks, *American Soldier*, p. 353. Franks also takes full responsibility for telling the president

to declare the end of major military operations in Iraq and claim on May 1, 2003 that, as the slogan went, the "mission was accomplished." See ibid., p. 524.

42   About the National Security Council counter-terrorism specialist (and future Bush detractor) Richard Clarke, Franks notes: "I suspected that Dick was better at identifying a problem than at finding a workable solution." Ibid., p. 211. For Franks' criticism of Secretary of State (and former Chairman of the Joint Chiefs of Staff) Colin Powell, see ibid., pp. 394–5.

43   Hardt and Negri, *Multitude*, p. 7.

44   To quote Franks once again: "Americans fight wars only when we are threatened. I wouldn't want it any other way." See Franks, *American Soldier*, p. 544.

45   The term "continuum" is one of Franks' preferred words when describing political–military relations. See ibid., p. 204.

46   Much of this self-incurred "blindness" of the state with regard to the violence and death caused by the war machine also has a lot to do with what Kennan Ferguson suggests takes place when "wars and acts of war are justified and excused through ordinary language." See Kennan Ferguson, "Three Ways of Spilling Blood," in François Debrix (ed.), *Language, Agency, and Politics in a Constructed World* (Armonk, NJ: M.E. Sharpe, 2003), p. 87.

47   Franks sometimes appears to confuse the need to defend the state with the need to maintain or even create a certain form of social life through war. For example, he writes: "The prize we seek in this time in history is a way of life." Ibid., p. 536.

48   See Hans Morgenthau, *In Defense of the National Interest* (Lanham, MD: Rowman and Littlefield, 1982).

49   For examples of recent (tabloid) realist critiques of the war in Iraq and the Bush administration's views on foreign policy, see Zbigniew Brzezinski, *The Choice: Global Domination or Global Leadership* (New York: Basic Books, 2004); John Lewis Gaddis, *Surprise, Security, and the American Experience* (Cambridge, MA: Harvard University Press, 2004); John Mearsheimer and Stephen Walt, "An Unnecessary War," *Foreign Policy*, Vol. 134 (January/February 2003), pp. 50–9; Joseph Nye, *The Paradox of American Power: Why the World's Only Superpower Can't Go It Alone* (Oxford: Oxford University Press, 2002); Kenneth Waltz, "Theory and International Politics: Conversation with Kenneth Waltz," Conversations with History Series, Institute of International Studies, University of California–Berkeley, February 10, 2003, available at globetrotter.berkeley.edu/. Perhaps the most sympathetic of these realists towards the Bush administration's grand strategy of preemptive force and war, John Lewis Gaddis, nonetheless finds fault with the US administration's handling of current American hegemony. Gaddis writes: "The rush to war in Iraq in the absence of a 'first shot' or a 'smoking gun' left a very different impression: a growing sense throughout much of the world that there could be *nothing* worse than American hegemony if it was to be used in this way ... [W]ithin a little more than a year and a half, the United States exchanged its long-established reputation as the principal *stabilizer* of the international system for one as its chief *destabilizer*." Gaddis, *Surprise, Security, and the American Experience*, pp. 100–1; author's own emphases.

50   Gaddis refers here to the Bush administration's military and geopolitical strategists. See Gaddis, ibid., p. 102, my inserts.

51   See, for example, Thomas Barnett, *The Pentagon's New Map: War and Peace in the Twenty-First Century* (New York: G.P. Putnam's Sons, 2004); David Frum and Richard Perle, *An End to Evil: How to Win the War on Terror* (New York: Random House, 2003); Samuel Huntington, *Who Are We? The Challenges to America's National Identity* (New York: Simon and Schuster, 2004); Lawrence Kaplan and William Kristol, *The War in Iraq: Saddam's Tyranny and America's Mission* (San Francisco: Encounter Books, 2003). See also Robert D. Kaplan, *Warrior Politics: Why Leadership Demands a Pagan Ethos* (New York: Random House, 2002) and Michael Ledeen, *The*

War against the Terror Masters (New York: Truman Talley Books, 2002) (these last two authors' volumes were discussed in the previous chapter).

52 Franks, *American Soldier*, p. 536.
53 Shapiro, *Methods and Nations*, p. 180.
54 Michel Foucault, "Right of Death and Power over Life," in Paul Rabinow (ed.), *The Foucault Reader* (New York: Pantheon Books, 1984), p. 266.
55 Giorgio Agamben, *Homo Sacer: Sovereign Power and Bare Life* (Stanford, CA: Stanford University Press, 1998), p. 3.
56 For more on the use of such a dialectic in international relations, see R.B.J. Walker, *Inside/Outside: International Relations as Political Theory* (Cambridge, UK: Cambridge University Press, 1993).
57 Agamben, *Homo Sacer*, p. 28.
58 Hardt and Negri, *Multitude*, p. 14.
59 Ibid., p. 20.
60 Ibid., p. 20.
61 As will be shown later through the analysis of Huntington's work.
62 Shapiro, *Methods and Nations*, pp. 181–2.
63 This is Shapiro's clarification of Agamben's concept of "bare life." See *Methods and Nations*, p. 181.
64 Agamben, *Homo Sacer*, p. 8.
65 Samuel Huntington, *Who Are We? The Challenges to America's National Identity* (New York: Simon and Schuster, 2004).
66 Ibid., p. 8.
67 Once again, see Victor Davis Hanson, *An Autumn of War*, discussed in Chapter 3.
68 Huntington, *Who Are We?*, p. 8.
69 Ibid., p. 11.
70 Ibid., p. 12.
71 Ibid., p. 12.
72 Ibid., p. 361.
73 Ibid., p. 361.
74 Ibid., pp. 361–2.
75 Ibid., p. 362.
76 Ibid., p. 362.
77 Ibid., p. 362.
78 Hardt and Negri, *Multitude*, p. 41.
79 Alain Joxe, *Empire of Disorder* (Los Angeles: Semiotext(e), 2002), p. 206.
80 Ibid., p. 208.
81 The very terms used by Joxe. See ibid., p 202.
82 See, for example, David Frum and Richard Perle, *An End to Evil: How to Win the War on Terror* (New York: Random House, 2003).
83 Lawrence F. Kaplan and William Kristol, *The War over Iraq: Saddam's Tyranny and America's Mission* (San Francisco: Encounter Books, 2003), p. 3. Lawrence Kaplan is the senior editor of the *New Republic* and William Kristol is the editor of the *Weekly Standard*. These two publications are traditionally conservative American print media outlets. From 2002 on, both Kaplan and Kristol used these two weekly publications, and their frequent appearances on cable news networks like Fox News, MSNBC, or CNN, to defend the need for the United States to go to war in Iraq.
84 George W. Bush, speech given at West Point on June 1, 2002. Quoted in Kaplan and Kristol, *The War over Iraq*, p. 74.
85 Bush, ibid., p. 74.
86 Kaplan and Kristol, ibid., p. 72.
87 Ibid., p. viii and p. 95.
88 This is Kaplan and Kristol's own term. See ibid., p. 120.
89 Ibid., p. 121 and p. 125.

90 See, in particular, Hannah Arendt, *The Human Condition* (Chicago: University of Chicago Press, 1973).
91 Seyla Benhabib, *The Reluctant Modernism of Hannah Arendt* (Thousand Oaks, CA: Sage, 1996), p. 125.
92 Ibid., p. 126.
93 Ibid., p. 126.
94 Ibid., p. 126.
95 Ibid., p. 127 and p. 130.
96 Arendt, *The Human Condition*, p. 193.
97 As Anthony Lang Jr. has noted, it is mainly in the politics of military interventions that agonal action and agency manifest themselves in international relations. See Anthony F. Lang Jr., *Agency and Ethics: The Politics of Military Intervention* (Albany, NY: State University of New York Press, 2002).
98 Dana Villa, "Beyond Good and Evil: Arendt, Nietzsche, and the Aestheticization of Political Action," *Political Theory*, Vol. 20, No. 2 (1992), p. 275.
99 Ibid., p. 276.
100 Ibid., p. 276.
101 Alain Badiou, *Infinite Thought: Truth and the Return to Philosophy* (London: Continuum, 2003), p. 117.
102 Ibid., p. 117; my emphases.
103 Franks, *American Soldier*, pp. 306–7; my emphasis.
104 See, once again, Michael A. Ledeen, *The War against the Terror Masters*.
105 Badiou, *Infinite Thought*, p. 120.
106 Ledeen, *The War against the Terror Masters*, p. xxiii.
107 Ibid., p. 213; my inserts.
108 Or, as Ledeen put it, "creative destruction is our middle name, both within our society and abroad. We tear down the old every day, from business to science, literature, art, architecture, and cinema to politics and the law." Ibid., p. 212.
109 Or, to put it somewhat differently, at no point do those agonal theorists of war and war's destruction pause to reflect on Bacevitch's warning that "the marriage of military metaphysics with eschatological ambition is a misbegotten one, contrary to the long-term interests of either the American people or the world beyond our borders." Bacevitch adds: "It invites endless war . . . As it subordinates concern for the common good to the paramount value of military effectiveness, it promises not to perfect but to distort American ideals." See Andrew Bacevitch, *The New American Militarism: How Americans Are Seduced by War* (New York: Oxford University Press, 2005), p. 7.
110 Here the colloquial saying "old warriors never die, they simply fade away" takes on an interesting meaning.
111 Deleuze and Guattari, *Nomadology*, p. 111.
112 Jean Baudrillard, "L'Esprit du Terrorisme" (The Spirit of Terrorism), *The South Atlantic Quarterly*, Vol. 101, No. 2 (Spring 2002), p. 407.
113 For an additional discussion of post-9/11 American moralities, their role and place in American culture, and their potentially disastrous and destructive effects, see Cynthia Weber, *Imagining America at War: Morality, Politics, and Film* (New York: Routledge, 2006).
114 Baudrillard, "L'Esprit du Terrorisme," p. 405.
115 The film director Quentin Tarantino is perhaps one of the few contemporary auteurs/ thinkers who has understood (and has sought to challenge) the power of contemporary war machines and their violence. His films *Kill Bill I* and *Kill Bill II* may be read as ironic revisitings and critiques of the cultural uses of sovereign agonal violence after 9/11. See, on this topic, François Debrix, "Kill Bill," film review, *Millennium: Journal of International Studies*, Vol. 34, No. 2 (2005), pp. 553–7.
116 Hardt and Negri, *Multitude*, p. 192.
117 Ibid., p. 192.

118 Ibid., p. 192.
119 For a more promising reflection on the human, bodies, and even body parts in the aftermath of 9/11 and its subsequent (American-led) wars, see Butler, *Precarious Life*. I return at length to Butler's more interesting argument regarding the precariousness of life in the concluding chapter. For another fruitful critical exploration of the relationship between life/lives and war violence today, see Rey Chow, *The Age of the World Target*.
120 Rowan Williams, "End of War," in Stanley Hauerwas and Frank Lentricchia (eds.), *Dissent from the Homeland: Essays after September 11*, Special Issue of *The South Atlantic Quarterly*, Vol. 101, No. 2 (2002), pp. 269–70; my inserts. Archbishop Williams' full quotation is: "[B]ombast about evil individuals doesn't help in understanding anything. Even vile and murderous actions tend to come from somewhere . . . But there is sentimentality too in ascribing what we don't understand to 'evil'; it lets us off the hook, it allows us to avoid the question of what, if anything, we can recognize in the destructive act of another. If we react without that self-questioning, we change nothing."

5 The sublime spectatorship of the Iraq war

1 Friedrich von Schiller, "On the Sublime (Toward the Further Development of some Kantian Ideas)," in F. Schiller, *Essays*, ed. Walter Hinderer and Daniel Dahlstrom (New York: Continuum Books, 1993), p. 29.
2 Quote from Frank "Dim" Dumphy (played by Luke Macfarlane) in the pilot episode of the *Over There* show, FX network, first broadcast July 27, 2005.
3 Jean-Luc Nancy, *Being Singular Plural* (Stanford, CA: Stanford University Press, 2000), p. 159.
4 Quoted in James Poniewozik, "Missing in Action: FX's Daring New Iraq War Drama is Violent and Provocative, but Filled with Clichéd Characters," *Time*, August 1, 2005, p. 58.
5 For an in-depth study of the connection between Bochco's cop shows and existentialism, see Philip J. Lane, "The Existential Condition of Television Crime Drama," *Journal of Popular Culture*, Vol. 34, No. 4 (Spring 2001), pp. 137–51.
6 Nancy Franklin, "The Yanks are Coming," *The New Yorker*, August 1, 2005, p. 86.
7 See Mike McDaniel, "Soldiers Walk the Walk, Talk the Talk," *HoustonChronicle.Com*, July 27, 2005, no page given. Available at www.chron.com/.
8 Poniewozik, "Missing in Action," p. 58.
9 Rob Owen, "TV Review: Gripping 'Over There' Displays War's Realities," *Post-Gazette.Com: A Service of the Pittsburgh Post Gazette*, July 24, 2005, no page given. Available at www.post-gazette.com/.
10 Jean-François Lyotard, *The Inhuman: Reflections on Time*, trans. Geoffrey Bennington and Rachel Bowlby (Stanford, CA: Stanford University Press, 1991), p. 98.
11 See, for example, Nicholas Mirzoeff, *An Introduction to Visual Culture* (New York: Routledge, 1999), p. 16.
12 Nancy, *Being Singular Plural*, pp. 159–76.
13 Immanuel Kant, *Critique of Judgment* (New York: Barnes & Noble, 2005), first published 1790 (see, in particular, "Second Book: Analytic of the Sublime"). Jean-François Lyotard, "Answering the Question: What Is Postmodernism?" in Lyotard, *The Postmodern Condition: A Report on Knowledge* (Minneapolis: University of Minnesota Press, 1984), pp. 71–82; and Lyotard, *The Inhuman*.
14 Lyotard, "Answering the Question," p. 77.
15 As Lyotard explains. See Lyotard, *The Inhuman*, pp. 136–7.
16 Lyotard, "Answering the Question," p. 78.
17 See Lyotard, *The Inhuman*, pp. 96–7.
18 Lyotard, "Answering the Question," p. 78.

19 Nicholas Mirzoeff, "What Is Visual Culture?" in Nicholas Mirzoeff (ed.), *The Visual Culture Reader* (New York: Routledge, 1998), p. 9.

20 Nathan Stormer, "Addressing the Sublime: Space, Mass Representation, and the Unpresentable," *Critical Studies in Media Communication*, Vol. 21, No. 3 (2004), p. 221.

21 Ibid., p. 222.

22 Ibid., p. 213.

23 Ibid., p. 214.

24 See Louis Althusser, "Ideology and Ideological State Apparatuses," in L. Althusser, *Lenin and Philosophy, and Other Essays*, trans. Ben Brewster (New York: Monthly Review Press, 1971), pp. 127–86.

25 Stormer, "Addressing the Sublime," p. 213.

26 Bernd Hüppauf, "Modernism and the Photographic Representation of War and Destruction," in Leslie Devereaux and Roger Hillman (eds.), *Fields of Vision: Essays in Film Studies, Visual Anthropology, and Photography* (Berkeley, CA: University of California Press, 1995), p. 105.

27 Marcel Saba (ed.), *Witness Iraq: A War Journal, February–April 2003* (New York: Power House Books, 2003).

28 See, for example, Robert Sullivan (ed.), "In the Land of the Free, September 11 – and After," *Life Commemorative*, November 12, 2001; Christopher Sweet, David Fitzpatrick, and Gregory Semendinger (eds.), *Above Hallowed Ground: A Photographic Record of September 11, 2001* (New York: Studio Books, 2002); and Magnum photographers, *New York September 11* (New York: Power House Books, 2001).

29 For more on the history and use of documentary photography, particularly in times of war, since the mid-nineteenth century, see Derrick Price, "Surveyors and Surveyed: Photography Out and About," in Liz Wells (ed.), *Photography: A Critical Introduction* (London: Routledge, 1997), pp. 55–102.

30 Saba, *Witness Iraq*, Paolo Pellegrin, Basra, 04/07/03, pp. 81–2.

31 Saba, *Witness Iraq*, Faleh Kheiber, Baghdad, 04/06/03, p. 69.

32 Saba, *Witness Iraq*, Jean-Marc Bouju, An Najaf, 03/31/03, pp. 59–60.

33 As Giroux puts it, these sublime images are about immersing the US public into "a visual culture of shock and awe," a culture that is "devoted to representations of the horrific violence associated with terrorism [in general], ranging from aestheticized images of nighttime bombing raids on Iraqi cities to the countervailing imagery of grotesque killings of hostages." See Giroux, *Beyond the Spectacle of Terrorism*, p. 21; my inserts.

34 Gregory, *The Colonial Present*, pp. 210–13.

35 It is of course ironic that the US government and military claimed that the Arabic news network Al Jazeera had violated the Geneva Conventions when, in the early days of the US military offensive, it showed the faces of US soldiers who had been taken prisoner by the Iraqi military (this was the episode that led to the capture, and later escape, of US female private Jessica Lynch).

36 In this sense, my reading of young Ali's photo is in line with Susan Sontag's interpretation of the Abu Ghraib pictures. About these photos of torture, Sontag claims that, far from being seen as shameful displays, they are actually "treated as souvenirs of a collective action." See Susan Sontag, "Regarding the Torture of Others: Notes on What Has Been Done – and Why – to Prisoners by Americans," *New York Times Sunday Magazine*, May 23, 2004, p. 27.

37 Saba, *Witness Iraq*, preface; my emphasis.

38 These troubling war images also remind us that, as Virilio has claimed, there probably cannot be any successful war machine without an accompanying "watching machine." Together, the war machine and its sublime imagery form what Virilio calls "the magical spectacle." See Paul Virilio, *War and Cinema* (London: Verso, 1989), pp. 3 and 5.

39 Thus, Bush thought that the acts of US soldiers depicted in the Abu Ghraib photos were just "mistakes." Bush was quoted as saying that "those mistakes will be investigated, and people will be brought to justice." George W. Bush, quoted in Joanne Mariner, "Rumsfeld and Abu Ghraib," *Find Law's Legal Commentary*, April 25, 2005; available at writ.news.findlaw.com/. As for Defense Secretary Rumsfeld, he absolutely refused to refer to the actions at Abu Ghraib as matters of torture, not only because it might have been difficult to ignore the blatant violation of humanitarian law and human rights if torture was admitted, but also because individuals capable of acts of torture cannot be excused, redeemed, or reformed. Torture is not just some temporary "illness," some passing wrong, or some "mistake." Rumsfeld stated: "I don't know if it is correct to say what you just said . . . that torture has taken place, or that there's a conviction of torture, and therefore I am not going to address the torture word." Donald Rumsfeld, quoted in David Folkenflik, "Dodging Using Words like 'Torture'," *The Baltimore Sun.Com*, May 26, 2004; available at www.baltimoresun.com/entertainment/.
40 Stormer, "Addressing the Sublime," p. 231.
41 Ibid., p. 231. Stormer gets to the idea that the sublime is at its most effective when it presents images that appear to "fail" a concept or idea through an analysis of the landscape photographic work of Ansel Adams. Some of Adams' photos have revealed natural sceneries that have been damaged, disrupted, or even destroyed by the work of man. Yet, as Adams put it, "the fact that [Man] has fouled his nest and seems certain to continue with his destruction seems now more of an illness than an expression of evil intent" (Ansel Adams, quoted in Stormer, ibid., p. 231). Thus, Stormer intimates, what Adams' non-nature glorifying photos still reveal is the belief in "a decadent civilization [nonetheless] finding its true, pure self again in primitive wilderness." See Stormer, ibid., p. 231.
42 See Jean-François Lyotard, *Lessons on the Analytic of the Sublime*, trans. Elizabeth Rottenberg (Stanford, CA: Stanford University Press, 1994), p. 70.
43 Slavoj Zizek, *The Sublime Object of Ideology* (New York: Verso, 1989), p. 206.
44 Ibid., pp. 206–7; my inserts.
45 To use Hinnant's own formulation of Schiller's thought on the sublime. See Charles Hinnant, "Schiller and the Political Sublime: Two Perspectives," *Criticism,* Vol. 44, No. 2 (2002), p. 125.
46 Nancy, *Being Singular Plural*, pp. 159–76.
47 As Nancy puts it, "the event is the interruption of process" (ibid., p. 172). It is "that which admits nothing presupposed" (ibid., p. 171).
48 Ibid., p. 174.
49 Florian Tréguer, "L'événement et l'éventualité: les formes du sublime dans l'oeuvre de Don DeLillo" (Event and Eventuality: The Forms of the Sublime in DeLillo's Work), *Revue Française d'Études Américaines*, Vol. 99 (February 2004), p. 65; my translation.
50 Ibid., p. 65; my translation. Obviously, as the title of Tréguer's essay indicates, it is through an analysis of DeLillo's novels that Tréguer is able to theorize the "sublime event" and relate it to Nancy's thinking.
51 Jacques Derrida, *Rogues: Two Essays on Reason*, trans. Pascale-Anne Brault and Michael Naas (Stanford, CA: Stanford University Press, 2005), p. 84.
52 Ibid., p. 42.
53 Nancy, *Being Singular Plural*, p. 172.
54 Derrida, *Rogues*, p. 87.
55 Ibid., p. 144; my inserts.
56 Ibid., p. 147.
57 See Gary Younge, "Bereaved Mother Camps outside Bush Ranch," *The Guardian*, August 10, 2005, available at www.guardian.co.uk/. See also Elisabeth Bumiller, "Turning out to Support a Mother's Protest," *New York Times*, August 18, 2005,

available at www.nytimes.com/2005/. The *Time* magazine chronicler Joe Klein best captures the meaning and force of Sheehan's protest and its moment of ideological arrest. Klein writes: "[Sheehan] represents all the tears not shed when the coffins came home without public notice. She is pain made manifest. It is only with a public acknowledgment of the unutterable agony this war has caused that we can begin a serious and long overdue conversation about Iraq, about why this war . . . is still worth fighting and why we should recommit the entire nation to the struggle." See Joe Klein, "The Danger of Yellow Ribbon Patriotism," *Time*, August 29, 2005, p. 23.

58 With her initial irruption into the US cultural war landscape (both over there and at home), Cindy Sheehan recalls another motherly figure, Lila Lipscomb, another mother of a US soldier killed in Iraq, who was featured in Michael Moore's film, *Fahrenheit 9/11* (released about a year before Sheehan's own intervention in Texas). At some level, and as Weber has put it in her reading of Moore's film, Lila Lipscomb represents "the unruly feminine who, in her determination to (re)secure the US home (front), is willing to destabilize not only US state practices but the US President himself." See Weber, *Imagining America at War*, p. 144.

59 The Sheehan protest is also reminiscent of another surprising – and to some shocking – display that took place in the US media in 2004. Shifting the discourse and representation away from what happened in the war "over there" to the situation "here," at home, on the so-called home front, and also wishing to shed light on the "return home" of dead US soldiers at a time when the Bush administration had imposed a media censorship that prevented the US public from seeing images of soldiers' coffins getting back to the United States, the late-night ABC channel news show *Nightline*, hosted by Ted Koppel, decided to display the faces and recite the names, for about one hour, of the soldiers who had died in Iraq. This show, "Faces of the Fallen," was reprised one month later for those US troops who had died in Afghanistan. In a manner reminiscent of the *Over There* show, "Faces of the Fallen" was intended to be, beyond politics, a tribute to those who served and died and to their families. Although announced and, in a sense, somewhat representative of a media coup (some locally owned ABC channels refused to air the show, though), this media event was far from spectacular and, for a while only, introduced a few questions in the midst of the otherwise dominant ideology of the US war. For more on the controversy over the "Faces of the Fallen" show, see Foreign Desk, " 'Nightline' to Read off Iraq War Dead," *New York Times*, April 28, 2004, p. A9. See also Bill Carter, "The Struggle for Iraq, the Media: Some Stations to Block 'Nightline' War Tribute," *New York Times*, April 30, 2004, p. A13.

60 One must note, however, that when Cindy Sheehan and other mothers went to Washington, DC, to protest the war in October 2005, the demonstrations gave rise to a few physical confrontations with the police, and Sheehan herself was forcefully removed and temporarily arrested.

61 Tréguer, "L'événement et l'éventualité" (Event and Eventuality), p. 60.

62 Ibid., p. 59.

63 I am of course referring here to Hardt and Negri and their argument in *Multitude* already discussed in Chapter 4.

64 The idea of a "necessary" or "lesser" evil was brought up by the Harvard University Human Rights Policy Professor Michael Ignatieff. See Michael Ignatieff, *The Lesser Evil: Political Ethics in an Age of Terror* (Princeton, NJ: Princeton University Press, 2004). Ignatieff refers to the possibility of turning the US wars in Iraq and Afghanistan into what he calls "a democratic war on terror" (ibid., p. 23). Moreover, and in apparent contradiction to his professed human rights concerns, Ignatieff goes on to justify the US government and military's interrogation techniques, which, he clarifies, should never be confused with torture. Ignatieff writes: "The interrogation methods of which the Americans have been accused since 9/11 are held to include nothing worse than sleep deprivation, permanent light or permanent darkness, disorienting noise,

and isolation. If this were true . . . it would amount to coercion rather than torture, and there might be a lesser evil justification for it" (ibid., p. 138). Thus, behind the covers of ideological moderation, ethical balance, and political correctness, Ignatieff and other democracy-promoting US intellectuals like him make themselves the apologists of an ideology whose very purpose it is to abuse democracy and negate democratic questioning. Along the same line of analysis, see also Michael Walzer's unwillingness to condemn the US war in Iraq on the ground that Saddam Hussein's own policies and war tactics for decades have been unjust and downright murderous. Walzer rejects the anti-war position and, instead, prefers to worry about finding ways of making the US invasion of Iraq a just war, a war that, Walzer goes on to affirm, the United States must win. See Michael Walzer, "So, Is this a Just War?," *Dissent Magazine*, Web Exclusive, Spring 2003, available at www.dissentmagazine.org/.

65 My Derrida-influenced thinking in terms of a "democratic interruption" or a "democratic event to come" is possibly another way of evoking what Sparke (also referring his critical analysis to a certain reading of Derrida) calls a "deconstructive geographical responsibility." As Sparke puts it, such a deconstructive responsibility (to come, I might be tempted to add) consists of "attempts to open up . . . unconnected connections that underwrite particular anemic geographies [i.e., geographies that are built upon the desire to conceal their own complex, polysemic, and heterogeneous writings]." See Sparke, *In the Space of Theory*, p. xvi; my inserts. Yet, similarly to what I suggest with regard to the radical sublime event to come, Sparke adds that such deconstructive geo(political) writings or graphings "can never be fully finalized." See Sparke, ibid., p. 312.

Conclusion

1 Judith Butler, *Precarious Life: The Powers of Mourning and Violence* (New York: Verso, 2004), p. xviii.
2 Bill O'Reilly, *Who's Looking Out for You?* (New York: Broadway Books, 2003), p. 139.
3 O'Reilly's style of news and/or truth reporting has led to the creation of a popular spoof show on the Comedy Central network, *The Colbert Report*. On this show, comedian Stephen Colbert mimics O'Reilly's mode of thinking, ideological beliefs, and populist antics. Colbert came up with the term "truthiness" to describe his approach (and by extension O'Reilly's) to fact telling and information-reporting. "Truthiness" can be defined as the ability to speak a language of truth in the absence of any referential support for such truth claims.
4 O'Reilly, *Who's Looking Out for You?*, pp. 2 and 3.
5 Ibid., p. 4.
6 Many pundits have tried to replicate O'Reilly's style. Other popular tabloid news shows on American TV include *Scarborough Country* (with pundit Joe Scarborough as host) on the MSNBC network, *Hannity and Colmes* (with rightist and leftist commentators Sean Hannnity and Alan Colmes) on Fox News, and the *Glenn Beck* show (hosted by former radio opinion/news talk-show guru Glenn Beck) on CNN Headline News among many others.
7 The full range of O'Reilly's media intrusions is visible on his website, www.billoreilly.com, sort of a crossroads where all his media ventures meet and connect. On the website, his followers can also purchase all sorts of Bill O'Reilly products, from coffee mugs and tote bags to posters and T-shirts.
8 O'Reilly, *Who's Looking Out for You?*, p. 79.
9 Ibid., p. 79.
10 Ibid., p. 79.
11 As O'Reilly puts it. See ibid., p. 2. This unabashed patriotism of Fox News, O'Reilly claims, explains why the network has become so popular among American audiences.

It also explains that what is good for Fox is necessarily also good for the United States. Thus, O'Reilly argues, "this country is a better place because Fox News has succeeded." See Bill O'Reilly, "Bill O'Reilly Quotes," available at www.brainyquote.com/quotes/authors/b/bill_oreilly.html.

12 In this manner, O'Reilly's task was very similar to the one that Victor Davis Hanson assigned to himself in his volume *Between War and Peace: Lessons from Afghanistan and Iraq*. In this book, Hanson (like O'Reilly in his shows during the war in Iraq) chose to celebrate the warriors and the wars they were fighting. No distinction between the soldiers and the strategy of going to war in Iraq was permitted. Refusing to support the war simply meant refusing to support the troops (thus, it also meant betraying them, Hanson suggested). Instead, as I argued in Chapter 4, a quasi-mythical aesthetic glorification of the US wars and warriors ("our" agonal heroes) was imposed in the tabloid media. As Hanson declared: "the American soldier is asked to do what no other could do – and yet does so with grace under fire." Hanson concluded: "On July 4th we should remember all this and the rare breed who, thank God, are on our side." See Victor Davis Hanson, *Between War and Peace: Lessons from Afghanistan and Iraq* (New York: Random House, 2004), p. 282.

13 O'Reilly, *Who's Looking Out for You?*, p. 146.

14 Ibid., p. 146.

15 Ibid., p. 144.

16 Ibid., p. 139.

17 Ibid., p. 143.

18 Ibid., p. 141.

19 Ibid., p. 50.

20 Ibid., p. 50. In his most recent book, O'Reilly's aggressive tabloid imperialism continues and desperately tries to explain why, despite the obvious fiasco, a continued military presence in Iraq and throughout the Middle East is required. This time, it is not just about avenging 9/11 but about supporting the Bush administration's fight (on behalf of America and all Americans) against "Islamo-fascism." It is also about every American becoming their own warrior to defend their "family and country." O'Reilly writes: "I believe that if the United States demonstrates the slightest weakness in the face of Islamo-fascism, we will be attacked more readily. I point to the appeasement of the fanatical Third Reich about seventy years ago to back up my opinion. There is no difference in attitude between the Nazis and the jihadists . . . The secular-progressive movement [in America] wants the United States to decline in power. It wants a new world order where global consensus would rule . . . It is now time to get back to basics: to develop a personal strategy designed to keep your family and country protected from those who would do us harm." See Bill O'Reilly, *Culture Warrior* (New York: Broadway Books, 2006), pp. 193–4.

21 O'Reilly, *Who's Looking Out for You?*, p. 145.

22 Quoted in Media Matters Action Network, "One Day after Smearing Protester Cindy Sheehan, O'Reilly Claimed He and Malkin Were 'Respectful' to Her," *Media Matters for America*, August 11, 2005, no page given. Available at http://mediamatters.org/; my inserts.

23 O'Reilly's program on Cindy Sheehan involved a dialogue with right-wing pundit and blogger Michelle Malkin. O'Reilly and Malkin's dialogue was a succession of short, lapidary statements that built upon one another and confirmed each pundit's views (which were essentially the same). Thus, a pretense of information or truth finding was provided by means of an exchange of ideas that was no exchange at all. This method is commonly used on *The O'Reilly Factor* where guests in agreement with O'Reilly are frequently given ample airtime. Guests who disagree with O'Reilly's positions are invited too. But they are often extreme caricatures of the argument O'Reilly wants to reject (and O'Reilly makes their views appear as if they are widely held). Or, if they are more sedate views, they nonetheless have no choice but to partake of the

ranting, simplistic, and sensationalistic format that O'Reilly has created for his show. Thus, the trap is not so much to find a way to argue with O'Reilly but to agree to appear on his show in the first place. The more an appearance of dialogue is provided by O'Reilly, the more limited the range of views actually is. In the O'Reilly media-scape, discourse is a trap. Silence is perhaps the best recipe against O'Reilly's noise. Another similar strategy is to refuse O'Reilly's semblance of dialogical engagement (the late night talk-show host David Letterman recently used this technique by simply responding to O'Reilly: "How come I have the feeling that at least 60% of what you say is pure crap?" See David Letterman, *The Late Show with David Letterman*, January 3, 2006).

24 It must be said, though, that Sheehan's decision to visit the Venezuelan President and US detractor Hugo Chavez in January 2006 in Caracas during the World Social Forum did not help her cause and, in fact, diminished the credibility of her challenge to the Bush administration in the eyes of many in the United States (and not just O'Reilly's supporters). On Sheehan's meeting with Chavez, see "Sheehan, Chavez Join to Bash Bush, Iraq War," *Associated Press*, January 30, 2006, available online at www.msnbc. msn.com/.

25 See Media Matters Action Network, "One Day after Smearing Cindy Sheehan . . . ," no page given.

26 Put somewhat differently, tabloid geopolitics excels at producing what Allan Pred has called "situated ignorance." Pred writes that "the discursive promotion of the invasion and occupation of Iraq, and the post-9/11 'War on Terror' more generally, has relied heavily on the production of widespread forms of anxiety-ridden 'situated ignorance,' on the successful production of fear-filled forms of situated knowledge that are in-fused with distortions, misrepresentations, and disinformation, and otherwise largely comprised of gaping holes." See Allan Pred, "Situated Ignorance and State Terrorism: Silences, W.M.D., Collective Amnesia, and the Manufacture of Fear," in Derek Gregory and Allan Pred (eds.), *Violent Geographies*, pp. 364–5. What Pred should add, though, is that this so-called situated ignorance is the result of discourses that aim at saturating people's domains of perception, cognition, and interpretation through a daily bombardment of "facts," "truths," and "realities" (as happens on O'Reilly's program for example) that are never meant to be doubted or questioned.

27 Butler, *Precarious Life*, p. xix.

28 Henry Giroux, *Beyond the Spectacle of Terrorism: Global Uncertainty and the Challenge of the New Media* (Boulder, CO: Paradigm Publishers, 2006), p. 3.

29 Butler, *Precarious Life*, p. xix.

30 Giroux, *Beyond the Spectacle of Terrorism*, p. 1.

31 Butler, *Precarious Life*, p. xx.

32 Once again, the term "tabloid imperialist" is partly borrowed from Dalby's work. See Dalby, "The Pentagon's New Imperial Cartography: Tabloid Realism and the War on Terror," in Derek Gregory and Allan Pred (eds.), *Violent Geographies* (New York: Routledge, 2006), pp. 295–308.

33 Alain Badiou, *Ethics: An Essay on the Understanding of Evil* (London: Verso, 1998), quoted in Giroux, *Beyond the Spectacle of Terrorism*, p. 5.

34 Butler, *Precarious Life*, p. 144; author's emphasis.

35 Among such critical, sometimes purportedly "leftist" or non-conservative, tabloid geopolitical discourses of the botched US military invasion of Iraq and other Bush administration disasters, see Craig Unger, *House of Bush, House of Saud: The Secret Relationship between the World's Two Most Powerful Dynasties* (New York: Scribner, 2004); Anonymous, *Imperial Hubris: Why the West Is Losing the War on Terror* (Washington, DC: Potomac Books, 2005); Thomas Ricks, *Fiasco: The American Military Adventure in Iraq* (New York: Penguin Press, 2006); Frank Rich, *The Greatest Story Ever Sold: The Decline and Fall of Truth from 9/11 to Katrina* (New York: Penguin Press, 2006); or Bob Woodward, *State of Denial: Bush at War, Part III* (New York: Simon & Schuster, 2006).

36 See, for example, Michael Moore, *Dude, Where's My Country?* (New York: Allen Lane, 2003); or his compendium of letters from US soldiers in Iraq and Afghanistan (whom he invited to write to him about their experiences and feelings "over there") in Michael Moore, *Will They Ever Trust Us Again? Letters from the War Zone* (New York: Penguin Books, 2005). For another blatant attempt on the American cultural left to provide a (fairly humoristic) counterpoint to *The O'Reilly Factor* in particular, see Al Franken, *The Truth (with Jokes)* (New York: Dutton, 2005).

37 As Weber notes, in his documentary film *Fahrenheit 9/11*, Moore claims to "let the images speak for themselves," particularly images that are supposed to demonstrate the irrefutable "fact/truth" that Bush was never in control of the post-9/11 geopolitical landscape, that before the terrorist attacks Bush and the neo-conservatives had already decided to invade Iraq, or that prominent members of the Bush administration never cared to protect American lives from terrorists but only wanted to fulfill their own political or financial ambitions. But Weber astutely shows that, in a typically tabloid fashion (one that is not so different from O'Reilly's own way of presenting reality to his mesmerized audience, for example), Moore actually speaks for the images that he claims his camera objectively captures and broadcasts. In so doing, like most tabloid pundits of statecraft, Moore constructs visual/representational meaning. Or, as Weber puts it, "he has to speak for them [the images], all the while presenting himself as if he is speaking through them." See Weber, *Imagining America at War*, p. 140.

38 A case in point is David Harvey, who directly associates what he calls the new "paranoid style" in American politics to neo-conservatism. As Harvey puts it, "after 9/11, the neo-conservatives had had their 'Pearl Harbor'," which allowed them to "harness" a "new-found nationalism" to "the imperial project of regime change in Iraq." Harvey concludes that American "neo-conservatives are, it seems, committed to nothing short of a plan for total domination of the globe." See David Harvey, *The New Imperialism* (Oxford: Oxford University Press, 2003), pp. 194–9. In this crude, conspiracy-laced mode of geopolitical analysis, the "new imperialism" Harvey speaks of is the product of a simple explanation: a few American neo-conservative ideologues and plotters have a plan for world domination.

39 Butler, *Precarious Life*, p. 146.

40 Roland Barthes, *Mythologies*, trans. Annette Lavers (New York: Noonday Press, 1972).

41 To borrow Weber's turn of phrase. See Cynthia Weber, *International Relations: A Critical Introduction* (London: Routledge, 2001), p. 6.

42 On the extension of the US war machine beyond Iraq and Afghanistan – and despite the apparent military difficulties in both countries – see the continued work of tabloid imperialist pundits, intellectuals, or politicians of terror and war such as Kenneth Timmerman, *Countdown to Crisis: The Coming Nuclear Showdown with Iran* (New York: Crown Forum, 2005); Curt Weldon, *Countdown to Terror* (Washington, DC: Regnery Publishing, 2005); Paul Sperry, *Infiltration: How Muslim Spies and Subversives Have Penetrated Washington* (Nashville, TN: Nelson Current, 2005); or O'Reilly's latest book, *Culture Warrior*. Perhaps one of the most representative illustrations of this ongoing attempt by tabloid imperialist discourses to not reconsider their premises after the Iraq war debacle but, instead, to viciously and somewhat desperately soldier on is the self-proclaimed "popular radio and television pundit" Tony Blankley's volume, *The West's Last Chance: Will We Win the Clash of Civilizations?* (Washington, DC: Regnery Publishing, 2005). In this book, Blankley (who sometimes appears on *The O'Reilly Factor*) seeks to redeploy the US war machine in the aftermath of the failed invasion of Iraq to send it to fight a global crusade against an expanding "radical Islam" (which, as he sees it, is already affecting Western Europe). To prevent the spread of what he calls "Eurabia" to the United States, Blankley calls for a World War II type of military engagement and support by the US population. This is, according to him, what it would take to "save our civilization," or, as he clarifies, "if Europe becomes Eurabia, it would mean the loss of our cultural and historic first cousins, . . . and the

source of our own civilization . . . An Islamified Europe would be as great a threat to the United States today as a Nazified Europe [was] . . . in the 1940s." See Blankley, *The West's Last Chance*, p. 185.

43 For an example of such a (perhaps premature) anticipation of change after the defeat of Bush's Republican party in the November 2006 midterm elections, see the British journalist and chronicler Simon Jenkins, "Republican Defeat Means the Iraqi Insurgency Has Won," *The Guardian*, November 9, 2006, available at www.guardian.co.uk/commentisfree/. Jenkins writes: "The ugly American mark two is dead. Overnight six years of glib European identification of 'American' with right wing fanaticism is over . . . Another McCarthy raised its head over the western horizon and has been slapped down. It is a good day for level-headed Americans." See ibid., no page given. On this topic, see also Peter Baker and Jim VandeHei, "A Voter Rebuke for Bush, the War and the Right," *Washington Post*, November 8, 2006, p. A01.

44 Giroux, *Beyond the Spectacle of Terrorism*, p. 14.

45 Emmanuel Levinas and Richard Kearney, "Dialogue with Emmanuel Levinas," in Emmanuel Levinas, *Face to Face with Levinas* (Albany, NY: SUNY Press, 1986), p. 23; also quoted in Butler, *Precarious Life*, p. 131.

46 Levinas and Kearney, "Dialogue with Emmanuel Levinas," p. 23; also quoted in Butler, *Precarious Life*, p. 132.

47 Butler, *Precarious Life*, p. 137; my inserts.

48 Ibid., p. 137.

49 Ibid., p. 137; author's emphasis.

50 Ibid., p. 133.

51 Ibid., p. 133.

52 Ibid., p. 137; my inserts.

53 As we saw at the very beginning of this book. See Fredric Jameson, "The Dialectics of Disaster," in Stanley Hauerwas and Frank Lentricchia (eds.), *Dissent from the Homeland: Essays after September 11*, Special Issue of *The South Atlantic Quarterly*, Vol. 101, No. 2 (2002), pp. 297–304.

54 These images of the faces of others we wish to kill, torture, abject, but also save can be placed in a larger visual and conceptual perspective that, following in the footsteps of the war machine, seeks to understand and capture the world as a target. As Chow argues, "to conceive of the world as a target is to conceive of it as an object to be destroyed." See Chow, *The Age of the World Target*, p. 31. On the combination of the machinery of war destruction and the visual apparatus, see Paul Virilio, *War and Cinema: The Logistics of Perception* (London: Verso, 1989).

55 Butler, *Precarious Life*, p. 143.

56 On this question of hope, I part company with Giroux, who believes that the challenge to the terror of today's "image-based society must also include a politics of hope." See Giroux, *Beyond the Spectacle of Terrorism*, p. 16.

57 Emmanuel Levinas, *Time and the Other*, trans. Richard Cohen (Pittsburgh: Duquesne University Press, 1987), p. 76.

58 Ibid., p. 77.

Index